YOUR MONEY
OR
YOUR LIFE

YOUR MONEY
OR
YOUR LIFE

How to Save Thousands on Your Health-Care Insurance

Donald Jay Korn

COLLIER BOOKS
Macmillan Publishing Company, New York

Maxwell Macmillan Canada
Toronto

Maxwell Macmillan International
New York   Oxford   Singapore   Sydney

Copyright © 1992 by Donald Jay Korn

Collier Books
Macmillan Publishing Company
866 Third Avenue
New York, NY 10022

Maxwell Macmillan Canada, Inc.
1200 Eglinton Avenue East
Suite 200
Don Mills, Ontario M3C 3N1

Macmillan Publishing Company is part of the Maxwell Communication Group of Companies.

Library of Congress Cataloging-in-Publication Data
Korn, Donald Jay.
    Your money or your life: how to save thousands on your health-care insurance / Donald Jay Korn.—1st Collier Books ed.
       p.   cm.
    Includes index.
    ISBN 0-02-080441-5
    1. Insurance, Health—United States.   2. Insurance, Disability—United States.   3. Insurance, Long-term care—United States.
    I. Title.
    HG9396.K67   1992   91-35827
    368.3'8'00973—dc20   CIP

Macmillan books are available at special discounts for bulk purchases for sales promotions, premiums, fund-raising, or educational use. For details, contact:

Special Sales Director
Macmillan Publishing Company
866 Third Avenue
New York, NY 10022

First Collier Books Edition 1992

10 9 8 7 6 5 4

Printed in the United States of America

To Marilyn, Michelle, and Alex,
in order of appearance

Contents

Acknowledgments

I'd like to thank all the people who helped make this book possible. To begin with, thanks to Howard Recht, my own health and life insurance agent, whom I would recommend without hesitation. In addition, thanks are due to:

Bob Bland and Bill Thoms of Quotesmith Corp., Sidney Madlock of IDS Financial Services, Ed Emerman of A. Foster Higgins & Co., Rosanne Hennessey of The Travelers, and Tom Goddard of the National Association of Insurance Commissioners for providing much-needed information;

Marty Kelman, Ron Lazarov, and Charles Auerbach, financial planners who helped me discover how things are in the real world;

Joseph Spieler and especially my agent, Lisa Ross, for all their effort and encouragement;

Natalie Chapman, my editor, for her kind words and sharp pencil;

Dr. Ed Janowitz, Dr. Jerry Lowenstein, Steve Ogilvy, Chuck Polle, and Les Winter, who not only keep me healthy but also contributed in their unique ways;

And, last only in this listing, Marilyn, Michelle, and Alex Korn, for whose health I'd pay any price.

YOUR MONEY
OR
YOUR LIFE

Introduction

Leo George thought he was covered. After all, he owned an office-supply company, and he had picked out the health insurance policy himself. So when 60-year-old Leo was scheduled for open-heart surgery, the least of his worries was the cost.

Surgery was a success, for the physicians as well as for Leo. The surgeon sent him a bill for over $15,000; the anesthesiologist valued his services at $5,000. Leo turned the bills over to his company's bookkeeper to let the insurer settle up.

When the insurer replied, Leo almost needed another operation. The surgeon would be reimbused $2,500; the anesthesiologist, $1,250. The balances were still due, but from Leo. Nor would his insurance company pay for all the nursing and postoperative treatment. Altogether, Leo was out of pocket nearly $50,000.

What's more, now that Leo realizes he needs better health insurance, he can't get it. Insurers aren't eager to cover 60-year-olds who already have had open-heart surgery.

If it's any consolation to Leo, he's not alone. Many people assume that the health insurance coverage they have through their employer, or their spouse's employer, is all they'll need. By the time they find out otherwise, it's too late.

Take the case of Jan Herbert, wife of a successful attorney. She had a radical mastectomy for breast cancer, followed by extensive chemotherapy. Again, she figured that her husband, a savvy guy who knows a "whereas" from a "herein," had selected a comprehensive health insurance policy.

Twenty-five thousand dollars later, she realized her mistake. Her husband, the lawyer, never read the policy and didn't realize it was inadequate. Again, now that Jan seeks better coverage, she's uninsurable.

Such examples abound. Many people—maybe most—don't have adequate insurance coverage. Moreover, they don't realize it's inadequate. In a true worst-case scenario, these people could lose their life's savings, their home, all their worldly goods.

It doesn't have to be that way. With an investment of a little time, you can discover what you already have and what you still need. Rocket-science expertise is not necessary. What's more, "adequate" doesn't have to mean "expensive." When you know what kind of insurance you really need, you probably can buy it for thousands of dollars less than you're paying now.

That's the purpose of this book. Step by step, it's designed to take you through the basic types of health-care insurance. You'll learn, in plain language, what you need and what you don't. You'll pay for what you need, and no more. You can save money and protect your assets at the same time.

SELF-STARTING

Where did Leo and Jan go wrong?

They made the mistake of depending on employer-provided insurance. They assumed that someone else had made the right decisions and that they were "covered."

Well, they weren't. Now that their health has deteriorated, they may never be able to get the right kind of health insurance.

No one is going to be as concerned about your welfare as you are. If you want the best coverage, you need to shop carefully and make the decisions yourself.

Few people get up in the morning with a craving to go out and buy health insurance. It's not one of life's pleasures.

To get yourself started, realize that you're never going to be younger and healthier than you are today. The sooner you buy insurance, the cheaper it will be. If you buy now, and buy right, you can lock in quality coverage at a less than outrageous price. You may wind up with your wealth as well as your health.

YOUR MONEY OR YOUR LIFE

Those are the words you fear hearing from muggers. Now they're likely to come from the white-clad guardian at the gates of your doctor's office or the hospital reception area. Yes, you can have the best medical care in the world. All you have to do is pay for it.

Health-care costs are rising faster than your cholesterol count after a weekend of cheese steaks and milk shakes. Who's going to help you write the checks?

Your employer? Big companies are so desperate to cut back that they're putting up with employee strikes to get out from under health-care obligations. Chances are whatever coverage you still have isn't comprehensive. Small-company health insurance is usually even skimpier, if it exists at all. And if you're self-employed, you have to pay your own way.

The government? There's been a lot of talk about health care in Washington recently, but the politicians aren't about to ride to your rescue. State governments as well as Washington are so awash with red ink they look like operating rooms. The catastrophic-care fiasco showed that everybody loves government-backed health programs as long as they're not taxed to pay for them.

We already have Medicare and Medicaid; they pay more and more each year, yet doctors complain they can't afford to see Medicare or Medicaid patients because of low payments. Do you really believe the government that brought you Medicare and Medicaid can cure the health-cost disease?

Dr. Louis Sullivan, secretary of health and human services,

has said, "In an era of federal fiscal constraints, government dollars will never supplant private insurance."

CRACKING THE CODE

That leaves the burden squarely on you, Mr. or Ms. Middle America. Not only do you have to worry about your own fiscal health: with the aging of America, you increasingly have to bear your parents' health-care costs.

Insurance is available, but whoever invented health-care-coverage plans designed them to make comparisons impossible. Who knows how to evaluate health maintenance organizations (HMOs) and preferred provider organizations (PPOs)? Who knows what to look for in a Medigap policy?

This book is an easy-to-follow guide through the health-care money maze: It shows you how to make sure you'll get the best health care for the least money.

THE THREE LEGS OF THE STOOL

There are essentially three ways in which failing health can dent your wallet:

1. You (or a family member) can get sick or suffer an injury, leading to huge medical bills.
2. You (or another wage earner) can lose your ability to work, reducing or eliminating your income.
3. A member of your family, while not truly sick, may no longer be able to care for him- or herself. Someone will have to provide care, perhaps for the long term.

Thus, for true financial security, you need to have all these bases covered.

1. In case of sickness or injury, you need insurance coverage to pay the medical bills. If your existing coverage—through your employer or another source—good enough? If not, you need supplementary insurance.

2. You need some financial backup in case of a long-term disability that keeps you from working. Again, you may have "disability income" (DI) insurance from your employer, which may or may not be adequate. If you don't have such coverage or if it's inadequate, you may have other resources (an investment portfolio, spouse's income) to see you through. If all of these fail, you may need to buy your own DI insurance.

3. You need some resources to pay for long-term care (LTC) in case it's needed. One of your parents, for example, may need to stay in a nursing home or require an in-home companion. Or you may be concerned that you or your spouse will one day need LTC, and you don't want to burden your children or use up your life's savings. Again, you may need to buy specialized LTC insurance.

Don't think that this book is dedicated to the insurance agents of America. You may not need another insurance policy, or perhaps you'll need only a small supplement to your existing coverage to be reasonably secure. In fact, you may be able to cut back on the insurance you're already paying for. Once you understand the purpose of insurance and the relative merits of your options, you can buy the coverage you really need, no more and no less.

INSURANCE-POOR

The experiences of Leo and Jan show how not having the right kind of insurance can wipe out your net worth. But it's possible to go the other way, too, and bankrupt yourself by paying too much for unnecessary coverage.

Carol and Dan Stillman never paid much attention to their health-care insurance. She was a rising young executive at a local bank, while he taught art in a high school. Between their two employers, they had ample health insurance and group DI insurance. They paid around $200 a month for the former, while the latter was "free."

While in their 30s, they had two children. Carol, tired of

juggling job and motherhood, never found day care that pleased her, so she quit her job to stay home with the kids. Dan, unable to support the family as a schoolteacher, went to work as an independent manufacturer's representative selling sportswear to clothing stores.

Under federal law, both Dan's and Carol's former employers had to let them continue their health insurance coverage. They chose Carol's, which they had been using, but they have to pay the full, unsubsidized premium now, around $500 per month.

Dan's DI insurance, on the other hand, didn't travel with him when he left his job. Now he has no coverage. But what happens if he's in an accident or suffers a serious illness and no longer can drive 2,000 miles a month, showing his lines to buyers? How will the Stillmans make up for the lost income? Dan asks his agent about DI insurance and discovers it will cost around $2,000 per year.

At the same time, Dan is worried about his 70-year-old widowed mother. Living alone, with neither a job nor a large group of friends, her mind seems to be wandering. What if she has to go into a nursing home? At her age and her present good physical health, she might be there 10 or 15 years.

Dan's mother lives comfortably now, in a paid-up house with income from a $150,000 investment portfolio to supplement her Social Security checks. But nursing homes in her area cost over $30,000 a year and are heading still higher. A long nursing-home stay could literally push her into poverty (and, not unimportantly, deprive Dan and Carol of any inheritance).

So Dan asks his agent if there's any kind of insurance that will protect his mother's assets. There is LTC insurance, he learns, but the annual premium is over $3,000 a year. Dan's mother, already spending $1,000 per year on a health insurance policy to supplement Medicare, can't afford that extra policy.

So Dan feels overwhelmed. He knows he needs health insurance, currently priced at $6,000 per year. He *should* carry DI insurance, at $2,000 per year. And, for the sake of his mother and his own future financial well-being, he feels obliged to come up with another $3,000 per year for her LTC insurance.

That's $11,000 per year—in addition to what he's already

paying for life insurance and auto insurance and homeowner's insurance. Dan makes a nice living as a manufacturer's rep, but not a fortune. How can he possibly afford all this with anything left over for luxuries, such as food, clothing, housing, and gas for his car?

DRIVE A CHEVY, DODGE THE LEVY

He can't. And, as you'll see later on, he doesn't have to. He can buy adequate insurance for less.

Dan drives a Chevrolet when he's selling fashions. It may not have all the features of a Cadillac, but that's what he can afford. His Chevrolet gets him there.

It's the same with health-care insurance. He can buy coverage that will meet his needs. The policies he winds up with may not have all the latest options, but stripped-down versions cost less. For $6,000, $7,000, or $8,000 per year, rather than $11,000, he can buy health-care insurance that will get him where he wants to go.

As you go through this book, you'll see how to cut nonessentials—and costs—from your health-care insurance.

DON'T SWEAT THE SMALL STUFF

There's a "top down" theory of investing in the stock market. First, you figure out whether the broad market is going up or down.

If things look favorable, you look for the industry groups (technology stocks, energy stocks, food stocks) with the best prospects.

Then, within each industry group, you pick the likely winners: You decide to invest in IBM or Exxon or Heinz.

According to long-term studies, over 90% of stock-market profits can be traced to the first two steps—finding the right time to buy and the right industries. Selecting individual stocks has a much smaller effect on the investment results.

Similarly, you need to take a top-down approach to buying

any type of health-care insurance. The purpose of insurance is to cut risks, so you should start with your greatest risks:

- What happens if I'm hospitalized and run up a huge bill for a series of operations?
- What happens if I'm injured or so ill that I can't work any longer and never earn any more income?
- What happens if I go into a nursing home and stay there, alive but not well, for 10 years or longer?

Any of these situations can be financially ruinous. Those are your greastest risks when it comes to health-care finances. So those are the risks you must have covered when you buy insurance.

After you have your "top" risks covered, you can move down the pyramid. In order to save money, check the available policy features to see which ones you can do without. To cut your annual out-of-pocket costs, adjust deductibles and coinsurance and stop-loss points. It's fine to save money on health insurance as long as you know you're protected in case of a catastrophe.

BUZZ WORDS

You don't need to become an insurance expert to buy the right policies. However, you need to know a few key words and insurance-related expressions:

- *Deductible.* What you pay first. A "$100 deductible" means that you pay the first hundred dollars before the insurance company pays anything.

- *Coinsurance or copayment.* What you pay next. Typically it's a share of subsequent expenses. With a $100 deductible and a 20% coinsurance, for example, you pay the first $100 and 20% of all subsequent medical bills.

- *Stop-loss.* Your maximum exposure. With a $2,000 stop-loss clause, you wouldn't have to pay more than $2,000 for medical expenses in any one year. After you've paid $2,000, the insurance company picks up the tab.

• *Waiting period.* How long you must pay before the insurance policy takes effect. A disability policy with a 60-day waiting period, for example, means that you have to be out of the work force for 60 days before you can start to collect.

There's a simple rule for all these features: The better they are, the more they cost. You pay more, for example, if the waiting period is only 30 days, not 60 days. You also would pay more for a 10% as opposed to a 20% coinsurance provision.

TAX-BRACKET BINGO

When you're insuring for medical care or DI or LTC, buy real insurance. In insurance lingo, skip "first-dollar" coverage and go for "last-dollar" protection.

First-dollar protection, or something close to it, is provided by some companies and government agencies. Virtually all of your health-care costs are covered. You go to the doctor for a $50 checkup, and your employer's health insurance policy picks up the tab.

So when you're looking for your own insurance policy, you may expect the same kind of coverage. If that's the case, you're going to wind up disappointed. First-dollar coverage works, when it's provided by an employer, because of the tax advantages. Employers deduct the premium cost, while the benefits received by employees are not counted as taxable income.

To understand how an employer can afford to provide first-dollar coverage, look at the kind of health insurance that pays for every checkup and aspirin, with all the dollars coming from the employer or an insurance company—the kind of insurance you're sure your neighbor has, so you want the same. (Even if employees pay a token amount, a few hundred dollars per year, they essentially have first-dollar policies.)

Suppose you make $40,000 per year working for a company

with no health insurance coverage. You ask for, and your company says you deserve, a $5,000 raise.

What happens? Suppose you're in the 30% income-tax bracket (including federal, state, and local income taxes):

Increase in income	$5,000
Increase in taxes (@ 30%)	1,500
Net increase in income	3,500

Now, suppose your total health-care expenses are $4,000 per year. So, instead of a $5,000 raise, your company gives you first-dollar health insurance coverage. Because this is considered a tax-free fringe benefit, you owe no income taxes on the benefits you receive under this policy. All of your medical expenses are paid.

Here's the comparison:

A. A $5,000 raise, no health insurance: You increase after-tax income by $3,500 but pay $4,000 in medical costs.
B. No raise, first-dollar health insurance: Your after-tax income is flat, but you pay nothing in medical costs.

As you can see, you're $500 ahead by taking option B. To give you a first-dollar insurance policy, your employer may buy a policy (pay a "premium") from an insurance company. Say that the policy costs $4,500 per year, giving the insurance company a $500 markup for paying your medical bills and shuffling the paper.

This is truly win-win-win:

• You're $500 ahead because your medical costs are all covered.
• Your employer is $500 ahead, paying an insurance company $4,500 rather than giving you a $5,000 raise.
• The insurance company is $500 to the good, receiving $4,500 in premiums and paying $4,000 in medical bills for you.

Who loses? The IRS, which never sees the $1,500 it would have received if you had been given a $5,000 raise. (As you can see, first-dollar health insurance, along with all fringe benefits, isn't really "free." Employees get it instead of cash compensation.)

That's a highly simplified way of how employer-provided health insurance works. Employers and insurers make certain assumptions, which may or may not prove to be accurate. Even if the assumptions are accurate, in the aggregate, they won't hold up for every single employee. Healthy employees wind up subsidizing those with large medical bills.

In the aggregate, though, the premise is that employers pay less, while employees receive more, with the insurance company making money in the middle. First-dollar or near-first-dollar coverage is as much about tax shelter as it is about health insurance.

STICK TO YOUR LAST

The picture changes, though, if you go shopping for your own health insurance. No insurance company is going to sell you a policy for less than it expects to pay out on your behalf. If the insurer expects you to have $4,000 worth of medical bills this year and you want first-dollar coverage, it will charge you more than $4,000, probably much more. Now you're the one out of pocket.

If you need to buy health-care insurance, buy insurance. Pay attention to the last dollar, not the first dollar. Buy protection against physical and financial catastrophes. You want to ensure that you won't get wiped out in an emergency.

Real insurance will have a large deductible, perhaps a couple of thousand dollars, or a long waiting period before the policy takes effect. You're paying the ordinary medical bills, just as you pay ordinary food or housing bills, and carrying an insurance policy in case of unforeseen health-care costs.

Here's how real insurance should work:

1. You, not the insurance company, pay the first dollars, probably the first few thousand dollars.
2. After the insurance kicks in, you pay a certain portion of all the costs.
3. After you reach your stop-loss amount, you're off the hook and the insurance company steps in. For example,

a health insurance policy may cap your family's annual medical expense at $2,000. Once you've spent that $2,000, the insurance company pays the rest, no matter how much it costs. A medical catastrophe won't be compounded by a financial catastrophe.

Why is this kind of insurance better than first-dollar coverage or near-first-dollar coverage? Because it's cheaper. If you want to buy a policy that will pay all of your medical bills, it certainly will be more expensive than a policy that calls for you to pay up to $500 per year.

If you're liable for up to $1,000, your policy will cost even less. And so on. The way policies are priced, you're better off paying a low premium and assuming a certain amount of your medical expenses a year rather than paying a much higher premium for first-dollar coverage.

Dan and Carol, for example, might choose a high-deductible health insurance policy rather than the low-deductible policy from Carol's employer. Or they might join an HMO, which has what amounts to a fixed yearly cost. Instead of paying $6,000 per year for health insurance, they'd likely pay $3,000 or $4,000 a year. The extra $2,000 or $3,000 can be used to buy disability insurance and perhaps to help Dan's mother with nursing-home insurance.

How can you cut your insurance costs and still buy real protection?

1. For health insurance, take the highest deductible you can bear. If you can afford to pay up to $2,000 per year in medical costs, take a $2,000 deductible, for example.

2. The same principle holds in case of a waiting period for disability or LTC. If you can afford to pay your own way for 90 days, take a 90-day waiting period. The higher your deductible and the longer your waiting period, the lower your insurance cost.

3. In health insurance coverage, be sure there's a stop-loss. After you spend a certain amount of money, the insurance company pays the rest. That's the type of insurance protection you really need.

4. In DI or LTC insurance, buy long-term protection. Dis-

abilty benefits should be payable until age 65; LTC benefits, for at least three years.

5. Avoid costly "extras." The insurers create them because they're profitable. That means you pay more than they pay. Only buy policy options truly necessary for disaster protection.

The $50 bill for an office visit should be your responsibility; the $50,000 bill for bypass surgery should be paid by your insurance company.

A Road Map to the
Information You Need
in This Book

Making the right decisions about any kind of insurance isn't easy, and that's especially true for health-care insurance. Some insurance companies want you to be confused; that way, you're more likely to buy whatever they have to offer.

But health-care insurance isn't theoretical math or abstract philosophy. Like all insurance, it's a contract: You pay so much to the insurance company, which will pay out certain sums in certain circumstances. As long as you can figure out those circumstances—when they'll pay and when they won't—and the amounts involved, you'll know how a health-care policy works.

That's what's in this book—the information you need to make decisions on health-care insurance. But not everyone needs to read every word, riveting as they all may be. To help you truly "Save Thousands on Your Health-Care Insurance," here's a step-by-step walk-through of what you need to know:

There are three main sections in the book, each one dedicated to a specific type of health-care insurance you may need to prevent a financial catastrophe.

I. Health Insurance

II. Disability Income (DI) Insurance

III. Long-Term-Care (LTC) Insurance

Each one needs to be considered separately, for there's no automatic connection. You may, for example, work for a company that provides you with superb health insurance, but you may have skimpy DI insurance and no coverage at all for LTC. Therefore, you need to approach this book one section at a time.

HEALTH INSURANCE

Everyone, no matter what his or her personal situation, needs adequate health insurance. Without the right card in your wallet, you probably won't make it past the receptionist at your hospital or doctor's office.

Situation 1: You're an employee of a company or some other organization that provides you with health insurance (or you're covered through your spouse's employer).

Start with chapters 1–5. You'll learn what you've got and what you haven't got. You may, in some cases, find that your employer provides you with first-rate health insurance: You may be vulnerable for a few hundred or a few thousand dollars a year, but your coverage protects you against a catastrophic loss. If that's the case, you can skip the rest of this section and move on to DI insurance (although you may want to see whether your parents' Medicare coverage is adequate, in chapters 11–13).

Situation 2: You find out, after reading chapters 1–5, that the health insurance you have from your employer, or your spouse's employer, doesn't cover all possible emergencies.

Situation 3: Your employer doesn't offer health insurance, or you've decided not to pay for the coverage that's offered. Either way, neither you nor your spouse is covered by health insurance from an employer or by any other group coverage.

Situation 4: You're self-employed and therefore responsible for lining up your own health insurance.

If you're in situations 2, 3, or 4, go on to chapters 6–8, which show you how to shop for health insurance, whether you need full coverage or just a policy to supplement what you have from your employer. The idea is to buy the least (and least expensive) amount of health insurance you'll need to protect you against disaster. You'll also want to read chapter 14, which has tips on dealing with health insurance paperwork.

Situation 5: Your employer (or your spouse's employer) asks you to choose between a traditional "fee-for-service" or "indemnity" plan, a health maintenance organization (HMO), or preferred provider organization (PPO).

In situation 5, you should read chapter 9, on HMOs, and chapter 10, on PPOs. The same is true if you're in situation 3 or 4, shopping for your own health insurance. For some people, an HMO or PPO can be a sensible alternative to traditional health insurance.

Situation 6: You're 65 or older, eligible for Medicare.

Situation 7: You're going to be eligible for Medicare within the next few years.

Situation 8: You have a parent (or someone else you're concerned about) in situation 6 or 7.

If you're in any of these three situations, go right to chapters 11–13. They explain what you'll get—and what you won't get—from Medicare. Because Medicare doesn't cover everything, supplementary coverage ("Medigap" insurance) is needed. You or your parent may have Medigap coverage from an employer or another group. If not, these chapters explain how to buy genuine protection. The Medigap area has been marked by scandal, which has led to federal regulation, but you still need to be careful not to get ripped off. In these chapters, you'll learn how to spot the bad guys.

DISABILITY INCOME (DI) INSURANCE

After you've finished reading about health insurance, you can turn to DI insurance. Everyone should read chapter 15, which explains how DI insurance works and how to determine whether you need it. Most people are unfamiliar with DI insurance, which has a different purpose from that of health insurance. Instead of payments going to a doctor or a hospital, the money goes directly to you, to make up for income you lose when you can't work.

You may think that you don't need DI insurance because you're covered by workers' compensation, or you may think that Social Security will take care of you. As you'll see in chapter 16, that's probably not the case. Neither workers' compensation nor Social Security is likely to fully make up for lost income, even if you qualify, which is unlikely.

Situation 9: You have substantial liquid assets (hundreds of thousands of dollars you can put your hands on).

Situation 10: You have a sizable pension plan you can tap, if disabled, before you reach retirement age.

Situation 11: Your spouse has a substantial income.

In these three situations, you probably don't need to worry very much about disability, so you can move on to the next section, on LTC insurance. But what if your cash flow isn't so secure?

Situation 12: You rely on DI coverage from your employer.

In chapter 17, you'll learn how to evaluate the coverage you have from your company or organization. Group plans often have severe disadvantages. Nevertheless, if you're satisfied with that coverage, go on to the section on LTC.

Situation 13: You decide your employer's DI coverage is inadequate.

Situation 14: You don't have any DI coverage, and you decide you need it.

In these two situations, turn to chapters 18–20. There you'll find a buyer's guide to DI insurance as well as suggestions for cutting the cost.

After you've resolved your concerns about DI insurance, you can turn to the next section, on LTC.

LONG-TERM-CARE (LTC) INSURANCE

The expression "long-term care" generally refers to care for the elderly when they can no longer take care of themselves. Older people may need someone to help them in their daily lives, even if they're not sick enough to be hospitalized. And such care may be needed for many years.

There are two basic varieties of LTC. One is at-home care, either in the home of the older person or in the home of a middle-aged son or daughter, niece or nephew, or other relative. The middle-aged person can provide care by himself or herself and thus save on direct costs.

But that's not always a feasible solution. Middle-aged relatives often have their own families or jobs (or both), so they can't—or don't want to—provide full-time care for an aging parent. At that point, professional help is needed, full- or part-time. That's when expenses begin.

In some families, at-home care isn't possible, so the older relative has to go into an institution, generally known as a nursing home. Nursing homes vary, from the purely custodial to those that provide skilled medical care. Expenses vary, too, but you can expect the costs to run over $25,000 per year for any kind of decent nursing home.

If your parents are no longer alive, you have no other elderly relatives to care for, and you yourself are many years from retirement age, you probably don't need to bother with LTC insurance. You're better off devoting your efforts to making enough money so you can afford your own nursing-home bills, if that time comes.

Most people, though, are concerned with LTC, either for their aging parents or, in a few years, for themselves. If you're in that category, you should read chapter 21, which explains why more and more people wind up in nursing homes and why the resources you may have been relying on—Medicare, Social Security, health insurance—probably won't do much to help you with LTC.

Indeed, the options most people have are bleak. They can pay for their own LTC, at $25,000 per year and up. Or they can give away their assets (impoverish themselves) so they can qualify for Medicaid, which is a federal-state welfare program that often buys inferior care.

> *Situation 15:* You or your parents are so comfortably fixed that spending $25,000, $30,000, or more per year for an indefinite time period won't bother you. And you or your parents aren't concerned about how doing so might deplete the estate that will be passed on to the next generation.

If you're rich enough, paying for LTC isn't a major concern. You can skip the rest of this section. But most people probably will find it hard to come up with $25,000 per year, or more, for nursing-home care.

> *Situation 16:* You're 65 or older, an age when you may soon be a candidate for LTC. You don't want to burden your children, but you don't know how you'll come up with $25,000 or more every year.

> *Situation 17:* You'd like to leave whatever assets you've accumulated to your children, not to some nursing-home operator.

> *Situation 18:* You're approaching the age when LTC will be a possibility, with no relatives likely to take care of you. You'd like to assure yourself a comfortable stay at a reputable nursing home.

> *Situation 19:* You're caught between your aging parents and your school-age children. You want to provide for your parents, whose means are modest, but you can't spare the time for personal at-home care or the money for institutional care.

> *Situation 20:* Although you're a long way from your own retirement, you don't want to burden your own children with your LTC, when the time comes.

In any of these situations, 16–20, LTC insurance is worth looking into, so you should read chapters 22 and 23. They describe policies designed specifically to cover LTC costs. If LTC is never needed, you'll never collect on these policies. They are "insurance" policies in the purest sense, just like health insurance policies designed to cover catastrophic costs.

Although LTC policies are relatively new, they've already provided newspapers and magazines with any number of juicy exposés. These chapters not only serve as a buyer's guide; they tell you how to avoid fraudulent schemes.

Chapter 24 is a companion piece to chapters 22 and 23. You may not want to buy an LTC policy that may never pay off. Instead, you may be able to buy life insurance with a "long-term care rider." This policy allows you to siphon off some of the life insurance benefits that otherwise would be paid to your beneficiaries on your death and use that money for your LTC. Of course, it also reduces the life insurance eventually paid to your beneficiaries.

Finally, read chapter 25 on Medicaid planning. There you'll find a strategy that uses insurance to keep your assets in your hands as long as possible, yet enables you to use Medicaid in case of a long nursing-home stay.

After you've completed all three sections, you'll likely realize that you need some kind of health-care insurance. Where do you go next?

There's no one in a better position to help than an agent who knows about health and DI and LTC insurance. Unfortunately, very few insurance agents really understand all these areas; many just want to sell policies, and the bigger the better.

So turn now to appendix A. There you'll learn how to find the good agents. More than that, you'll find out what you need to tell your agent so you'll be sure to wind up with the right coverage.

Appendix B is optional. If you're a do-it-yourselfer when it comes to financial matters (you research your own no-load mutual funds, for example, or you book your own travel reservations), this appendix is for you. It lists the names and phone numbers of selected insurance companies for each of the three sections in this book. You can comparison shop on your own and decide which policies make sense for you.

But if you're not so diligent, you don't need to read this appendix. Just give it to the agent you've chosen, after reading appendix A, and let him or her do the investigation and earn the commissions you're going to pay. Why should you do all the work yourself?

Part I

HEALTH INSURANCE

Chapter 1

No More Mr. Nice Guys

Recently, it has become fashionable to talk—with either nostalgia or derision—of the "Ozzie and Harriet 1950s," when Dad worked outside, and Mom worked inside, the house. When discussing health insurance, though, the better image is the "Archie Bunker 1970s." Just 20 years ago it was widely assumed that anybody who worked had health insurance. Archie and Edith and Gloria and Meathead were all covered by their employer or their spouse's employer when they went to the hospital or to a doctor's office.

Employer-provided health care, however, is a recent and, as it is turning out, short-lived phenomenon. For most of our nation's history, few people had any health insurance at all. Fortunately, few people needed any. If you went to see a doctor, he or she would examine you and perhaps give you an injection or a prescription. The charge would be a relatively few dollars, and you would probably pay in cash.

About the only way you could run up a much larger bill was to be hospitalized for any length of time. Some fraternal orders, such as the Masons, provided insurance against disasters of this nature. In the 1930s, the first Blue Cross organizations were founded. These nonprofit groups, formed by doctors and hospitals, were mainly in the business of providing insurance against expensive hospital stays.

A TAX SHELTER EVEN THE *IRS* COULD LOVE

The seeds of the new era were sown in the early days of World War II. Wages were frozen, so some labor unions suggested they receive health insurance instead. The federal government agreed, and the idea of employer-provided health insurance, rather than cash compensation, was born.

After World War II and into the mid-1960s, employer-provided health insurance grew slowly. Most policies were simply protection against hospital bills; Blue Cross (and, later, Blue Shield) continued to dominate the field.

Then two major events changed the landscape. First, employers and employees negotiated contracts in which *all* forms of health care, not just hospital bills, would be insured under employer-provided health insurance plans. Increasingly, health insurance became a savvy way to beat the tax code.

Suppose General Motors gave John Jones a $100 raise. John might owe $40 in income taxes, leaving him only $60 to spend. If he went to see a doctor and the doctor charged him $80, John was $20 behind.

Now suppose GM gave John a health insurance policy that would pay that $80 doctor's bill in full. Even if the insurance cost GM $90, the company was still $10 ahead—better to pay $90 to an insurance company than to pay John $100 in extra wages. Health insurance, moreover, is a tax-free fringe benefit under the Internal Revenue Code. So John was better off with $80 worth of health insurance than with a $60 after-tax raise.

Everybody—GM, John, the insurance company—was happy with the new system. GM, and thousands of companies like it, began providing their John and Jane Joneses with more and more health insurance instead of salaries and wages. Government agencies, too, found that they could cut labor costs by giving employees tax-free health insurance, not taxable cash.

What did the IRS say about all this? Nary a discouraging word. After all, IRS agents and policymakers work for the government, so they enjoy tax-free fringes as much as anyone. Besides, most of the money not paid in taxable salaries or wages was diverted to doctors, who made so much money they all wound up in the top tax bracket, anyway. That's who the IRS collected from.

UNCLE SAM PAYS THE BILL

About the same time as employers were substituting health insurance for compensation, the second major event was unfolding in Washington, D.C. As part of President Lyndon Johnson's "Great Society," Medicare and Medicaid were created in 1965. The former provides health insurance for the elderly, paid for by the federal government, while the latter is a poverty program funded by state governments as well as by Uncle Sam.

The creation of Medicare and Medicaid, in addition to the spread of employer-provided health insurance, meant that most Americans had health-care coverage. Now nearly 75% of the population is covered by Medicare, Medicaid, or an employer's plan. What's more, these plans cover most forms of health-care treatment, not just hospital bills. Through the late 1960s and most of the 1970s, Americans got used to the idea that they're entitled to health insurance, paid for by someone else.

Not all health insurance plans were the same, of course. Some were "first-dollar" plans. You just waved your card at the doctor's receptionist and had carte blanche to all available services. The insurance would pay all the bills, from the first dollar on, or nearly so. These plans tended to be offered by the biggest employers, including governments, and by employers who negotiated with the most powerful unions.

Other plans weren't so generous. Some employees had to put out dollars of their own through deductible or coinsurance (cost-sharing) or partial-premium payments. But, on the whole, these contributions were modest. Basically, if you were employed, or your spouse was employed, your family was protected against health-care expenses.

ABOUT-FACE

That's no longer the case. In 1991, the *New York Times* reported that 33 million Americans—13% of the population—have no health insurance. No employer-sponsored coverage, no private insurance, no Medicare, no Medicaid. "Most of the uninsured are jobholders and their family members," according to the *Times*. (Some estimates of the number of uninsured Americans are as high as 37 million, in 1992.)

Moreover, even those who are covered may not be as well covered as before. With few exceptions, first-dollar coverage has practically disappeared, and those exceptions likely will become even fewer. Employees are paying more. A. Foster Higgins, an employee benefits firm, reports that single employees paid an average of $35 per month—over $400 per year—in health insurance premiums in 1991. For family coverage, the average monthly contribution was $101, or over $1,200 per year. Instead of a tax-free fringe benefit, even the best employer health insurance plans have become a cash drain.

The *Wall Street Journal* reported that "Benefits Must Go, Not Grow." William F. Wayland, executive vice-president, human resources, Textron, Inc., told the *Journal* in 1990 that health care is the "single most important cost issue" facing employers and employees. "We are paying $3,200 or $3,300 or $3,500 a year per employee and the Japanese are paying virtually nothing. . . . From basic health-care coverage, prescription drugs were added, and mental health was added, and then dental was added, and then hearing was added. . . . Then they started peeling them away again."

In other words, companies aren't just going to add $50 to your deductible or raise your coinsurance from 10% to 20%. In addition, they're going to strip away benefits employees have come to count on.

Suppose you have a teenage child with a drug- or alcohol-abuse problem. Many companies provide coverage now for treatment in a hospital's psychiatric unit. In the future, you may have to foot those bills yourself, if your employer "peels away" mental-health coverage. Average cost per admission: $18,000.

A DOLLAR FOR DEFENSE, TWO DOLLARS FOR HEALTH CARE

Why is health insurance coverage shifting into reverse? Because costs have gone out of sight. Health-related spending in the United States now accounts for around 12% of our gross national product (GNP), up from 5% in 1960. At more than $660 billion in 1990 and an estimated $800-plus billion in 1992, health care consumes twice as many dollars as the entire federal defense budget. In 1991, federal budget director Richard Darman forecast that health-care spending will reach 17% of GNP by the year 2000, as much as we spend on defense, education, and recreation combined.

Health insurance has had to pay a good deal of those hundreds of billions per year, driving up the costs of such insurance. Depending on whose statistics you use, corporate medical bills are rising anywhere from 14% to 22% per year, with more of the same in sight. In 1990, the average cost was about $3,200 per employee per year (see table 1), escalating to more than $3,600 in 1991. That was the average. For some companies, costs topped $4,000 per employee per year.

Looking at it from the companies' perspective, health benefits now cost 14% of total payroll, on average, up from 5% in 1980. For some firms, health insurance may top 20% of payroll—they're paying workers $20,000, for example, plus another $4,000 for health insurance.

Naturally, rising health insurance costs squeeze profits. In 1965, health-care costs were 8% of pretax corporate profits. In 1989, the last year for which data are available, health-care costs were 56% of pretax corporate profits.

WHY HEALTH-CARE COSTS CONTINUE TO SOAR

Why has health-care inflation persisted? Consumers—patients—have no reason to cut back. They pay little or nothing for health care, with "third parties" (employers, insurance companies, government agencies) paying the bills. For employees,

Table 1: GROWTH IN TOTAL HEALTH PLAN COST*
(1985–90)

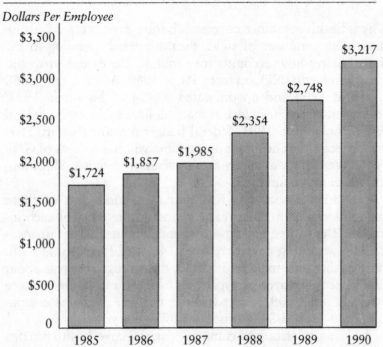

Dollars Per Employee

*Includes employer and employee costs for indemnity plans, HMOs, dental plans, and vision/hearing plans.
Source: A. Foster Higgins & Co., Inc.

if part of their compensation is in the form of health care, there's an incentive to use more, not less, health care.

Doctors, hospitals, and other health-care providers certainly aren't going to turn away business. They'll see as many patients as they can, providing ample treatment and charging as much as the payers will bear.

In addition to this odd "I buy but someone else pays" structure, other factors contribute to runaway health-care costs:

• *High tech.* An experimental bone-marrow treatment might cost $100,000; emergency care for a premature baby might top $400,000; hooking a patient up to a full array of intensive-care electronics might cost $5,000 per day.

Magnetic resonance scanners, marvelous devices that allow physicians to detect abnormalities in the brain, the spine, and other parts of the body, cost from $1 million to $2 million apiece. If you've bought one, you need to charge $600 to $1,000 per visit to recoup your cost. If you're a doctor who has invested in such a scanner, there's a natural inclination to send patients to the clinic where your scanner is, whenever possible.

The latest device, now coming on stream, is the positron emission tomography (PET) scanner, which can observe chemical changes inside your body—it can spot Parkinson's disease at an early stage, for example. The price tag, though, is $5 million; Congress's Office of Technology Assessment says insurance companies will have to pay at least $2,500 per scan.

• *Spillover*. Even the uninsured get sick and see doctors and wind up in hospitals. They may pay something or nothing, but doctors and hospitals still want to get paid for services. They do so by increasing fees to insured patients, boosting the cost of insurance. The National Association of Manufacturers contends that hospitals overcharged employers by $10.8 billion in 1991 to make up for losses on unpaid bills.

At the same time, Medicaid doesn't fully cover the costs of treating the poor. The American Hospital Association puts the annual shortfall at more than $4 billion, which finds its way onto the bills of people who can pay. In New Jersey, for example, every hospital bill contains a surcharge to make up for those bills that don't get paid.

• *Litigation*. Million-dollar malpractice awards barely make the news in these days of $10 million judgments. The surge of suits filed against medical providers drives up costs in two ways. First, doctors and hospitals have to pay huge premiums for malpractice insurance, increasing the overhead that must be covered. Second, "defensive" (read: cover-your-anatomy) medicine has to be practiced, with batteries of extra tests performed, more to protect practitioners against future lawsuits than to diagnose patient ills.

• *Fraud.* With so many billions at stake and so many third parties paying bills long distance, fake billing is inevitable. A 1991 federal investigation found improper, abusive procedures in 20% of the bills submitted by 8,000 doctors who filed Medicare claims for surgery.

When it comes to long distance, it's hard to beat the $9,800 bill for treatment of "severe left-side lobar pneumonia," submitted from a Nigerian hospital to Blue Shield of California. A month later, Blue Shield of California received another bill, for another patient, from another hospital in Nigeria: The treatment and the dollar amount were exactly the same! After an investigation, Blue Shield discovered that a patient and a doctor there had agreed to split the proceeds from a false claim.

Counting everything from international scams to checkups listed as flu treatments, the National Health-Care Anti-Fraud Association, an insurance-industry group, estimates the cost of medical fraud as high as $37.5 billion per year.

• *Demographics.* Modern medicine has been so successful in keeping people alive that the U.S. population is tilting toward the over-65s, over-75s, even over-85s. The over-75s, for example, have grown from 5.6 million in 1960 to 13.2 million in 1990. As people get older, they need more health care. Often the elderly need the most expensive operations.

FUTURE SQUEEZE

The above trends are unlikely to be reversed. Therefore, employers are cutting back on health insurance benefits not only to reduce today's costs but to prevent tomorrow's expenses from going off the charts. In addition, an obscure change in corporate accounting rules is making employers reconsider health insurance benefits.

Many corporations' health-care plans include a promise to pay medical costs for retirees. Historically, companies deducted these expenses as they came due. But in 1990 the Financial Accounting Standards Board (FASB) ruled that companies must estimate future retiree health-care costs and deduct them beforehand. The total cost has been estimated at anywhere from $200 billion to $1 trillion in lower profits. IBM, for example, took a $2.26 billion loss in the beginning of 1991 to account for this obligation, while General Motors estimates its ultimate writeoff at $20 billion! Concern over this issue is so great that CIGNA, a major insurance company, has been taking magazine back covers to advertise, "Will it [new FASB regulations] cost your company your company?"

Corporations generally don't want to report lower profits—that hurts the price of their stock and impairs their ability to borrow money. So you can expect companies to cut back on health benefits for retirees as well as for active employees in order to keep profits from plunging.

UNKIND CUTS

In response to all of the factors, employers have trimmed their health insurance exposure in several ways:

1. Making employees pay more. Not only are employees sharing the premium costs; they now have higher deductibles and greater coinsurance obligations. That is, they have to spend more of their own dollars on medical treatment before the health insurance takes effect. Moreover, even after that point, employees usually pay a portion of the fee.

2. While employees pay more, they're getting less coverage. One area in which cutbacks have been particularly severe is "mental health," which covers psychotherapy and substance-abuse programs. Expenses rose 50% from 1987 to 1989, and employers now pay nearly $20 billion per year on such treatment. Stories are rife of private psychiatric hospitals where the employee's copayment share is winked at or surreptitiously returned so the family will keep the patient in a $600-per-day bed. Therefore, companies are putting annual or lifetime limits on an employee's health-care benefits.

Now, you may think that mental health is one area

that can be cut back without causing a lot of anguish. But suppose your teenage son has a long bout with depression or drug abuse and your health plan has a $25,000 lifetime cap. That's what happened to one Atlanta executive whose son ran up a $200,000 bill in just one 14-month hospital stay. He and his wife have gone through $50,000 in savings and a $60,000 home-equity loan to pay those bills.

3. Many employers are steering employees into "managed care." Here an employer or insurance company cuts a deal with certain doctors or hospitals: We'll send our employees to you if you give us discounts. Employees are encouraged (through lower deductibles and lower co-payments) to use the doctors and hospitals in the network. For the employer, this means lower costs. For employees, it may mean seeing a doctor who's not their first choice or paying more to see their favorite physician.

Many managed-care plans now call for hospital certification, disdainfully known to physicians as "1-800-Captain-May-I?" That is, in 80% of managed-care programs, a doctor has to call the insurer and ask permission before committing a patient to a hospital or recommending a nonemergency operation. Doctors don't like the idea of someone looking over their shoulder, but insurers say it serves notice that doctors need a good reason for hospitalizing patients.

As for employees, if you don't play the managed-care game and get preapproval for major operations, you may wind up paying for all or part of the bill out of your own pocket.

IN BRIEF
- Ten or 20 years ago, most American workers could rely on their employers for solid protection from health-care expenses.
- Since then, health-care inflation has raged, imposing tremendous costs on employers and insurers.
- As a result, employers are making employees pay more for health care.

- Employers also are limiting coverage, excluding psychiatric care, treatment for substance abuse, etc., in some cases.
- Managed-care plans steer employees to selected doctors and hospitals that promise to charge lower fees.

Chapter 2

Why Small Companies Have Big Problems with Health Insurance

Even the largest American corporations are scaling back on the medical benefits they provide to employees. Take Rockwell International, for example. Rockwell is a huge company ($12.5 billion in annual sales, 350,000 employees), exactly the kind you'd expect to provide full health insurance. In the 1970s, in fact, Rockwell paid virtually 100% of its employees' health bills.

Not anymore. Most Rockwell employees now pay $500 a year for their health insurance, plus the first $500 of their family's medical bills. After that, employees pay around 30% of all medical costs, up to an additional $4,000 per family. Thus, a Rockwell employee with family coverage, who might be earning $25,000 or $30,000 per year, may wind up paying as much as $5,000 per year out of his or her own pocket.

Moreover, there are expenses that Rockwell won't cover at all: certain artificial fertility procedures, for example, or radial keratotomy to correct nearsightedness. Employees must pay these costs themselves.

Singling out Rockwell doesn't mean it's the only company with such practices. Far from it. Virtually all large companies, threatened by rising health-care costs, are asking employees to share more of the burden. From 1980 to 1990, employees' portion of the costs paid for health insurance rose from 20% to 31%.

NAKED BUNCH

Nevertheless, if you work for a large corporation or government agency, chances are you have decent health insurance. If you work for a small company, chances are that you don't.

Small companies typically face higher costs for health insurance than large ones because they don't have the negotiating clout. Moreover, in a small company, one high-risk employee can cause an enormous increase in premiums. One Salt Lake City couple, for example, had their health insurance through a small music company they own. The husband was in an auto accident in 1988 and needed two back operations. When the company's health insurance policy came up for renewal, premiums for the couple went from $600 per month to $1,200 a month—over $14,000 per year.

As you'd suspect, some small companies meet this sort of problem by not offering health insurance at all, leaving workers and their families exposed to medical costs. According to the latest statistics, among firms with 1,000 or more employees, 72% of employees have employer-provided health insurance. Among companies with fewer than 25 employees, employers provide health insurance to only 29% of their workers.

But small companies have to compete with large ones for employees, so many of them would like to offer health insurance. How can they offer it without busting their budgets? A few tactics have been tried.

Bare-Bones Insurance

Prodded by associations representing small companies, some states have relaxed their laws to permit stripped-down plans. Suppose a state has a law requiring that all company health plans offer, at the least, benefits A–G. This "full-service" plan may be rather expensive.

However, that state may pass another law saying that small companies can offer health plans with only A, C, F, and G. These plans give workers some coverage, and they're less expensive for the companies. Both the Health Insurance Association of America and the Blue Cross & Blue Shield Association have proposed small-company plans (for companies with up to 25 employees) that would include basic doctor visits and surgery but not mental-health, substance-abuse, or high-tech infertility treatments.

At least 24 states have already eased their rules in order to allow bare-bones health insurance, with more sure to come. In Virginia, where the average health insurance cost for an employer is about $130 per employee per month, bare-bones coverage is expected to average $80 per employee. In Oklahoma, the range is expected to be from $25 to $125 per employee, depending on age. Missouri Blue Cross/Blue Shield offers a plan for $30 a month that covers $50 worth of emergency-room costs, $50 of prescription drugs, 10 hospital days, well-baby care, and $500 worth of doctors' bills (after a copayment of $10 per visit).

How do bare-bones plans stack up? Their very name indicates their limits. To get a lower rate, employers provide less coverage. If that cutback is something you need—treatment of a child's drug-abuse problem, perhaps—you may have a major hole in your safety net through which all your assets could fall. Some bare-bones plans have caps on coverage as low as $50,000. That won't provide much protection in case of a medical catastrophe.

Joining Forces

Another tack for small employers is to join a pool. Why does IBM get such a good deal on insurance? Because insurers expect to make money administering a plan with thousands of workers. So if 100 small companies get together and they each have 50 workers, that's 5,000 workers to cover, enough to tempt insurance companies that wouldn't be interested in 50-worker companies one at a time. Thus, small companies have banded together to join MEWAs (multiemployer welfare associations) for strength in numbers.

Employee Leasing

Taking the pool idea one step further is the idea of employee leasing. If you're an employer, you have more things to worry about than health insurance. You have to handle all the book-keeping for your employees, including payroll taxes and with-holding. You may have to pay workers' compensation insurance. For a small company, which probably can't afford a full-time employee-benefits manager, all of this responsibility is usually dumped on the shoulders of an already overworked clerk or manager.

That's why such companies turn to employee leasing. Take the Johnson Press, which employs 20 people. As of tomor-row, all of those 20 employees no longer work for Johnson Press; they work for Smith Lease-A-Body. Outwardly, there's little difference. The 20 employees show up at Johnson Press every day for work, and they do whatever jobs they had before.

On paper, though, Johnson Press no longer has any em-ployees. Instead, it sends one check every week or two weeks or month to Smith Lease-A-Body. Now the employees' pay-checks come from Smith Lease-A-Body. Smith, in turn, handles all the paperwork.

As you can see, Smith is another small-company pool. Per-haps it has similar arrangements with 50 companies and a couple of thousand employees on its payroll. Smith now can negotiate health insurance and workers' compensation for all of these employees, getting big-group rates. Although the cost ultimately is born by Johnson Press and 50 others like it, the rates are lower than what Johnson Press could negotiate on its own. Plus, Johnson avoids all the aggravating and time-consuming paper-work.

Employee leasing sounds exotic, but it isn't. The *Wall Street Journal* reports that thousands of small companies use leased employees and as many as 2 million U.S. workers are on lease.

PIPE DREAM

Each of these ideas has some merit, at least in theory. The practice, though, may not be so admirable. Take employee leasing, for example. At least some employee-leasing firms are fraudulent: They take money but never place insurance with any insurance companies. Claims may be paid out of the money received from client companies. At some point, though, these phony leasing firms walk away, and employees are left holding a stack of medical bills no one will pay.

That's what seems to have happened to Tony McGehee, an Oklahoma oil-derrick worker. Back in 1988, hundreds of pounds of drilling pipe fell on him, damaging his spine. His employer, he learned, was not the oil-drilling company but an Oklahoma City leasing firm.

The leasing firm, it turned out, had "bought" insurance from an insurance company based in Barbados that had no other customers; the head of the leasing firm was a director of the insurance company. The insurer, moreover, wasn't even licensed to sell insurance in Oklahoma.

CHECKUP

How can you check on a MEWA or leasing firm that's carrying your health insurance?

1. Find out who's running it and what business experience they've had. Look into their reputations.
2. Ask to see its financial statements. (They should be audited by a reputable accounting firm.) Look for profitability and substantial net worth.
3. Check the policy or ask your company's insurance agent exactly who is providing the insurance.
4. Find out if there are knowledgeable outsiders on the MEWA's or the leasing firm's board of trustees to keep an eye on operations.
5. Call your state's insurance department to find out if the firm is licensed and contributing to a state guarantee fund.

Before Tony McGehee could collect any benefits, the leasing company filed for bankruptcy. Three years after his accident, he had lost his home, his truck, his wife (who left him), and his child, and he couldn't afford surgery to ease his pain. According to state insurance regulators, many injured or ill workers around the United States suffer from similar conditions.

Certainly not all employee-leasing firms are frauds. But if you work for a company that now leases you instead of employs you, you may be vulnerable to chicanery or incompetence on the part of the leasing firm.

The same is true of situations in which you're still employed by your company but the health insurance has been farmed out to a MEWA. Many MEWAs are legitimate, but there are more than a few exceptions. One insurance commissioner says that "many employers haven't a clue what they bought," while another says some MEWAs "keep taking people's money and not paying claims." Recently, the federal government has filed charges of MEWA abuses in North Carolina and Florida. According to press reports, hundreds of thousands of workers and their families have been stuck with tens of millions of dollars in unpaid medical bills.

Federal law permits MEWAs to be established but does not regulate them. No federal law forces a MEWA to register or set aside reserve funds. That's left up to state regulators, who often don't know that a MEWA exists until consumer complaints start to come in. Sometimes federal and state regulators point fingers at each other, but no one effectively addresses reported problems.

Therefore, if your employer-provided health insurance is through a MEWA, you may not have the health protection you thought you had. That's especially the case if the MEWA or employee-leasing firm is "self-insuring" health care. You may receive a great-looking card from the Travelers Corp., say, which is administering the plan, but the real insurer may be another entity with few assets. The Travelers Corp., in fact, was caught up in such a situation, with millions of dollars in question and three executives of Cap Staffing, a North Carolina leasing firm, pleading guilty to mail fraud, embezzlement, and conspiracy.

CHECKUP

How can you find out if your employer self-insures for health care?

1. Don't assume your health insurance is from New York Life or Prudential or a similar big-name insurer just because you receive a glossy booklet with that insurer's imprint on it. Many self-insurers hire insurance companies to administer health-care plans but not to provide coverage. Ask to see a copy of the policy to find out who the insurer really is.

2. If you find you're in a self-insurance plan, look into your employer's finances. Check the latest income statement for profitability and the balance sheet for substantial net worth. If you have doubts, discuss the situation with your employer and with someone you know who's savvy about financial matters.

3. Ask for evidence of catastrophic coverage. If your employer has bought stop-loss protection, an insurance policy exists. You should see it, or a copy of it. Just to make sure it's been renewed, ask to see the policy each year.

4. If you can't derive comfort from your employer's financial condition and a stop-loss policy, consider buying your own insurance or covering your family through your spouse's employer.

DOING IT THEMSELVES

Self-insurance is by no means limited to employee-leasing firms or MEWAs. If you have health insurance from your employer, chances are the insurance actually is provided by your employer rather than Aetna or Equitable or Metropolitan Life. As of 1990, over half of all U.S. employees with employer-provided health insurance work for companies that self-insure benefits.

Whan a company self-insures, it simply holds on to the insurance premiums rather than paying them to an insurance company. When claims are made, the employer pays them. Employers that self-insure enjoy certain advantages, especially an exemption from state-mandated benefits.

For example, your state may have a law that all health insurance policies must include chiropractic care. (Some states mandate hair transplants, herbal therapy, or sperm-bank deposits.) Your employer wants to offer you a package without chiropractic care, which it thinks costs more than it's worth. By self-insuring, it can offer you a chiropractic-free health insurance plan.

In most cases, self-insurers are allowed such exemptions, even if they take out insurance against catastrophic claims. Peerless Pumps might pay The New England a relatively small premium, for example, for catastrophic coverage with a $100,000 stop-loss. If one of its employees contracts a rare blood disease and runs up more than a million dollars' worth of hospital bills, The New England will pay the excess $900,000. But if no catastrophes of this magnitude occur, Peerless Pumps will pay all of the health insurance claims out of its own pocket.

For the employee, you can see the risk involved. Your health coverage may be backed only by your employer's promise. If the company goes out of business, you may be out of health insurance. Or, in case of a catastrophe, you may not collect if your employer has neglected to buy stop-loss protection.

IN BRIEF
- Small companies have higher health insurance costs than big companies.
- As a result, many small companies don't offer health-care insurance. Other small companies are turning to bare-bones insurance, employee leasing, and multiemployer groups to reduce premiums for health care.
- Your coverage may have gaps that will expose you to huge medical bills. That's especially true if your coverage is provided by a small company.
- Many employers "self-insure" health-care plans.
- If your health insurance is from an employer that self-insures or is provided by a MEWA or an employee-leasing firm, you need to check the plan's financial strength.

Chapter 3

Traditional Employer Policies: Fee-for-Service

Just because your employer provides you with health insurance doesn't mean you're well covered. There may be dangerous gaps in the policy you're offered.

In many cases, your company will split the cost with you. That is, you'll be asked to pay part of the premium, a cost that may be as much as a few hundred dollars per month. Should you pay it? Not if you can get better coverage for less elsewhere.

You may have a choice of health insurance plans from which to select. Or you and your spouse both may be employed and have a choice of two health-care plans. How can you decide where you're going to get the best coverage for the lowest cost?

No matter what your specific situation, you need to check over your employer's policy carefully before deciding if you want to pay (or continue to pay) the premiums. The first step is to look at the policy. If you're already enrolled in the plan, you probably have a policy tucked away next to your 1987 tax returns. If you don't already participate or can't find your policy, ask whoever administers the health insurance plan at your company for a copy you can inspect. (If you can't get hold of a policy to inspect, that's not an encouraging sign.)

Most companies (75% of large and midsized employers) offer traditional "fee-for-service" or "indemnity" health insurance. You go to the doctor of your choice, and the insurer helps pay the bill. (Health maintenance organizations [HMOs] and preferred provider organizations [PPOs], in which your choice of physicians is limited, are covered in chapter 10).

After you have the policy, read it. The policy shouldn't require a law degree to decipher. If the coverage is worth paying for, you should be able to determine what it is.

WHAT'S COVERED

In a traditional plan, the major points to look for are hospital and doctor benefits. Obviously, they are the heart of your health insurance.

Hospital Benefits

If you're admitted to the hospital, you should be covered for:

• Room and board. A good policy will specify a semiprivate room, paid in full. There should not be a cap, such as $300 or $400 per day. There may, however, be a time limit (perhaps 30 days) on how long a policy will pay if you need physical therapy or rehabilitation in a hospital after an operation.

• Miscellaneous charges, including nursing care.

• Surgeon's fees, including anesthesiologists and assistants.

• In-hospital doctors's visits.

• Intensive care. Sometimes this care is capped. A policy might pay, for example, three times the rate for a semiprivate room in the hospital.

If you expect to have children (or more children), maternity care obviously is important to you. So look closely at this coverage when you inspect your policy.

Childbirth expenses may or may not be treated the same as other medical costs. A trend recently has been to provide health care for problem pregnancies but not for routine deliveries. If you want coverage for these deliveries, you'll need a "rider," a special feature added to the basic policy.

Maternity-care riders have some drawbacks. They may be expensive and include caps on coverage. Perhaps you'll pay $1,000 per year for a rider with a $2,500 cap. Considering that a routine delivery can cost $4,000 or more, you may wind up paying most of this cost.

Few insurance policies are going to extend maternity coverage if a pregnancy is already under way. To the insurer, that's a sure claim. Often maternity riders call for no benefits the first year, 50% of the cap the second year, and full coverage thereafter.

Another point to check: Does your policy cover "well-baby care" in the hospital and after childbirth?

Doctor Benefits

Outside of a hospital, routine doctor visits and checkups probably won't be covered. If they are, you're probably paying for them through superhigh premiums. However, a good health-care policy will cover doctor visits in connection with accident or illness. It also may cover:

- Diagnostic X rays and lab tests.
- Presurgical testing and second opinions.
- Ambulatory surgery in approved facilities.
- Mammography screening. Recently, the national Blue Cross & Blue Shield Association announced it would offer coverage for breast cancer tests as well as some other screening procedures (high blood pressure, Pap smears, cholesterol, and so on). The estimated extra cost is $36 per year per person, $90 for a family. Other health insurers likely will offer similar plans.
- Nursing-home stays. It's doubtful that any health insurance policy will cover "custodial" nursing-home stays, where care mainly consists of maintaining regular living

functions (see page 225). However, a health insurance policy may cover up to a year's stay in a "skilled-care" nursing home, where medical treatment is necessary, following discharge from a hospital.

- Chemotherapy and radiation therapy.
- Kidney dialysis.
- Prosthetic devices.
- Organ transplants. There may be limits on this coverage.
- Physical therapy. Outside of a hospital, coverage may be expanded to 90 visits.
- Home health care. Even without a hospital stay, some policies will cover visits by a nurse, physical therapist, etc. Home health care costs about half as much as a hospital stay, so many insurance companies encourage such care.
- Private-duty nursing. Some policies will cover, say, up to $5,000 per year.
- Chiropractic care. A policy might pay, say, 50% of costs, up to $40 per visit, up to $1,000 per year.

Other Coverage

In addition to hospital and doctor coverage, traditional fee-for-service insurance may cover most or all of the following:

- *Mental and nervous.* There are often two separate coverages here. Patients admitted to a hospital or other institution may be covered only for a certain number of days per year, with coverage limited to a certain dollar amount per year. Plus, there may be a lifetime cap of $10,000 or $20,000 per individual.

An outpatient (someone visiting a psychiatrist, for example) may have an entirely different schedule—perhaps the insurance will pay 50% of the cost, up to $50 per visit, up to $1,000 per year.

This category often covers treatment for drug and alcohol addiction.

- *Dental.* Some policies will cover routine office visits; others will cover orthodontia. You may find a separate deductible here (say, $50 per year) and a maximum on payments (perhaps

$1,000 per year). For some major dental procedures, you may have to wait 12 months after the policy is in effect to have the work done if you want insurance to pay for it.

• *Prescription drugs.* Often there is some sort of cost-sharing arrangement.

• *Accidents.* Some policies will pay several hundred dollars if you're injured in an accident, regardless of deductibles or coinsurance.

• *Disability coverage.* Most health insurance policies are not intended to provide a replacement for lost income if you can't work. For that, you need separate disability income (DI) insurance (see part II). However, some health-care policies pay a limited amount, say, $350 per week for 26 weeks.

Major Medical and Hospital-Surgical Policies

Often a policy will be called either a "major medical" or "hospital-surgical" policy. Hospital-surgical policies, as the name implies, mainly cover costs incurred in a hospital. There may, moreover, be significant expenses incurred in a hospital that are not covered by these plans. Some policies have fairly low caps on coverage.

Major medical policies are more far-ranging: They often cover doctor visits, assistant surgeons' fees, and other costs not included in hospital-surgical plans. However, major medical plans tend to be more expensive and impose charges such as deductibles and coinsurance. The best hospital-surgical plans require no deductible and little coinsurance.

WHAT'S NOT COVERED

You definitely should look for the section on "Exclusions and Limitations" in your policy, because that will tell you what's *not* covered. Usually, the main limit will be on the following:

Preexisting Conditions

A preexisting condition is a health problem you had when you bought the policy. If you need a carotid endarterectomy (surgery on neck arteries that can cost $9,000), you can't expect to buy health insurance on Wednesday and get reimbursed for a procedure that takes place the next Thursday.

Generally, a health insurance policy defines a preexisting condition as one that was treated within a certain period of time (12 months, 6 months) before you bought the policy. Usually, if you didn't seek treatment but *should* have sought treatment, that will count as a preexisting condition. In some policies, a preexisting condition never will be covered. (It will be specifically excluded.)

Other policies require a waiting period of around a year for preexisting conditions. That is, if you have a hernia when you buy the insurance, you have to wait for a year before the operation to get coverage.

Read this section carefully, because policies vary widely in their treatment of preexisting conditions. In some cases, if you fully disclose your condition on the application form and there's no specific exclusion, there won't be a waiting period. Also, sometimes a replacement health insurance policy will pick up coverage from the preceding policy, eliminating or reducing the waiting period.

Preauthorization

Often a policy won't cover surgery, or even a nonsurgical hospital stay, unless it's authorized in advance by a representative of the insurance company. Effectively, that's another way to limit costs.

WHAT TO CONSIDER
WHEN YOU COMPARE POLICIES

Let's look at some of the points you need to keep in mind when you compare policies, beyond what they cover.

Deductible

How much will you have to pay before the insurance kicks in? A "$250 deductible," for example, means that you pay the first $250 of medical expenses. After that, the insurance takes effect. Generally, the deductible starts over at the beginning of each calendar year. In some plans, though, deductibles are "per cause," so each health condition has its own deductible.

Suppose you have a calendar year $250 deductible and you spend $2,000 on health care in 1992. You would pay $250; the next $1,750 would be covered by insurance. (That doesn't mean that the next $1,750 would be *paid* by the insurance company; usually you'd be responsible for 20% of the covered costs.)

In 1993, though, you'd start over, paying the first $250 of your medical costs. If the deductible is "per cause," though, you may not have to pay a new deductible for continued treatment of the same condition. The 1993 deductible would kick in only if you sought treatment for medical conditions you didn't have in 1992.

If you're insuring for a family, you have to know how the deductible works for the various members. If it's $250 per person, it might be $500 or $750 for the entire family. Say it's $500 (calendar year) and Dad uses his $250 for treatment of a kidney stone, while Mom spends $250 treating a sprained ankle. That's the family's $500 deductible: If Junior comes down with pneumonia that year, his treatment would be covered without a further deductible.

In some policies, though, each person has his or her own deductible: You pay for Dad's first $250 each year, Mom's first $250 each year, Junior's first $250, etc. Only then does the insurance coverage begin.

Coinsurance

The percentage you'll pay of covered medical costs is called coinsurance. The norm is 20%, so if you choose 10% coinsurance, or even 0%, you'll pay markedly higher premiums. (Sometimes the industry lingo is "80%" or "90%" coinsurance, but that refers to the company's obligation, not yours.)

A policy may have different deductibles and different coinsurance for different aspects of health care. The basic "major medical" coverage may call for a $500 family deductible and 20% coinsurance. However, psychiatric care in a hospital might only cover 50%, and the insurance will stop paying after $3,000 per year or $10,000 in a lifetime. Prescription drugs might require a $5 deductible on each prescription.

Stop-Loss

This is one of the most important questions to ask when you shop for health insurance. A stop-loss is designed to protect you from steep financial losses.

Today it's not unusual to run up a $100,000 bill for, say, a bypass operation. Even if the insurance company picks up 80%, your 20% share could hit you with a $20,000 bill.

Let's say that your policy contains a "$5,000 stop-loss." That can be read two ways. It may mean that you pay your deductible plus your 20% coinsurance of the next covered charges until your total expense for the year is $5,000. After that, the insurance coverage will be 100%.

Or it may mean you pay your coinsurance on $5,000 worth of medical bills. Thereafter, the insurance company pays everything. As you can imagine, it's vital to understand whether your family's maximum financial exposure for a year is $1,500 or $5,000.

Again, you need to know what the *family* stop-loss is. If one person's maximum exposure is $1,500 per year, is the stop-loss for a family of four $6,000? Sometimes it is, but sometimes it's only $3,000 or $4,500 per family per year.

Maximum Coverage

Good plans will pay up to $2 million per individual or family. A $1 million limit probably is adequate. If your plan has only a $500,000 limit, though, a real catastrophe could run through that and force you to pay the excess.

PUTTING IT ALL TOGETHER

Let's look at a simple health-care policy. Suppose you have a $250 deductible, 20% coinsurance, and a $5,000 stop-loss (i.e., you pay 20% on up to $5,000 worth of medical bills). You incur $10,000 in covered medical expenses this year. Here's how the costs would be split:

	You Pay	Insurance Company Pays
First $250	$250 (deductible)	$0
Next $5,000	$1,000 (20% co-insurance)	$4,000
Next $4,750	$0	$4,750
Of the $10,000 total	$1,250	$8,750

Of course, you're also paying the health insurance premiums, which might be a couple of thousand dollars per year. But you can see why you have health insurance, especially with a stop-loss. When you run into a health emergency and incur $10,000 worth of costs in a year—$10,000 that you might be hard-pressed to put your hands on at one time—the insurance coverage winds up paying nearly 90% of the bills.

IN BRIEF
- If you are covered by an employer's plan or are thinking about accepting coverage, you need to know if it's adequate. That's especially true if you're required to pay part of the premium, which increasingly is the case.
- Make sure you see a copy of the policy. Don't accept anyone's word on what's in the policy or that it even exists.
- The first thing you need to do is check the covered benefits. There are myriad ways to run up medical bills in or out of a hospital.
- Major medical policies generally cover more than hospital-surgical policies.
- You usually pay more for a major medical policy through higher premiums, deductibles, and coinsurance.

- Some policies have a waiting period for coverage of pre-existing conditions.
- It's extremely important to know if a policy has a "stop-loss" (your maximum financial exposure per year) and exactly what the stop-loss is.
- A good health-care policy will be structured so that the insurance company picks up most of the tab for expensive medical emergencies.

Chapter 4

Protect Your Personal Assets from Overexposure

After you've seen your employer's health insurance policy and know what's in it, you can begin to evaluate it. You need to know how much you're likely to pay for what levels of coverage.

The first thing you need to know is the extent of your exposure. That is, are there any circumstances that could strip you of your assets? In a real medical disaster, could you lose everything to pay the bills?

DANGER ZONES

Fake Insurance

Your company's insurance policy could say, "We'll cover everything, all the time." But when you go to collect, there may be no one to collect from.

As mentioned, some employee-leasing firms and multi-employer pools have been scams, not providing any real health insurance. So you need to know if the insurance really is in place (see the policy) and if the insurer is for real.

If your coverage is actually provided by CIGNA or John Hancock or some other company that advertises on prime-time TV, that's not a problem. Legitimate claims will be paid. But what if your coverage is from First World Fidelity Life, or some other company you've never heard of? It may be a perfectly sound small insurer, or it may be nothing more than a few papers in a bank vault in the Bahamas.

Or you may get a brochure from a AAA insurance company, leading you to believe it's the insurer. In reality, this giant insurer is being paid to administer the plan; the coverage is actually self-insured by your employer, a multiemployer welfare association (MEWA), or an employee-leasing firm. If the insurance is self-insured, you need to know the self-insurer's financial strength and whether a stop-loss policy exists to protect against catastrophes.

You can find out without too much difficulty. Ask someone in your company's benefits department for evidence of the insurer's financial strength. If your company doesn't have a benefits department, or even an executive responsible for benefits, ask to speak to the life insurance agent who sold the health insurance policy to your company.

What are you looking for? Some evidence that the company actually exists and that it has been paying benefits for years. You probably don't want to examine reams of financial statements, but you can piggyback on the efforts of financial analysts who spend their days doing just that. Several companies— A. M. Best, Moody's, Standard & Poor's, Duff & Phelps—rate insurers. Ask to see, on paper, the current rating from any of them. As long as there's a rating, you're dealing with a real company.

If you find that the rating is A, A+, AA, etc., you can breathe easily. As far as anyone can tell, this company will be able to pay your claims.

But what if your insurer is rated B or C? That's a tough call. Weak insurance companies are "dropping like flies," as one agent puts it. More than 100 life and health insurers failed between 1985 and 1990. Just ask the people who work at Mid-Cities Honda in Paramount, California, where an insurer went bankrupt and stuck employees for thousands of dollars in unpaid medical bills. Your state may have a health insurance "guaranty fund" to back up failed insurers, but do you really want to find out how effective it is?

There may, then, come a time when you'll pass up coverage through your company's low-rated insurer and seek out your own policy from a sound one. If you're not satisfied with the financial strength of your employer's insurer, you should at least shop the market to see what you can buy on your own. To help you determine an insurer's financial strength, call Weiss Research at (800) 289-9222 and ask if it rates the company. For $25 ($45 for a more detailed report), Weiss will send you a one-page report on any of 1,700-plus insurance companies that may help you decide.

Areas Not Covered

Even if you are covered by a bona fide, solid insurer, your policy may have gaps. Go over the list of coverage areas in chapter 3 and match it with your policy. What's missing? What's excluded? Are those missing links likely to bankrupt you?

Suppose there's no coverage for "mental and nervous" conditions, including alcohol and drug abuse. Such treatment may run into many thousands of dollars.

People Not Covered

Most family insurance policies will cover children up to age 19. But what happens if your 20-year-old daughter gets sick while in college? Some policies will cover students up to age 23, but you need to be certain. (Some insurers, such as Golden Rule Insurance Co., offer a six-month major-medical policy for recent college graduates to provide coverage until they find a job and acquire their own health insurance.)

If you're in a family situation that's not strictly Mom and Pop and the kids (you're not married to the other parent of your children, you're remarried with stepchildren, etc.), check to see who is specifically covered.

No Stop-Loss

Is there a stop-loss? Say you have 80–20 coinsurance. If you run up a $500,000 hospital bill (intensive care for a premature baby, for instance), your 20% share will come to $100,000.

Therefore, you need to know what your "worst case" is. After you've spent $1,000 per year, $5,000, or whatever, on deductibles and coinsurance, does the insurance company step in and pay everything after that? Keep in mind that different policy areas may have a separate stop-loss for psychotherapy, for dentistry, etc.

Low UCR Levels

Your "worst case," though, isn't necessarily the worst case. To see why your costs may exceed the stop-loss, you need to understand the concept of "UCR" (usual, customary, and reasonable) costs. In many insurance policies, the company will set UCR rates for each medical procedure in every area. For all costs over the UCR rate, you're responsible regardless of the coverage.

For example, say an insurance company sets $800 as the UCR rate for a surgeon's fee for performing an appendectomy. You have an appendectomy, and the surgeon charges you $700. No problem. Assuming 20% coinsurance, you pay $140 and the insurer pays $560.

Suppose the surgeon charges you $800. Now you pay your 20% share, $160, and the insurer pays $640.

However, if the surgeon goes over $800, you pay the excess. If it's $900, $1,000, $1,100, etc., the insurance company's share is frozen at $640—80% of the UCR rate. If the fee is $1,200, you'll have to pay $560, which is nearly 50%.

Doctor charges		$1,200
Rate is	$800	
Insurer pays 80% coinsurance		640
Your share is		560

Suppose you run into your annual stop-loss limit, after which your insurance company is on the hook. Still, you're responsible for excess costs over the UCR limit. For the $1,200 appendectomy, for example, you'd have to pay $400, while the insurer pays its share of the $800 UCR limit.

Some insurers, though, base their coinsurance on 80% or 90% of the UCR cost. That's even more expensive for you.

Doctor charges		$1,200
UCR rate is	$800	
Insurer bases claim on 80% of UCR	640	
Insurer pays 80% coinsurance on $640		512
Leaving you to pay		688

Therefore, you should ask if your insurer pays 100% of the UCR cost, because such policies are the best.

Some insurers publish lists of "participating physicians" or "preferred providers," doctors who agree to charge no more than UCR limits. If you stick with these physicians, you won't have to worry about paying excess fees.

Low Cap on Benefits

Is there a cap on the benefits a policy will pay? Again, a stop-loss doesn't mean you're home free. Suppose a policy has a $500,000 "lifetime cap" on benefits. You pay your coinsurance to, say, $5,000. After that, the insurance company pays everything. However, after the company has paid a total of $500,000 on your policy, it effectively steps aside and says, "It's all yours from here." Now you have virtually unlimited exposure for future bills. And with a health history that includes half a million dollars' worth of medical expenses, it's unlikely you or your family will be attractive to a different insurer.

Good policies will have at least a $1 million cap on benefits, perhaps $2 million. Some have $5 million or unlimited caps.

THE 95% SOLUTION

If you've got all that—real policy, strong insurer, full coverage, stop-loss, 100% UCR payment schedule, high cap—you likely have a good policy. Real insurance. But how can you really tell?

One way is to come up with "doomsday scenarios" and ask your company's benefits department or life insurance agent how much would be covered by your policy and how much would come out of your pocket. A good policy will pay 95% or more.

If you can't come up with your own nightmare scenarios, try these:

- You have a difficult pregnancy and run up a hospital bill of nearly $20,000.
- Your 13-year-old daughter loses 40 pounds. Severely anorexic, she weighs 75 pounds. Over the course of the next few months, psychiatry and hospital bills run to $25,000.
- After a heart attack, you go through open-heart surgery and a three-week hospital stay. Total cost: $50,000.
- Someone else in your family suffers serious weight loss. After weeks of hospital tests, colon cancer is diagnosed, and surgery is performed. The hospital bill comes to over $100,000. Plus, ongoing chemotherapy is necessary, at $700 per week.
- Another family member is hit by a car driven by an uninsured motorist. As a result, the injured person loses the use of his legs. Doctors, hospitals, wheelchairs, etc., cost $300,000. Plus, a home health aide is needed every day, at a cost of $1,500 per month.

Suppose your policy would pay virtually all of these costs. In all likelihood, you have an excellent health insurance policy. You're very fortunate. Now all you have to do is keep your eyes and ears open in case your employer announces a change in insurance companies or a change in coverage.

HOLD ON TO WHAT YOU'VE GOT

If you have full coverage, chances are your policy is expensive. What's more, you're probably being asked to pay some of the price through sharing of the premium, deductibles, and coinsurance, and that cost may be considerable. If you have a choice and your expenses are great, should you opt out? Should you choose not to participate?

Definitely not. Today a health insurance card is your ticket to health care. If you don't have one, you're definitely relegated to second-class service, no matter how many laws are passed saying otherwise.

Should you pass up your employer's plan and shop for your own coverage? Probably not. It's doubtful you can buy a better policy than one that has passed these tests. Even if your company pays only half the cost, it's better than your paying everything.

Suppose you and your spouse work for two different employers. Both provide health-care insurance with a family-coverage option. You can use these tests to decide which coverage provides the best protection for your family.

Or suppose your employer offers a choice of plans. Perhaps you can choose between a fee-for-service plan (the kind described above), a health maintenance organization (HMO), or a preferred provider organization (PPO). Before you make that choice, you'll need to know what an HMO or a PPO is and how they work. After you've read about them (pages 105–120), you can research the HMO or PPO that's offered and make that decision.

For the most part, if your employer provides you with quality health-care coverage, consider yourself blessed, no matter what the cost.

COMING UP SHORT

Increasingly, though, you're likely to find that your employer's plan not only costs more than it used to; it won't provide as much coverage. There may be unprotected areas, no stop-losses, or low caps on benefits. If you run into this problem, you essentially have three choices.

1. Do nothing. Hope that you'll never be hit with a catastrophic expense in an uncovered area. This is a high-risk strategy.
2. Pass up your employer's plan. Instead of paying something for inadequate coverage, buy a good plan with your own money. Later, you'll see how to purchase adequate coverage at the least cost.

   Your employer may offer "cafeteria" benefits. That is, you choose your own fringe benefits up to certain cost limits. If that's the case and the health insurance isn't up to standard, you might choose other benefits (i.e., more life insurance, child care, tuition reimbursement) and pay for your own health care.
3. Supplement your employer's plan. Perhaps your employer's plan will permit you to spend a few dollars more for complete coverage. If so, those may be dollars well spent.

   Or you may decide to purchase another, supplemental health-care plan. Some insurers offer major medical plans, perhaps with unlimited benefits, that have deductibles of $2,000, $5,000, $10,000, or more. Because the deductibles are so high, costs are relatively low. You might use such a policy to cover expenses not insured by your employer's plan. In case catastrophe strikes and the benefits from your employer's plan run out, your own coverage will kick in and protect you from severe losses.

IN BRIEF
- There are several tests your employer's health insurance needs to pass.
- There must be a real policy in force from a real insurance company.
- The insurer should be in strong financial condition.
- There should be no significant gaps in coverage.
- "Stop-losses" should limit your out-of-pocket exposure.
- Insurance company "caps" on benefits should be at least $1 million.

- Policies that meet these tests provide strong protection. If your company offers such a policy, you probably should participate.
- If your company's policy can't meet these tests, you probably need more coverage. Your options include bypassing your company's plan and buying your own insurance or supplementing that plan with extra coverage.

Chapter 5

Dealing with Two Employer Plans— Or with None

If you and your spouse are both employed, you may each be offered health-care plans at work. Depending on the options you're allowed, you may be able to juggle things so you get the most coverage for the least cost.

For example, some health insurance plans give you the option of whom to cover: yourself, yourself and spouse, yourself and spouse and kids. It doesn't make sense to duplicate coverage, so you should choose one plan as your primary insurer.

When you're deciding which plan to select, evaluate the coverage as described above. Which plan covers the most possible expenses, which plan has the higher cap on benefits, which plan has a stop-loss, etc. If the plans are similar, see which has the lower deductible and the lower coinsurance requirements. Generally, that's the plan to choose for family coverage. The other spouse can choose not to pay for coverage, so you can save that expense.

FLEX YOUR MUSCLES

Increasingly, large companies offer "flexible-benefits plans." The idea is that each employee is allowed a certain amount of tax-free fringe benefits. Selections are made from a "menu." One worker might choose to participate in a 401(k) retirement plan; another might pick auto insurance at a special group rate. In these situations, one spouse might choose the health insurance, while the other spouse fills in with other needed benefits.

Out of the companies offering flexible plans, nearly 75% give employees the chance to decline health insurance coverage. The cost of the health insurance can be used to buy other benefits. On average, employees who decline medical insurance have over $600 they can divert each year to other tax-free fringe benefits.

Chuck and Jane, for example, have two children. Chuck's employer offers an extremely comprehensive health-care plan that covers himself and the children at a cost of $35 per month, or $420 per year. Jane's employer offers an inferior plan, but the company pays all the premiums. Based on recent experience, their family medical expense for the year will be the health insurance premiums plus another $750, including deductibles, coinsurance, and items (such as checkups) not covered by either plan.

Thus, their annual medical budget looks like this:

Chuck's health insurance premiums	$420
Jane's health insurance premiums	0
Uncovered expenses	750
Total cost	1,170

In addition, they're vulnerable to a catastrophic illness or accident that strikes Jane, because her coverage isn't thorough.

Chuck's company offers to include Jane for another $25 per month, bringing the family total to $60 per month. Jane's company says that she'll get a $600 credit if she "opts out" of the medical plan. That is, if she chooses not be covered by her company plan and the company is relieved of that expense, her employer will allow her to choose other benefits worth up to $600 per year.

Therefore, Jane's coverage is switched to Chuck's employer. At her own company, Jane chooses to use her credit for an account that will pay for unremimbursed health-care expenses. Now the annual budget looks like this:

Chuck's health insurance premiums	$720
Jane's health insurance premiums	0
Uncovered expenses	750
Total cost	1,470
Health-care reimbursement by Jane's company	(600)
Net cost	870

As you can see, the family health-care expense is cut by $300 per year, while Jane's protection has increased.

However, before Jane decides to pass up her company's health-care plan, she should be sure she has the right to sign up again if her situation changes (e.g., if Chuck loses his job).

TWO HALVES MAKE A WHOLE

There are other ways to shop at a fringe-benefit "cafeteria" to get the most tax-free dollars. Often dental plans limit reimbursement to 50% of the expense incurred. If each spouse has such a dental plan, you may be able to cover all of your dental bills.

A variation on flexible-benefit plans is the "flexible spending" or "flexible reimbursement" account. Here employees voluntarily reduce their pay (and their income taxes). Often you can choose how much you want to go into the account, up to, say $2,000 per year. The income you've passed by goes into an account that pays for certain expenses, such as child care or health care.

Why would you want to cut your salary by $2,000? Suppose you're in a 35% tax bracket. On that $2,000 in salary, you'd owe $700, leaving you with $1,300 to spend. If you had $2,000 worth of unreimbursed medical bills to pay, you'd be $700 short. If you diverted that $2,000 into a tax-free flexible-spending account, you could cover all $2,000 worth of expenses and be $700 ahead of the game. In financial terms, you're covering your health-care expenses with pretax rather than after-tax dollars, always a desired outcome.

The drawback: At the end of each year, unspent amounts

in these accounts go back to the company, not to you. So be sure not to put too much in these accounts and to spend whatever is in there. For example, if you're approaching year-end and there are still several hundred dollars in your flexible account, use them for some health-related expense, perhaps one that won't be covered by health insurance. Get a mammogram if you need one; buy new prescription sunglasses. (Unfortunately, cosmetic surgery isn't a valid expense for these tax-favored plans.)

COBRA CAN BE CHARMING

As you can see, two-income couples can play the health insurance game to their best advantage as long as both employers provide decent coverage. But what if you become a no-income household? Thanks to COBRA (the Consolidated Omnibus Budget Reconciliation Act), a 1985 federal law, you can continue your group coverage. Basically, COBRA allows you to extend your group coverage for up to 18 months after losing your job. COBRA is expensive—you have to pay 102% of the total premium—but at least you and your dependents will have some interim coverage while you search for a new job or new health insurance.

One New York City structural engineer, for example, recently lost his job. He had been paying $170 per month for family coverage. His company, though, had been paying $510

TAX TIP

If you can choose, a spouse earning below $55,000 should fund the flexible-spending account. Not only will you reduce income taxes; you'll escape the 6.2% + paid to Social Security on the money set aside. (If you reduce income from, say, $65,000 to $60,000, you'll still pay the maximum to Social Security, so you won't get that savings.)

per month. That's a total of $680 per month. Under COBRA, the engineer had the option of continuing his coverage if he was willing to pay $693.60 ($680 times 102%) per month.

COBRA applies to companies with 20 or more employees. Basic COBRA coverage lasts 18 months. If you're eligible for Social Security disability, you can get an extra 11 months, but you pay 150% of the premium in the excess time period. If you lose spousal coverage because of death, divorce, or separation, you can get 36 months of COBRA coverage at 102% of the premium.

The COBRA provisions are complicated, but here are some examples:

Case 1: You work as an advertising assistant for ABC company, which has 20 or more employees. You leave to establish your own free-lance photography business. You're entitled to COBRA coverage for at least 18 months.

Case 2: You've been a forklift operator for a metals distributor, but a wrenched back makes it impossible for you to work anymore. Now you're collecting disability benefits from Social Security. You're entitled to COBRA coverage for 29 months. For the last 11 months, you may pay as much as 150% of the total premium costs, up from 102%.

Case 3: Your spouse, a partner at a large accounting firm, has been providing you with health insurance through his or her group coverage. You get divorced, and your ex drops you from coverage. You're entitled to up to 36 months of COBRA coverage.

Case 4: You switch jobs from one computer company to a rival. Under your new employer's plan, any recurrence of your colon cancer wouldn't be covered for 12 months. However, you can keep COBRA coverage for the next 12 months, protecting yourself until your new policy kicks in, as long as you pay the premiums.

Case 5: You get laid off from your job as an investment banker. Your former employer, a large brokerage firm, self-insures its health coverage rather than buying a policy from an insurance company. You're still eligible for COBRA coverage.

What if you leave a company with fewer than 20 workers? About two-thirds of all states require some type of COBRA-type coverage, anywhere from 3 to 18 months.

COBRA is not the ultimate answer to your health insurance needs, but its provisions can give you some time to make more durable arrangements.

CONVERSION FACTORS

COBRA can provide excellent short-term protection until you get a new job and new health coverage or until you reach Medicare eligibility. If you can't sail into either of these safe harbors, you may have to buy your own health insurance.

But what if you're in poor health? You may not be able to get individual health insurance, or the cost may be too high. In such cases you may be able to get a "conversion" policy from your former employer after you leave your job or after COBRA benefits run out.

Conversion policies are simply individual health insurance policies. Insurers can't turn you down because of poor health, but they can limit benefits. Instead of major medical coverage, a conversion policy might cover only hospital stays, with a $250-per-day maximum. What's more, premiums for conversion policies commonly run twice as high as premiums for standard individual health insurance policies. (In some cases, you may be able to cover one family member in poor health with a conversion policy while the others get standard policies.)

Therefore, consider conversions as health insurance of the last resort. They're worthwhile only if you can't buy anything else. In most states, you have to choose a conversion policy within 31 days after losing your job or after your COBRA benefits run out.

If you find yourself out of work and out of employer-provided health insurance, COBRA should be your first line of defense, followed by a conversion policy, until you can find other coverage. However, if you or a family member is in poor health and there's no state law guaranteeing you a conversion policy after COBRA but you can get a conversion policy directly after losing coverage, you should take the conversion policy right away (if available), after losing your coverage.

IN BRIEF

- If two spouses work and both are offered health insurance plans, they should choose only the better plan to avoid duplicate coverage.
- Many companies now offer "flexible-benefits plans." If you and your spouse have this opportunity, one can choose the better health-care plan, while the other can select other desired benefits.
- "Flexible-spending plans" offer you a chance to pay uncovered medical bills with pretax rather than with after-tax dollars, a much better deal.
- If you have a flexible-spending account, be sure to spend all the money in it each year.
- COBRA, a federal law, may require your employer to continue your group health-care insurance for at least 18 months after you leave the company.
- You'll have to pay 102% of the full cost—employer and employee shares—for COBRA coverage.
- If you or a dependent is in poor health and not able to get health insurance after leaving a group plan, you may qualify for a "conversion" policy, with no health requirements. Such plans, however, have high costs and skimpy benefits.

Chapter 6

Your Health Insurance Card: Don't Leave Home Without It

THE NEED FOR INSURANCE

Who needs health insurance? In a word, everyone. Suppose you or a member of your family gets sick or injured. Your local hospital, clinic, or doctor's office likely contains the latest in state-of-the-art medical technology, from scanners to wonder drugs to organ-transplant expertise. If you have a little card in your wallet, one that shows participation in a health insurance plan, that technology—along with skilled practitioners to implement it—is at your service. Afterward, you can sort out who owes what to whom.

Without a little card, though, you're a nonperson. For a moment, put yourself on the other side of the receptionist's desk. You're a doctor, with a decade of college and med school and internship and residency behind you, tens of thousands of dollars in debt. Now you have rent and staff to pay, supplies to buy, liabilty insurance to pay, and probably more debt for expensive new equipment you needed to buy to keep up with your practice.

When you work, you want to be sure you get paid promptly

and in full. Already you're seeing Medicare and Medicaid patients, with your fees effectively capped by the government. That makes your other patients even more important to your financial well-being.

A patient comes in with no health insurance. What's your impression? You, the doctor, may think this person can't afford health insurance. Or else this is a person in such poor health that he or she can't qualify for health insurance, so a huge bill likely will be run up, with no insurance-company reimbursement. Or else the patient cares too little about his or her health—and paying for care—to bother to obtain insurance.

With those impressions, how are you going to treat this patient? And if that's your attitude, won't it filter back to your receptionist and your other employees, all of whom depend on your continued prosperity for their salaries?

Second-Class

Now go back to the patient's side of the reception room. Sure, there are some saintly doctors who'll take all patients and treat them to the best of their ability. But at many hospitals and doctor's offices you're likely to get second-class treatment if you can't produce a health insurance card. Uninsured patients, if they're admitted at all, may face long waits, impersonal care, and a "referral" to some specialist who may or may not treat you any better.

Recently, for example, the Harvard School of Public Health studied thousands of Massachusetts patients who complained of circulatory disorders or chest pains. Patients with health insurance were 80% more likely to receive angiography, 40% more likely to receive bypass grafting, and 28% more likely to receive angioplasty (three forms of sophisticated medical treatment), compared with uninsured patients. Similarly, a University of California study found that sick newborn babies not covered by insurance received services costing 28% less and were discharged two and a half days sooner than sick newborns covered by private insurance.

Therefore, you need some kind of health insurance, even if it's not the full-protection policy you'd like. If you have a family, the need is even more pressing that someone in the family have a policy that covers everyone.

Supplemental Coverage

What if you have employer coverage but you fear it's inadequate? Judging from the standards discussed in chapter 4, your health-care plan has

- Big gaps in coverage.
- No stop-loss.
- A low cap on the benefits the policy will pay.

With any of these prevalent inadequacies, you're vulnerable. Even a minor health crisis could cost you thousands. According to *Consumer Reports*, a fractured finger can cost $6,500 to treat. And if you're unlucky enough to encounter a catastrophe, all of your assets can be lost.

Therefore, if you have subpar employer coverage, you should replace it or supplement it to cut your exposure to health-care costs. The better your coverage, the better your treatment. Your doctor won't hold back, fearing he or she won't get repaid. And you won't be reluctant to seek treatment because you won't be able to pay for it.

Press Your Advantage

The younger and the healthier you are, the less you feel you need health insurance. However, that's the ideal time to buy health insurance. A policy that's "guaranteed renewable" can't be canceled if your health deteriorates. Next best is a policy that's "conditionally renewable," because the only way for the company to cancel your coverage is to cancel all similar policies throughout the state.

"Optionally renewable" policies aren't in the same league. Here the option belongs to the insurance company. If it decides you're a poor risk, your coverage can be canceled.

So if you don't have adequate coverage from your employer, get some now, while your health is as good as it's going to get.

You don't need to buy the most expensive coverage, but you want a policy with real financial protection.

SHOPPING FOR HEALTH INSURANCE

In a sense, shopping for your own health insurance (individual or family policies) is like evaluating an employer's group plan. The best policies are those with broad coverage, stop-losses, and high benefit caps. After those criteria are met, the best policies have the lowest deductibles and the lowest coinsurance obligations.

However, there is a crucial difference between the two situations. When you're evaluating an employer plan, you're looking at a given policy, trying to decide if it merits thumbs up or thumbs down. (In some companies, you may have to decide between a few different plans.)

When you're shopping for your own coverage, on the other hand, you may have to choose among several insurers—even dozens—offering health insurance in your state. From each of those insurers, there's a full range of options. Out of all those choices, you have to come up with an affordable policy that provides real insurance—certainly a daunting task, especially if you, like many people, don't rank talking with insurance agents among your favorite pastimes.

So there's risk here: You may choose a policy that's too expensive or one that doesn't give you adequate coverage. But risk usually is the flip side of opportunity, and this is no different. Because you're the consumer, you can pick out a policy that suits your needs, not one that some multinational corporation picked out for its "average" employee. You can shop among all the suitable policies for the one that's least expensive. And if that policy or that company pushes its rates too high, you're free to take your business elsewhere, if you can find a more competitive policy.

Consider Health Hazards

With all these possibilities, how do you start to shop for health insurance? First, make sure your expectations are reasonable.

Health insurance is hard to get if you have cancer, AIDS, or some other serious illness. As you'll learn later, there are some "open enrollment" insurers who'll take everyone who applies. But if you're critically ill, you have to realize that health insurance will be expensive and possibly limited in scope.

That makes a certain amount of sense. After all, what insurance company wants to take $5,000 of your money in the certainty it will pay out $50,000 in medical bills? Taking it one step further, insurers typically avoid certain occupations and professions in the belief that large claims will be filed. Doctors and lawyers, for example, may find it hard to find coverage, apparently in the belief that they'll be more adept in pushing the right papers than the average policyholder. Truck drivers, exterminators, barbers, beauticians, and people who work in bowling alleys, theaters, gas stations, cleaners, restaurants, bars, farms, logging camps, coal mines, or oil wells—for one reason or another, insurance companies are unwilling to cover them. Or coverage is available only at a higher premium. So if you work in one of these businesses, be prepared to look hard for coverage and to accept whatever may be available.

Get a Good Agent

After you realize whether you're in a high-risk or low-risk category and consequently have few or many options, you can begin the search for health-care insurance. Now, you probably don't care to make it your business to discover the best health-care policies, so you probably should join forces with someone whose business it is. That is, you need to work with a first-rate insurance agent.

Where do you begin to find such a paragon? Few insurance agents make a living selling individual or family health insurance policies. Such policies generally are sold by life insurance agents, just as most health insurance issuers are primarily life insurance companies.

So the best place to start is with your own life insurance agent, assuming this person is someone you can rely on. The agent who isn't "captive" to one company can screen policies offered by several companies and recommend the one that looks best for you.

What if you don't have a life insurance agent or you're not wild about the one you have? Find a different agent. There's one simple way to go about this: Ask. Ask your friends and business associates, those whose judgment you trust, for the name of a good insurance agent. Find a relationship that goes back several years, not a recent chance meeting at an alumni luncheon. Then arrange a meeting with that agent to see if you get along.

It may be that an agent will expect you to buy your life insurance as well as your health insurance from him or her. If you find an agent you really like ... well, you should have a good life insurance agent, too.

Find a Good Company

Agents can help you find good life insurance, but don't expect them to do everything. It's up to you to tell your agent precisely what you want and to make the crucial decisions.

The most crucial decision is the selection of the insurance company. Say you can buy a family health insurance policy from Xanadu Mutual that covers everything—no exceptions—with no deductibles and no coinsurance. The annual premium is $200 per family. Naturally, you sign up.

Just as naturally, you and your family make the complete rounds of pediatricians, obstetricians, internists, ophthalmologists, dentists, etc., rolling up thousands of dollars of bills, which are all submitted to Xanadu Mutual. Nothing happens. No claims are paid. A year later, you read in the newspaper that Xanadu Mutual has gone bankrupt.

You thought you had the world's greatest health insurance policy, but you really had the world's worst. You're out the $200 premium, and you're liable for all the other bills you incurred. You'd have been better off with a not-so-great policy from a solid insurer, which would have provided you some bona fide insurance.

Therefore, you need to set a standard, and the easiest way to do it is by using the ratings agencies. Tell your agent, for example, that you'll only consider health insurance policies from companies rated A or A+ by A. M. Best, plus an A or better rating from Standard & Poor's, Moody's, or Duff & Phelps. No rating system is perfect, but you'll certainly increase the chances of buying insurance from a company that will be around to pay off.

Singing the Blues

When you're shopping for a reliable insurer, consider the "Blues": your local Blue Cross and Blue Shield plan. However, the more than 70 Blue Cross/Blue Shield plans in the United States vary from one to another, just as commercial insurers do, so they need the same kind of scrutiny.

Created back in the 1930s, Blue Cross and Blue Shield were nonprofit organizations, exempt from federal income taxes. Thanks to the tax break and to the large discounts they were able to negotiate with hospitals, the Blues could offer affordable hospital insurance to everyone. In some cases, nonhospital expense also were covered.

Originally, the Blues offered coverage for everyone, regardless of health. This was called "open enrollment." Premiums, too, were the same for everyone. With this "community rating" practice, healthy people effectively subsidized unhealthy ones, who paid the same premiums but used more health services.

This changed in the 1960s as health insurance became a form of tax-free compensation rather than just protection against major expenses. Insurance companies lured away major employers with full-scale insurance; small groups and individuals, seeking the same comprehensive coverage, turned to insurance companies offering lower premiums for healthy people. As a result, the Blues' customer base, in many cases, became skewed toward poor health risks.

Now the Blues have gone in two directions. Most have stopped their open enrollment and community rating policies, acting more like commercial insurers. In fact, some have given up their nonprofit status and have become mutual insurance companies (in effect, owned by policyholders). Others have kept to their original path but have to charge high rates because the pool they insure is so risky.

Most states have their own plans for in-state residents (e.g., Blue Cross and Blue Shield of Maryland, Blue Cross and Blue Shield of Oklahoma). In some cases—Blue Cross of Washington and Alaska—two states will be covered. Blue Cross and Blue Shield of Rochester (N.Y.), on the other hand, focuses on one metropolitan area.

Contact your local Blue Cross and Blue Shield and ask what it offers. Empire Blue Cross Blue Shield, for example, offers three different plans to New Yorkers. One is a hospital-only plan (not hospital-surgical), open to everyone at a relatively modest premium. There's no deductible, no coinsurance, and no cap on the benefits the plan will pay. However, there are large gaps in the coverage.

For nearly twice as much money, Empire has a major medical plan that covers most expenses, open to everyone. However, this plan has its shortcomings: There is a $1,000 deductible, a 20% coinsurance requirement, no stop-loss, and a $500,000 cap on benefits.

If you want major medical with a stop-loss and a $1 million cap on benefits, Empire has yet another plan. But this one requires a health exam and it's pricey: over $6,000 per year for family coverage.

Therefore, you need to shop carefully for the right policy from your local Blues. Empire, by the way, gets high marks for its policies, along with the Blues in New Jersey (which offers at least five different plans), Minnesota, and Pennsylvania.

In addition, some Blues offer health maintenance organizations (HMOs) and preferred provider organizations (PPOs) that are highly regarded (see chapters 9 and 10).

Blues in the Red

Buying insurance from the Blues poses another problem: How can you judge the organization's financial condition? This is not an idle question. In late 1990, Blue Cross/Blue Shield of West Virginia collapsed and was combined with the Ohio plan (now called Mountain States Blue Cross & Blue Shield). Some West

Virginia policyholders were billed for medical expenses they thought were covered—one gas-line repairman who earns $23,000 per year told the press that he received $36,000 worth of bills. Plus, the new combined plan announced huge rate increases for many customers.

How can you avoid such catastrophes? You can ask for financial statements to see if the organization is reporting gains or losses, if net worth is positive or negative, and if its capital meets state requirements.

In early 1991, the *Wall Street Journal* reported that the Blue Cross/Blue Shield plans in New Jersey, Vermont, Rhode Island, New Hampshire, and western New York each had a negative net worth. Six others—in Massachusetts, New Mexico, Delaware, Maryland, Rochester, and New York City—had positive net worth but relatively low assets in comparison to the claims they regularly pay out.

As you can see, most of these financially weak plans are in the Northeast. In general, the Blues in the rest of the United States are in better financial shape.

Ultimately, though, politics must be considered. Will your state allow the Blues the rate increases they need to stay solvent? In case of a disaster, will there be a bailout? The Blues in the Northeast tend to be relied upon as insurers of last resort, so there may be state action to prevent a failure.

There are no hard-and-fast answers, but you need to keep a Blue Cross/Blue Shield's financial health in mind when you're comparing its insurance policies to those of a traditional insurance company.

If you're young and in excellent health, you might do better with a commerical insurer. But if you have had a difficult time finding coverage or have been burned by escalating health insurance premiums, your local "Blue" may be your best bet.

IN BRIEF
- If you don't have health insurance, you need it.
- Without insurance, you face poor treatment and financial disaster.

- If your employer has subpar insurance, look into replacing it or supplementing it with your own coverage.
- The younger and healthier you are, the easier it will be to find health insurance.
- If you work in certain occupations, you may find insurance hard to buy.
- Try to buy insurance that can't be canceled if your health declines.
- A good insurance agent can help you find the right coverage.
- Screen insurers so that you buy from a financially strong company.
- There are over 70 Blue Cross and Blue Shields in the United States offering health insurance.
- Originally, most of the Blues covered everyone at the same rate. Now some are turning down applicants and charging higher rates for higher risks.
- Some Blues are in poor financial shape.
- Blue Cross and Blue Shield organizations are worth considering for health insurance, but their coverage and financial stability must be compared closely with those of private insurers.

Chapter 7

Shop Before You Drop

When you're in the market for health insurance, the "back end" is more important than the "front end." That is, your first goal should be to find coverage that will protect you from steep medical bills. Once you're covered on the back end, you can worry about how to lower front-end costs, such as premiums, deductibles, and copayments.

In the last chapter, you saw the importance of finding the right agent, the right insurance company, and the right expectations regarding your health. Now you can look for specific policy features. The benefits described in chapter 3 on traditional health insurance provided by employers also are available in individual and family coverage, and the same comments generally apply.

WHAT POLICY FEATURES TO LOOK FOR

You definitely should get coverage for all hospital expenses, including room and board, surgery-related costs, intensive care, emergency-room care, lab tests, X rays, etc. Be sure to ask about coverage of organ transplants, which are becoming increasingly common at $50,000–$200,000 apiece. "Miscellaneous" hospital costs can mount fast, so be sure they're included. Akin to hospital coverage is "ambulatory surgery" you have done outside a hospital to save money. Those costs should be covered, too.

Other coverage—physicians' visits, stays in skilled nursing homes, "mental and nervous" disorders—is "nice but" insurance. These features are nice to have, but you have to evaluate if they're worth paying for. Treatment for mental and nervous disorders has become such a sore spot for insurers that you probably won't be able to get more than $50,000 worth of lifetime benefits on an individual or family policy.

Don't pay for coverage that you're unlikely to need. For example, policies that cover maternity costs are more expensive, so don't ask for this coverage if you're a single male or if you and your spouse are a couple in your 50s with no likelihood of having children. In the latter situation, you may prefer coverage for prescription drugs.

Major Medical

Generally, you're better off buying a major-medical policy rather than a hospital-surgical policy. Some hospital-surgical policies don't cover everything performed in a hospital; others have maximum amounts they'll pay for each procedure. Often those limits are on the skimpy side: $600 for a hysterectomy, perhaps, while the national average is nearly $2,000.

Some hospital-surgical policies are "first-dollar." They'll pay for all hospital room and board, for example, and "the full range of hospital services, supplies, equipment, and facilities." You pay nothing, or only a few hundred dollars as a deductible.

First-dollar policies sold to individuals and families usually don't make sense. To cover their risk, insurance companies charge huge premiums for this kind of coverage.

Look at it this way. If you go into the hospital, you're going to pay, one way or another, for the doctors, nurses, supplies, high-tech equipment, and the mortgage on the building. If you have a first-dollar policy with a high premium, you're going to pay every year, whether or not you're hospitalized. If you buy a major-medical policy with a high deductible and lower premium, you'll pay when—and if—you actually go into the hospital.

If you're buying major-medical coverage, you need to evaluate the following:

• *Deductibles.* Ask how much you'd pay for similar policies with $500 deductible, $1,000 deductible, $2,000 deductible, etc. You may want to take a higher deductible and pay a lower price.

If you're responsible for paying $1,000 worth of medical bills per year, out of your own pocket, you'd expect to pay a lower premium than someone responsible for paying only $100 per year. Coverage that calls for a $4,000 annual premium with a $100 deductible might cost you only $2,600 per year with a $1,000 deductible. In this example, a family staying in good health would save $1,400 per year by going from a $100 to a $1,000 deductible.

Charles Auerbach, an associate with Kelman-Lazarov, Inc., a Memphis financial planning firm, says that $100 or $250 or $500 deductibles don't make sense in today's market because premiums are so expensive. "You should expect to pay those costs yourself, as regular living expenses, and take at least a $1,000 deductible on your health insurance."

CHECKUP

How can you tell what you're buying?

1. Ask to see a copy of the policy.
2. Read it.
3. Look for the words "major medical." Hospitalization policies generally include—often on the last page—an explicit announcement that "this is not a major medical" policy.
4. If you see this kind of language, you may need more coverage. Ask about a major-medical policy.

• *Coinsurance.* You may be able to reduce your premium considerably by going from the standard 80–20 sharing arrangement to one in which you pay 30%, 40%, or even 50%. As long as you have a stop-loss in place, your exposure won't be increased.

If your stop-loss is $1,000 (plus deductible) and your coinsurance is 20 percent, you pay 20 percent of $5,000. Thereafter, the insurer pays 100 percent.

If you increase your coinsurance to 50 percent (and the stop-loss remains $1,000), you pay 50 percent of $2,000. Thereafter, the insurer pays 100 percent.

Ozzie Jones, a free-lance photographer, carries a health insurance policy for himself and his family with a $1,000 deductible, a $1,000 stop-loss, and 20% coinsurance. His daughter gets a serious eye infection from a playground sand-tossing incident that leads to $8,000 worth of medical bills. Ozzie has to pay the $1,000 deductible plus 20% of the next $5,000 worth of bills until he reaches his $1,000 stop-loss, for a total of $2,000. The insurance company pays the remaining $6,000.

The next year, Ozzie's health insurance premium is increased. To cut his premium, Ozzie agrees to increase his coinsurance from 20% to 50%. The next year, he sprains his back and requires surgery, incurring another $8,000 worth of bills. Now he pays his $1,000 deductible plus 50% of the next $2,000 in bills, until he reaches his $1,000 stop-loss. The insurance company pays the next $5,000 worth of bills, for a total of $6,000.

Thus, Ozzie has the same end result—he pays $2,000, the insurer pays $6,000—with 50% coinsurance, while he pays a lower premium than he would with 20% insurance. (However, if total bills were between $3,000 and $6,000, he'd wind up paying more with 50% coinsurance.)

• *Stop-loss.* All health insurance plans should have a point after which your exposure ends, or nearly so. It's important you understand how this is structured—per person, per family, or per illness or accident. The same is true of deductibles.

If the premiums are lower, you're probably better off with "per-cause" plans. Tragedies usually strike one family member at a time, so a deductible or stop-loss that applies to one incident should give you catastrophic coverage. (Some policies will adjust deductibles or stop-loss limits if more than one family member is injured in the same auto accident.)

Remember, even a stop-loss won't help if physicians charge more than the insurer allows per procedure. Try to find an insurer that will provide you with a list of physicians who won't charge fees higher than the usual, customary, and reasonable (UCR) limits.

• *Caps on benefits.* A $1 million cap is the minimum for good coverage.

UNEASY RIDERS

A "rider," in insurance lingo, usually means extra coverage at extra cost. If you insure your household goods, for example, you may have to pay a few hundred dollars extra for a rider that covers specific valuable jewelry items. In health care, you might buy a policy that usually has no maternity care but pay $1,000 for a rider that will cover up to $4,000 worth of the costs involved in a normal delivery.

In health insurance, some riders gallop in the opposite direction. That is, they subtract rather than add coverage. Thus, they're called "exclusion riders." With this type of coverage, you have regular health insurance except for the conditions spelled out in the riders. Usually, these are conditions you already have, anything from arthritis to varicose veins. A rider may expire after a year or so, giving you coverage for this condition, or it may be perpetual. If you need medical treatment for ridered conditions, you have to pay the bills yourself.

Another way you pay for not-so-perfect health is through higher premiums, if you have a condition—such as obesity— that indicates a high risk of future problems. Nearly half of all health insurance policies come with an exclusion rider or with an excess premium. However, insurers vary widely in their handling of medical conditions, so it may pay to do some comparison shopping.

HONESTY GETS THE BEST POLICY

If you have a health problem, buying insurance can be tricky. Most application forms will ask you if you've ever been denied health insurance. It's important to be able to answer no honestly. Once you answer yes to that question, red flags are bound to go up at the prospective insurer's office. But if you say no to that question and the insurer later discovers that you have been turned down, your coverage may not be honored.

How do you avoid this trap? If you get several calls from the insurer about a health problem of yours or if your physician gets such calls, tell your agent. He or she should be able to find out how likely it is that you'll be denied coverage. If it looks as though you're going to be turned down, withdraw your application before the coverage can be denied. Make another application with a different insurer. (Don't lie on your application, even if you're afraid of the results. If you falsify data and the truth is exposed, all your health-care coverage may be jeopardized.)

HIGH-PRICED SPREAD

Recently, a family of four went shopping for a health insurance policy and received several quotes. The best price quoted from a "name brand" insurer, a company you might recognize from its advertisements, was $371 per month from Guardian Life. That's nearly $4,500 per year.

However, if they were content with a lesser-known insurer—United Olympic Life—that has the same A+ rating from A. M. Best & Co., they could have found a policy that met their standards for $273 per month, or less than $3,300 per year. And if they were willing to do without dental coverage, John Alden Life, another Best-rated A+ company, had a policy that otherwise met their needs for $150 per month, or $1,800 per year.

Another option is to go down a bit in the insurer's rating. A comparable health insurance policy, with dental coverage, was offered by Boston Mutual Life, which is rated A rather than

A+ by A. M. Best, for $180 per month, or less than $2,200 per year.

The point isn't that you should buy your health insurance from John Alden or Boston Mutual. More expensive policies may offer more benefits. Rather, the point here is to let you know that there is a wide range of costs among the different policies from well-rated companies, so you should comparison shop before you buy. The price savings can be significant.

If you compare prices at the supermarket before buying a can of tuna for $1.09, why shouldn't you look hard for an insurance policy that will cost you thousands of dollars every year?

THE RATING GAME

Is there such a thing as a rate guarantee in health insurance? Not really. When you buy a whole-life insurance policy, for example, you can lock in a premium that you'll pay for your "whole life." That's not true in medical insurance, where costs are constantly going up and insurers pass along those costs to policyholders.

Before you buy health insurance, ask about rate increases over the past five years; be leery of companies whose rates have increased more than 12% per year. Often, when you buy a new policy, you can get a guarantee that the rate won't go up for six months, perhaps even one full year. Considering the way prices have been shooting up lately, a 12-month rate guarantee is a good buy, even if it costs an extra $25 or $50. After that period, if the insurer tries to jack your rate up, you can shop for another policy.

Don't forget, quoted rates usually assume standard health. If you have a certain health condition, such as migraine headaches, different companies have different policies. Some might exclude migraine coverage for a year or two; some might exclude it permanently; some might include it but increase the rate. You need to specify health conditions when you're comparison shopping to be sure you're weighing apples against other apples.

TAX BREAK—OR BROKEN PROMISE?

Employers can deduct from their taxes the costs of money spent to provide health insurance for employees. But what if you buy your own health insurance? Can you deduct the cost from your taxes?

Despite a lot of talk about tax cuts, under current law there are only a few ways to use the tax code. For example, if you itemize deductions, you can deduct health-care costs in excess of 7.5% of your adjusted gross income (AGI).

Your AGI is the number you wind up with at the bottom of the first side of your federal tax return. Suppose your AGI is $50,000. If you itemize deductions, you can deduct any medical costs over $3,750, which is 7.5% of $50,000.

Suppose your health insurance premiums come to $2,400 per year. You add that to the total spent on doctors, dentists, hospitals, etc., plus what you paid for eyeglasses, transportation for medical care, and other related expenses. (You don't include expenses for which you've been reimbursed.)

AGI		$50,000
Health insurance premiums	$2,400	
All other medical expenses	3,000	
Total		5,400
Threshold (7.5% times $50,000 AGI)		(3,750)
Deductible amount ($5,400 minus $3,750)		1,650

As you can see, if you didn't include your health insurance premiums, you would get no deduction. So, about two-thirds of your health insurance is deductible, in this example.

If you're self-employed, there may be another path you can take. The 1986 tax act included a 25% deduction for health insurance premiums. This provision lasted for three years but has since been extended one year or six months at a time. As of now, there is no knowing whether it will be in effect for the second half of 1992 or in subsequent years.

Assuming the provision stays alive, there are a few hurdles to clear. You must have earned income from self-employment (i.e., you must have a real business), and neither you nor your spouse can be eligible for a subsidized health plan offered through an employer. If you meet those tests, in the above example, you could deduct $600 (25% of your $2,400 premium) on page 1 of your tax form.

But at the same time you'd have to reduce your itemized deduction by the same $600, so it's a wash, right?

Not exactly. The way the tax form is set up, by taking the $600 deduction, you reduce your AGI to $49,400. Now 7.5% of your AGI is $3,705, not $3,750. So you increase your total writeoff by $45:

AGI		$49,400
Health insurance premiums	$2,400	
minus self-employed deduction	(600)	
net	1,800	
all medical expenses	3,000	
Total		4,800
Threshold (7.5 times $49,400)		(3,705)
Itemized deduction ($4,800 minus $3,705)		1,095
Self-employed deduction		600
Total deduction		1,695

If this seems like a lot of pain for little gain, you're right. However, many people can't qualify for any itemized deduction at all for medical expenses because their medical expenses don't add up to more than 7.5 percent of their AGI; it's a high threshold. If you're in that category, the self-employed deduction (if it's not buried by Congress) may be your only chance to deduct any of your health insurance costs.

IN BRIEF
- When you buy health insurance, look for catastrophic protection rather than first-dollar coverage.
- Major medical policies usually offer the broadest protection.
- Increasing your deductible and your coinsurance ratio can cut your insurance premiums.
- You should insist on a stop-loss.
- Stop-losses won't help if your doctor charges more than what an insurer allows. Try to find physicians who'll accept the insurer's allowance as payment in full.

- If you have a health problem, shop with care to find the insurer with the most generous coverage.
- There may be large price differences between health insurance policies, so it pays to shop around.
- Paying a few dollars for a "rate guarantee" can lock in health insurance premiums for 12 months.
- You may be entitled to a partial tax deduction for your health insurance premiums.

Chapter 8

The Computer Comes to Health Insurance

If you're going to take your family to Hawaii on a vacation, your travel agent undoubtedly will consult a computerized data base to find out the lowest air fares, the least restrictive terms, the most attractive hotel rates, and so on. You can even do this yourself, in many cases, if you have a home computer tied in to a telephone.

You might think, wouldn't it be nice to shop for health insurance as you can shop for trips to Hawaii? Well, to a certain extent, you can. A few services now track insurance via computerized data bases. These data bases are aimed mainly at insurance agents and financial planners who, in turn, use them to serve corporate accounts. But there are ways in which you can use them for yourself and your family.

So check with an independent insurance agent—one who's not locked in to one company. Or, if you use a financial planner, consult with your planner. If you're fortunate, your agent or planner will have access to one of the computerized health insurance data bases.

Data-base services include HealthQuotes, Quotesmith, and Group Benefit Shoppers. Each one includes many health insurers. If your agent or planner provides the details on the coverage you need, the data base will report on what's available and at what price. Often the cost differences will be huge.

Quotesmith, a company based in Palatine, Illinois, charges about $700 a year to insurance agents, financial planners, and others who wish to subscribe. (Besides health insurance, Quotesmith also offers quotes on term life insurance. Recently, it has added Medigap and nursing-home insurance to its data base.) When subscribers want information, they call Quotesmith on a modem–personal computer hookup. They tell Quotesmith the size of the group they're inquiring about, the number of dependents to be covered, and all the relevant ages.

Within hours, Quotesmith will report on all the insurance companies offering health insurance in that state. Rates will be quoted, depending on whether or not maternity coverage is desired, plus options for deductibles, coinsurance rates, and stop-loss limits. Then the agent can select the coverage that seems most promising, call the company, and work out specific details.

In 1990, *Financial Planning* magazine asked Quotesmith for the cost of a health-care policy for a New York company with 10 employees, ranging in age from 20 to 53. The company wanted a $5,000 per family stop-loss, 80–20 coinsurance coverage, and a $250 deductible with dental coverage. About a dozen companies offered such coverage, according to Quotesmith, with costs ranging from under $4,000 per month (for all 10 employees) to nearly $5,000 per month.

What's more, Quotesmith checked into coverage for an identical company based in Alabama. About five times as many insurers were willing to offer coverage there, and they were all less expensive than the costs in New York: from $1,600 to $3,200 per month.

AN INSIDE LOOK

To help in the preparation of this book, Quotesmith prepared real-life quotes for a family of four, consisting of two 45-year-old parents and two teenaged children, living in New Jersey. Desired coverage included (continued on page 93)

Table 2: PREMIUM SUMMARY PAGE*

Carrier Number	Nonmatching Reasons	Quotesmith Plan ID	Carrier Name/Best's Rating	Monthly Base Premium	Proposal Attached
174	R	HOSPITAL10	Fidelity Security Life A	160.30	
118	RC	GOLD B-10	Centennial Life	177.90	
174	MATCH	HOSPITAL10	Fidelity Security Life A	180.85	Yes
118	C	GOLD B-10	Centennial Life	193.80	
111	RC	INHOSP-10	Centennial Life	199.86	
160	R	COMP-10	Durham Life A+	213.96	
162	R S	VAN-1	Durham Life A+	221.55	
111	C	INHOSP-10	Centennial Life	226.66	
164	L	PLANB-10	Boston Mutual A	228.00	
164	S	PLANC-10	Boston Mutual A	242.10	
162	S	VAN-1	Durham Life A+	248.96	
120	L R S	780FS-10	Continental American Life A+	256.25	
120	L R S	780FS-10M	Continental American Life A+	261.25	
800	L R S	10INN-10	United Olympic Life A+	262.40	
120	R	80FS-10	Continental American Life A+	262.55	
121	R	80HM-10	Continental American Life A+	263.17	
118	RC	GOLD A-10	Centennial Life	264.17	
121	R	80HM-10M	Continental American Life A+	265.27	
120	R	80FS-10M	Continental American Life A+	267.95	
164	L	PLANA-10	Boston Mutual A	273.81	

111	RC		PRES-10	Centennial Life		274.54	
800	R S		5INN-10	United Olympic Life	A+	277.40	Yes
175	R		EXCEL-10	Fidelity Security Life	A	280.32	Yes
120	S	L	780FS-10	Continental American Life	A+	284.60	
118	C		GOLD A-10	Centennial Life		288.70	
120	S	L	780FS-10M	Continental American Life	A+	290.20	
164	MATCH		PLANA(5)10	Boston Mutual	A	291.55	
120	MATCH		80FS-10	Continental American Life	A+	291.66	
121	MATCH		80HM-10	Continental American Life	A+	292.35	
121	MATCH		80HM-10M	Continental American Life	A+	294.70	
160	R	I	COMP-10	Fidelity Security Life	A	297.34	
128	R		PRO-MED10M	Continental Assurance	A+	297.66	
120	MATCH		80FS-10M	Continental American Life	A+	297.70	
121	R	L	90HM-10	Continental American Life	A+	298.81	
121	R	L	90HM-10M	Continental American Life	A+	300.91	
160	R S		COMP-10M	Durham Life	A+	309.96	
111	C		PRES-10	Centennial Life	A+	312.55	
805	R S		PRIME-10	United Olympic Life	A+	324.12	
121	R S		100HM-10	Continental American Life	A+	330.26	
121		L	90HM-10	Continental American Life	A+	332.27	
121	R S		100HM-10M	Continental American Life	A+	332.35	
120	R S		100FS-10	Continental American Life	A+	333.39	
121		L	90HM-10M	Continental American Life	A+	334.62	
175	R		EXCEL-10M	Fidelity Security Life	A	339.32	
120	R S		100FS-10M	Continental American Life	A+	340.39	

Table 2: PREMIUM SUMMARY PAGE (continued)

Carrier Number	Nonmatching Reasons	Quotesmith Plan ID	Carrier Name/Best's Rating	Monthly Base Premium	Proposal Attached
173	R S	STAR2-10M	Fidelity Security Life A	353.70	
805	S	PRIME-10	United Olympic Life A+	354.93	
121	S	100HM-10	Continental American Life A+	367.50	
121	S	100HM-10M	Continental American Life A+	369.83	
120	S	100FS-10	Continental American Life A+	371.00	
120	S	100FS-10M	Continental American Life A+	378.84	
800	L R S	10INN-10M	United Olympic Life A+	382.40	
800	R S	5INN-10M	United Olympic Life A+	397.40	
805	R S	PRIME-10M	United Olympic Life A+	444.12	
805	S	PRIME-10M	United Olympic Life A+	486.81	

REASONS FOR NONMATCHING

L = stop-loss.   I = coinsurance.
C = carrier profile.   † = industry may be acceptable.
D = dental.   P = prescription drug card (PCS).
S = supplemental accident.   W = weekly disability income.
R = rate guarantee.

*Example only. Insurance may not be currently available at quoted prices.
Source: Quotesmith Corp.

- Deductible near $1,000 per person.
- Coinsurance of 20% or less.
- Stop-loss at $1,000 per person or less.
- Supplemental accident coverage.
- No maternity coverage.
- No dental coverage, disability income, or prescription card service.
- No takeover coverage from a prior insurance policy.
- Insurance company rating of A or A+ by A. M. Best.
- A rate guarantee of 12 months or longer.

The results are shown in table 2. More than 50 health insurance plans came close to the stated criteria, and 6 matched exactly. Now look at the range of costs: from $160 to nearly $500 per month. Of course, such lists will vary from time to time and from state to state, but you're likely to find a similarly wide spread among possible health insurance plans.

Suppose you wanted to use this sort of table to help you choose a carrier. The first thing you might notice is that the lowest-priced policy ($160 per month) and the lowest-priced matching policy ($181 per month) come from Fidelity Security Life. Quotesmith has more details on the matching plan (see table 3).

Table 3: BENEFIT ANALYSIS*

CARRIER: 174   FIDELITY SECURITY LIFE A
PLAN NAME: HOSPITAL PLUS (IN-HOSP)   NO MATERNITY
ID: HOSPITAL 10

Life Insurance/AD&D
  (minimum required) $10,000/$10,000

HOSPITAL AND DOCTOR BENEFITS
  Room and board   In-hospital only
  Miscellaneous charges   In-hospital only
  Surgical charges   In-hospital only†
  In-hospital doctor visits   In-hospital only
  Diagnostic X ray and
    laboratory   In-hospital only
  Maternity   Not covered
  Well baby/nursery charges   No/no

MAJOR MEDICAL
    Deductible—family $1,000/3 per family
    Coinsurance (insurance co./
        employee)   80/20 to $5,000
    Maximum out-of-pocket per
        insured $1,000 plus deductible
    Plan maximum $1,000,000

MENTAL AND NERVOUS
    Inpatient/lifetime maximum   80%/$10,000
    Outpatient/annual maximum   Not covered

OPTIONAL COVERAGES
    Supplemental accident   Yes—$500 included
    Coverage for prescriptions   Major medical

DENTAL BENEFITS
    Deductible/annual maximum $25/$50 per person/$1,000 max.
    Diagnostic/preventive   Paid at 80%
    Basic restorative   Paid at 80%
    Major restorative   Paid at 50%
    Orthodontia   Not available

WDI (WEEKLY DISABILITY INCOME)
    Disability benefits   Not available

UNDERWRITING   8 medical questions per appli-
                             cant

PREEXISTING CONDITION
    (MONTHS)   12/24 months
TAKEOVER COVERAGE   None
RATE GUARANTEE   12 months

COMMENTS
This is an in-hospital-only plan. This is an individual plan only.
†There is 80% coverage for eligible outpatient surgical procedures after deductible. Association dues of $3 are included in rates shown. Fifteenth of the
month effective date = $30 admin. fee & $6 association dues. Denial:
6-month wait for basic services; 12-month wait for major services.

Ineligible Industries and Occupations

The following industries are ineligible:

Attorneys
Doctors

Professional athletes
Professional drivers
Security guards
Entertainers
Individuals working in bars
Barber and beauty shops
Individuals with special industry/occupational hazards

EC and FF rates shown assume two children per family. One-child families will pay less.

* Example only. The policy illustrated may not be available at the quoted price.
Source: Quotesmith Corp.

Looking at the fine print under "Comments," you can see that this plan covers only in-hospital expenses, plus some out-patient surgical expenses. Thus, you're exposed to a wide range of nonhospital costs, but you probably have good catastrophic protection, up to $1 million in benefits. "If you know anyone who was wiped out financially by medical bills, it probably was from a long hospital stay," says Bill Thoms, a Quotesmith vice-president. "Several companies are beginning to offer hospital-only policies." (Mutual of Omaha is a prominent example.)

At any rate, the price of hospital-only coverage is attractive: If you want comprehensive coverage from the same insurance company, you'll have to pay at least $280 per month. That's an extra $100 per month, or $1,200 per year.

Two other matching plans were described in detail by Quotesmith. Both cost $292 per month, or about $3,500 annually for family coverage. One plan, from Boston Mutual, which has an A rating from A. M. Best, is seen in table 4. As you can see, under "Hospital and Doctor Benefits," most charges are covered by "Major Medical."

Table 4: BENEFIT ANALYSIS*

CARRIER: 164   BOSTON MUTUAL A
PLAN NAME: INDEPENDENCE PLAN A   NO MATERNITY
ID: PLAN A (5) 10

Life Insurance/AD&D
  (minimum required) $10,000/$10,000

HOSPITAL AND DOCTOR BENEFITS
  Room and board   Major medical
  Miscellaneous charges   Major medical
  Surgical charges   Major medical
  In-hospital doctor visits   Major medical
  Diagnostic X ray and
    laboratory   Major medical
  Maternity   Complications only
  Well baby/nursery charges   Not covered

MAJOR MEDICAL
  Deductible—family $1,000/3 per family
  Coinsurance (insurance co./
    employee)   80/20 to $5,000
  Maximum out-of-pocket per
    insured $1,000 plus deductible
  Plan maximum $5,000,000

MENTAL AND NERVOUS
  Inpatient/lifetime maximum   80%/31 days per year/$20,000
  Outpatient/annual maximum   50%/$30 per visit/1 visit per
                                           week

OPTIONAL COVERAGES
  Supplemental accident   Yes—$300 included
  Coverage for prescriptions   Major medical

DENTAL BENEFITS
  Deductible/annual maximum   See type of service/$1,000 max.
  Diagnostic/preventive   Paid at 80% after $25 ded.
  Basic restorative   Paid at 80% after $50 ded.
  Major restorative   Paid at 50% after $50 ded.
  Orthodontia   Not available

WDI (WEEKLY DISABILITY INCOME)
  Disability benefits   Not available

UNDERWRITING	6 medical questions per employee
PREEXISTING CONDITION (MONTHS)	12 prior/24 under
TAKEOVER COVERAGE	None
RATE GUARANTEE	12 months

COMMENTS

Precertification is required. List billing is available. Add one-time $10 enrollment fee per EE to rates shown. $5 association dues included in rates shown. Life insurance not available in Vermont and Pennsylvania. 6-month waiting period for restorative services/12-month for major services.

Ineligible Industries and Occupations

The following industries are ineligible:

Attorneys, law firms
Doctors (M.D., D.O.)
Hospitals
Extra-hazardous occupations and certain other occupations with a high incidence of exposure to diseases or injury.

Evidence of insurability is required from all members and their dependents, if applicable, when applying for coverage.

For groups of less than 10 employees, company will not accept anyone who is pregnant. For groups of 10 or more, company will accept one person who is at least seven months pregnant per each 10 employees.

Call 1-800-CAPPING for a list of CAPP CARE hospitals and doctors in your area. CAPP CARE is one of the largest PPO networks in the United States.

* Example only. The policy illustrated may not be available at the quoted price.
Source: Quotesmith Corp.

In essence, this means that the family will pay a $1,000 deductible per person (up to $3,000 per family). After that, the family will pay 20% coinsurance, until another $1,000 has been paid per person. After that, the insurance company will pay everything—up to a generous $5 million. No maternity or well-baby coverage is included, but this family is unlikely to need it.

"Mental and nervous" coverage is limited, but that's what you can expect from individual health insurance plans. In a hospital, the plan will pay 80% of the costs for up to 31 days per year. However, after the company has paid a total of $20,000 for in-hospital costs, no more will be paid. Out of hospital, the insurance will cover one visit to a therapist per week, paying 50% of the bill, up to $30 per visit.

As you can see, in case of an accident, the plan will pay $300 worth of expenses. Prescription costs are covered on the same terms as major medical, with the money spent counted toward the deductible and the stop-loss. Dental coverage is described, but that would cost an extra $30 per month.

Under "underwriting," you can see that everyone needs to fill out a brief medical questionnaire. Any preexisting condition that was treated (or should have been treated) in the preceding 12 months won't be covered until the policy has been in effect 24 months. There is no takeover coverage from previous policies, meaning that the 24-month waiting period is in effect for all conditions. And this rate—about $3,500—is guaranteed for the next 12 months.

Under "Comments," it says that precertification is required. That means your doctor will have to get permission from an insurance company rep before you can go into the hospital for nonemergencies and before you can have nonemergency surgery. Certain types of procedures, spelled out in the policy, have 6- and 12-month waiting periods.

You also can see that certain occupations (e.g., doctors, lawyers) are excluded from coverage. Plus, there's a phone number to call for a list of preferred provider organization (PPO) hospitals and doctors. PPOs are described in chapter 10; essentially, the doctors and hospitals on the list will give special prices to policyholders.

The other $3,500 plan comes from Continental American Life, rated A+ by A. M. Best. Actually, four plans from Continental American matched our criteria, but this one is the least expensive, so Quotesmith spelled out the details (see table 5).

Table 5: BENEFIT ANALYSIS*

CARRIER: 120 CONTINENTAL AMERICAN LIFE A+
PLAN NAME: FREEDOM SPIRIT NO MATERNITY ID: 80FS-10

Life Insurance/AD&D	
(minimum required)	$10,000/$10,000
HOSPITAL AND DOCTOR BENEFITS	
Room and board	Major medical
Miscellaneous charges	Major medical
Surgical charges	Major medical
In-hospital doctor visits	Major medical
Diagnostic X ray and laboratory	Major medical
Maternity	Complications only
Well baby/nursery charges	No/no
MAJOR MEDICAL	
Deductible—family	$1,000/3 per family
Coinsurance (insurance co./ employee)	80/20 to $5,000
Maximum out-of-pocket per insured	$1,000/$2,000 plus deductible
Plan maximum	$1,000,000
MENTAL AND NERVOUS	
Inpatient/lifetime maximum	50%/$10,000
Outpatient/annual maximum	50%/$30 per visit/$1,000
OPTIONAL COVERAGES	
Supplemental accident	Yes—$300
Coverage for prescriptions	NPA card—$5 copayment
DENTAL BENEFITS	
Dental benefits	Not available
WDI (WEEKLY DISABILITY INCOME)	
Disability benefits	Not available
UNDERWRITING	9 medical questions per employee
PREEXISTING CONDITION (MONTHS)	12 prior/24 under/12 free

TAKEOVER COVERAGE   None
RATE GUARANTEE   12 months

COMMENTS
This is an individual plan. List billing is available. Add one-time $23 enrollment fee per EE to rates shown. $1 Unitec dues included in rates shown. See ineligible list for special state provisions.

Ineligible Industries and Occupations

The following industries are ineligible:

Agriculture, marine, animal: crop dusters, divers, farms—other, hunting and trapping, logging operations, longshoremen, tanneries, underwater demolition and salvage. Construction: heavy construction, highway and road, underground, drywall applicators, excavating, insulation applicators, plant construction, shipbuilding, structural steel, building moving, building wrecking, seasonal. Entertainment: actors/entertainers/musicians, amusement parks, athletes—professional, carnivals/circus, dance halls/studios/schools—instructional, fraternal, or social organizations, gambling-related businesses, health and sports clubs, martial-arts instructors, massage parlors, racetracks, rodeos, ski lifts and tows, tanning salons, video arcades. Finance, professional, health: apartment management, attorneys and law firms, property management, chiropractors, clinics—medical and dental, dentists and oral surgeons, dental hygienists, home-health care, hospitals, hypnotists, labs—medical and dental, nursing homes, nurses, opthalmologists, opticians, physicians—general category, anesthesiologists, osteopaths, pediatricians, medical/physician/surgeon groups, podiatrists, psychologists, psychotherapists, rehabilitation centers, sanitariums, physical therapists. Food, hotel and liquor industry: bars and taverns, canneries, distillers of alcohol, food processors and packers, meat packing and processing, restaurants, nonfranchise—other. Government/nonprofit services: apartment and condo assocs., charity organizations, police depts., embassies/consulates, nonprofit organizations, public employee/schools, public transportation, Salvation Army, etc., union and welfare funds. Manufacturing: asbestos, batteries, chemicals, chemical petroleum, explosives, ammunition, fertilizer, fiberglass operations, foundries and smelters, natural gas (including transportation), paint, plastics and rubber. Mining: drilling—oil and gas, mining—underground, mining/coal—subsurface, oil refinery. Retail and wholesale trade: barber and beauty shops, car washes, drugstores, florists, junk and salvage yards, pawnshops. Service and miscellaneous: bail bondsmen, detective agencies/security guards, domestic—maids, chauffeurs, exterminators, mobile park homes, newspaper delivery, religious groups, clergy, sales—commission only, septic tank cleaners, social workers, tree maintenance. Transportation and public utilities: airlines and aviation firms, ambulance companies, bus companies, garbage or sanitation, limousine services, parking lots, taxi companies, trucking firms—long haul. Occupations that are seasonal in nature are not eligible.

Please note: This listing should be used only as a guideline. Other industries may be ineligible. Call the contact for further information.

Special state provisions: For IL and NH only: the preexisting-condition provision has been modified where necessary to comply with state regulations. Please refer to Certificate Booklet for details or call Pilgrim Health Applications. List billings not available in CT, IL, NH, and NC. NC has no additional charge for a 12-month rate guarantee.

* Example only. The policy illustrated may not be available at the quoted price.
Source: Quotesmith Corp.

The hospital and doctor benefits are virtually identical to the plan from Boston Mutual except that there's a $1 million cap on benefits, not $5 million. Mental and nervous coverage is even more limited, but family members will get a card for prescription drugs, enabling subscribers to pay only $5 per prescription.

Other conditions also are similar except that no precertification is required and there's no list of low-cost providers to choose from. However, Continental American has a huge list of excluded occupations, from crop dusters to long-haul truckers. (That's probably how it got to be rated A+.) So you may not be able to get coverage, depending on what you do for a living.

At this point, you might want to check back with table 2, to look at some other options. As you can see, one other low-cost insurance company, Centennial Life, didn't match because of "C"—carrier profile. That means the company doesn't have the A or A+ rating from A. M. Best that was requested.

Another insurer, Durham Life, has an A+ rating. However, it failed to match because of "R" (no 12-month rate guarantee) and "S" (no supplemental accident coverage). If you can do without these features, you can ask for a closer look at some of the Durham Life policies, which are priced at $2,500–$3,000 per year.

This information from Quotesmith may not be all-inclusive—Blue Cross and Blue Shield of New Jersey, for example, has some good major medical policies—but at least it can point you in the right direction, giving you an idea of the coverage available and the probable cost.

Other data-base companies, such as Dinan and Group Benefit Shoppers, offer a variation on the same theme. Here insurance professionals who participate get a new diskette each month. These professionals can manipulate the data, finding the best combination of features for their clients.

Ask your insurance agent or financial planner if he or she subscribes to such a service. If not, contact one of these services directly and tell them what you're looking for. They'll probably put you in touch with a participant in your area. Then you can work with that agent or planner to shop the market and seek out the best deal.

- Quotesmith: (800) 556-9393
- Dinan: (800) 346-2610
- Group Benefit Shoppers: (800) 231-8495

(In late 1991, Quotesmith introduced a medical insurance price comparison service for small-business owners, who can order a price comparison report for $15.)

CHEAPER BY THE DOZENS

If you're not covered by an employer health plan or not covered well by your employer's health plan, there's another option to consider while you're shopping for insurance. You might join a group.

Large employers, as mentioned, have an advantage over small companies when shopping for health insurance. Insurers prefer to administer a plan with hundreds, even thousands, of employees rather than one for Paul & Paula, Inc., with three clerical workers. More employees means more premiums, and the serious health risks are spread over a much larger population. Usually, large groups don't require that you pass a physical exam to be covered by the health insurance and pay the standard premium.

You can get the same size advantage by joining a group. What kind of group? The possibilities are virtually endless. It can be a professional society, a religious organization, a fraternal group, or a veteran's organization. Even some credit-card issuers put together groups for the purpose of obtaining health insurance.

The problem with group insurance is the same as the problem with employer insurance: Someone else puts together the coverage, which you can accept or decline. It's not tailored to your needs.

Some group coverage is comprehensive, while some is skimpy. Some requires health exams. Premiums and other cost factors (deductibles, coinsurance, stop-losses, benefits caps) vary widely. In some groups, for example, younger and healthier members can find health insurance for less money elsewhere. These groups tend to wind up with older and sicker participants, paying high premiums because of the insurer's experience with substantial claims.

Empire Blue Cross and Blue Shield, which serves New York State, has just dropped group coverage for more than 100,000 members of the State Bar Association, the Foreign Press Association, and other organizations because it was losing money on these people, even though it had increased premiums. One lawyer, who has AIDS, had been paying $3,000 per year through the bar association's plan; Empire has offered him an individual policy at $11,000 per year.

Don't sign up for group coverage just because it's there—read over the terms carefully and compare what you're getting for what you pay with the coverage you could buy on your own.

However, if you find it difficult to obtain health insurance at a reasonable cost, joining a group may be your best tactic.

THE LAST RESORT

About half of all states have a "high-risk" pool for people who can't buy health insurance. Terms vary, but in order to qualify you usually have to have been a resident of that state for at least six months and to have been denied coverage by at least one insurer. (Usually, if you can buy health insurance only with exclusion riders or only at a superhigh premium, you're eligible to jump in the pool.)

As you'd expect, you pay a lot for a little coverage, but high-risk groups are better than nothing. Pool participants might pay premiums around double the size of those a healthy person would pay to an insurance company. Plus, you might have to pay higher deductibles and higher coinsurance and live with a cap on benefits. So these plans usually are worth considering only after all your other options have been exhausted.

IN BRIEF

- Some computerized services will try to match your health insurance needs with the policies on the market. You probably will have to work with an insurance agent or financial planner to use these services.
- Although computerized services have their limitations, they can be valuable guides to finding out what's available at what price.
- If you're not covered by your employer, you may get good value in health insurance by joining a professional, religious, fraternal, or other group.
- As a last resort, many states offer pools where high-risk individuals can buy health insurance. Premiums are often high, and coverage is limited.

Chapter 9

HMOs Can Maintain Your Wealth as Well as Your Health

If you had basic economics in school, you probably remember supply curves and demand curves. In essence, demand for any good or service will decrease as the price increases. Conversely, as the price increases, so will supply as more suppliers come into the market. The intersection of supply and demand curves determines the end price.

For the past 25 years or so, that didn't seem to be the case in health care. The introduction of Medicare and Medicaid (in which government pays for health care) and the rise of tax-free health care as a form of compensation (in which employers and insurance companies pay for health care) distorted conventional economics.

You had an inexhaustible demand. Everyone wants all the health care possible, especially when one is paying little or nothing for it. On the supply side, doctors and hospitals were willing to supply all the health care anyone would want. There was no natural tension between suppliers and consumers to regulate prices, so prices went straight up.

But no tree grows to the sky. Soaring physicians' incomes have led to huge increases in the numbers of doctors. Often new doctors come into the world long on debt and short on patients. At that stage, they're ready to cut deals. Health-care payers— employers and insurers and government agencies—have made them offers they can't refuse: Give us a price break and we'll send you patients.

That's an oversimplification, of course, but there's no doubt that power is shifting to the payers, who are starting to wield that power. Just as certain, an oversupply of physicians and hospitals in certain areas has made them willing to deal with payers. Out of these deals has come the concept of "managed care," which includes health maintenance organizations (HMOs) and preferred provider organizations (PPOs). As recently as 1977, only 4% of the health-care bills in the United States were handled by HMOs, PPOs, and similar plans. By 1987, that figure was over 25%, heading toward an estimated 90% by 1997. An HMO or PPO probably is in your future.

ONE PRICE FITS ALL

HMOs have been around for decades, but cost pressures have increased their popularity in recent years. In an HMO you don't pay a premium for health insurance because you're not really buying insurance. Instead, you're paying a fee that's designed to cover most, if not all, of your health-care needs. Although individuals can join an HMO, most HMO memberships come through group plans, where no health exam is required. Membership in an HMO is usually slightly more expensive than paying health insurance premiums.

HMOs differ, but here's how a typical plan would work: The Adams family pays $60 per month, while John Adams's employer pays $200 per month. (Those figures are the national averages.) For this, they get to go to a limited group of doctors whenever they'd like. Routine checkups are included, as well as the usual round of colds, aches, and injuries. Each of these office visits is free, or there may be a token (say, $6) fee. Similarly, you may have to pay only $2 per prescription whenever you need medication. Although there may be exceptions, most HMOs don't impose sizable deductibles or coinsurance requirements.

There are two basic forms of HMOs.

• HMO Central. Technically called the "group model" or the "staff model," those HMOs work out of a central office building or several such buildings in different locations. When you need health care, you'll go to the office and see doctors there. Large HMOs may have a full range of specialists, X-ray equipment, lab facilities, even nutrition specialists to work out a diet with you.

• HMO Local. In "individual practice associations," an HMO will sign contracts with a number of doctors who have their own practice. Instead of going to the HMO office, you'll visit these doctors in their own offices, identifying yourself as an HMO member. A doctor might have just seen six patients who are not HMO members, billing them directly or sending the bills to Blue Cross. When it's your turn, the doctor will treat you and charge you perhaps a token $6, because he or she is being paid by your HMO to care for you.

TAKE A BITE OUT OF HEALTH COSTS

With either type of HMO, you and your family may well enjoy better health because all routine checkups, preventive testing, and screening are paid for. Your physicians have a real incentive to keep you healthy so you won't need expensive hospital care.

For example, Hewlett-Packard added HMO coverage for dental care for some of its employees in 1987. In its traditional fee-for-service plan, participants pay a $50 deductible for cleanings and 20% coinsurance for other care. In the dental HMO, there's no fee for cleaning and other preventive care. Remedial work (e.g., filling teeth) requires a $25 deductible.

Since then, the company has found, employees in the dental HMO are more likely to go to the dentist for routine care. Their teeth are healthier, and despite the fact that the HMO provides free cleaning, dental costs per employee actually fell, while dental costs for employees in the traditional health-care plan rose more than 25%.

If you need a specialist that the HMO doesn't have, you'll be referred to one who has a contract with that HMO. Again, your fee will cover the bill.

Similarly, if you need to go into a hospital, you'll go into one with a contract with the HMO, which will pay the hospital bills.

There are variations, of course, and some HMOs will demand out-of-pocket costs for some treatments, but the basic principle is that of an all-you-can-eat restaurant. You pay the fixed price and help yourself to the health care you want. Moreover, there are few if any claim forms to fill out and no need to pay up front and wait for reimbursement.

HMO, HEAL THYSELF

So far, HMO sounds as if it stands for win-win-win. Patients have all the health care they want for a fixed price, doctors have a steady stream of patients to provide a predictable income, and payers get to hold down the amounts they pay to doctors and hospitals because of negotiated fees.

Unfortunately, HMOs don't always work out so well. In fact, one danger you face is that your HMO will collapse, leaving you with no protection in case of an emergency. For an HMO, income is limited to what it receives from patients in monthly or quarterly fees. Some HMO costs—money paid to contracting doctors and hospitals—can be controlled, but not everything. What happens if outside specialists need to be called in or expensive operations are necessary or the number of lab tests exceeds expectations? What happens if the HMO expects 5% of its members to be hospitalized in a given year but the actual number exceeds 10%? Even at favorable hospital rates, the expense may be more than the HMO can bear.

Whether because of poor management or unexpected developments, many HMOs have gone under. Before you sign up, ask to see financial statements. If you're not familiar with how to read them, ask your CPA or your sister-in-law who works on Wall Street to help you.

CHECKUP

What should you look for in terms of an HMO's financial strength?

• A track record of at least three years.
• Reported profitability.
• Large enrollments. An HMO with over 20,000 members can afford the necessary support services.
• Sponsors. An HMO owned, in part or in full, by a "name-brand" corporation or institution likely will stay in business.
• Federal qualification. An HMO approved by the U.S. Office of Pre-Paid Health has demonstrated its financial reserves. Some states have similar standards. Check with your state insurance commissioner's office.

OUT OF CONTROL

In a traditional fee-for-service, or indemnity, plan, you pick out the doctors you want. If necessary, you go to the hospital chosen by you and your doctor. With an HMO, however, you're limited to the doctor the HMO wants you to see. Typically, you must see a "primary care" doctor, the "gatekeeper," before seeing any other doctor in order for the HMO to cover your costs. This gatekeeper may be the same doctor, time and again, or you may see a different one each time you go in. Many times, when you go to an HMO, you won't be treated by a doctor. Instead, a nurse or a physician's assistant will perform routine tests. There's not a lot of hand-holding involved. If you feel you need to see a specialist, the primary-care physician will refer you to one on the HMO's rolls—or may disagree that a specialist is required and treat you him or herself.

What happens if you don't play by the HMO rules? You have to pay the bills yourself. If you want to see the best specialist in town and your HMO doesn't preapprove the visit, you'll wind up paying the entire fee yourself. Or you may have a doctor you've been seeing for years to treat a specific condition. If you're offered a switch to an HMO and that doctor isn't in the network, you may be reluctant to sign up and start with a new doctor.

Sometimes location is a problem. One New York City business owner employs around 50 people. Recently, he switched from Blue Cross to a large local HMO, reducing his company's costs from over $200 per employee per month to around $120 per employee per month. "My production workers love the HMO," he says. "Before, they mainly went to clinics. Now they can call a doctor and get an appointment."

However, the business owner himself, who lives on Long Island, has kept his Blue Cross, and so have a few top executives who live in the suburbs. "The HMO has no doctors anywhere near where we live," he says. "Doctors in these areas usually do fairly well, and they're not interested in the terms this HMO is offering."

TOO SLOW, TOO FAST

Other HMO problems include long waits for nonemergency appointments and in the reception room, even after you have such an appointment. Also, when you're traveling and are unable to use the HMO network, your coverage may be limited to emergency care.

Perhaps more substantially, some critics charge that HMOs are so obsessed with cost control that the quality of care suffers. For example, about one out of every six HMOs engages in "therapeutic substitution," the use of similar but cheaper drugs. (Don't confuse therapeutic substitution with the use of generics instead of brand-name drugs, which may be appropriate and economical.) Often neither the patient nor the doctor is aware of this practice, which takes place at HMO hospitals or pharmacies. In some cases, problems may result when patients on multiple medications are subjected to therapeutic substitution.

HMO critics also charge that doctors do fewer tests than necessary. To hold down expenses, surgery may be done out of a hospital rather than in the hospital; any hospital stays may be cut as short as possible.

Now, this isn't necessarily a bad thing: Fewer tests and fewer days in the hospital may mean better care. A Johns Hopkins University study found the care at HMOs, on average, as good as or better than care from fee-for-service physicians.

OPEN-DOOR POLICY

Nevertheless, HMOs are different, especially for patients used to traditional care. Therefore, many HMOs are trying to respond to these perceived shortcomings. Hybrid HMOs are on the rise, offering you more freedom of choice in return for higher fees.

Recently, "open-ended" HMOs have become popular, with enrollment up nearly 40% per year. In these plans, members are allowed to see non-HMO doctors if they're willing to pay deductibles and coinsurance.

Wells Fargo, for example, offers its employees a hybrid HMO called "SelectCare." Patients start out with the HMO-style gatekeeper. However, if the primary-care physician assigns them to a specialist inside the HMO network, they can go outside and see a specialist of their choice. Outside, they pay a $400 deductible plus 30% of subsequent costs. They therefore have some freedom of choice if they're willing to split the cost with their employer.

CIGNA's Healthplan, an HMO offered to employers, gives members the choice of using their own doctors. Groups that want this option pay an extra 5%–10%. If you go outside, you pay a deductible ($150–$300) and coinsurance (20%–30% of the excess). So there's some coverage. Inside the HMO, there's only a token charge per visit.

PHYSICIANS HEAL THEMSELVES

Besides giving patients more freedom of choice, some HMOs are taking steps to shore up other perceived shortcomings. US Health-care, for example, sends out about 900,000 questionnaires to its patients per year, receiving around 200,000 responses. They ask the following types of questions: How long does it take to

CHECKUP

How can you check out an HMO? Obviously, you want to know what you'll pay and what services the HMO has to offer. You should also check into an HMO's financial strength, mentioned above. In addition, here are some of the things to ask about:

- Professional certification. Groups such as the Joint Commission on Accreditation of Healthcare Organizations, the Accreditation Association for Ambulatory Health Care, and the National Committee for Quality Assurance have standards for judging HMOs.
- Association membership. The Group Health Association of America and HMO-USA are the leading industry groups.
- Hospital affiliation. Ask which hospital(s) the HMO uses. If it's a well-known local hospital or one affiliated with a medical school, that's a good sign.
- Board of directors. Respected doctors should be on the board.
- Physician screening. Ask what the criteria are for signing up physicians, along with the average years of professional experience. The tougher the standards and the more years of practice, the better.
- Patient-doctor ratio. If there are 10 physicians responsible for 15,000 patients, you may not get much in the way of individual care. For self-contained HMOs (where doctors see no non-HMO patients), the patient-doctor ratio averages 200:1 to 300:1. Beware of HMOs where the ratio is significantly higher.
- Patient profile. If most of the members are old enough to be beyond pediatric care and too young for Medicare, the doctors are likely to have more time for you.
- Checkup on physicians. Is there a formal procedure for monitoring physician performance and patient satisfaction?
- Checkup on patients. Ask for the names of longtime members, then call them to ask their opinion of the HMO.
- Checkup on medicine. If therapeutic substitution is practiced, is it cleared with physicians and disclosed to patients?
- Appeals process. What if you and your gatekeeper don't agree on treatment? The better HMOs have a procedure for resolving these disputes.

get an appointment? How long is the average wait in the office? Does the physician return calls? Each of these questions has five answers, from poor to excellent. The answers are passed on to physicians to help them manage their practices. What's more, the results of the questionnaires, along with other factors—what percentage of children are immunized on a given schedule, what percentage of adults over age 40 have had cholesterol tests— are used in determining incentive pay for physicians. According to US Healthcare executives, 1%–2% of the physicians on its roster are dropped each year because of poor ratings.

Other HMOs use similar surveys, by mail or by phone, to judge physicians' overall performance and adjust compensation. In fact, the Group Health Association of America, an HMO trade association, has developed a model survey of patient satisfaction that many HMOs use. According to the *New York Times*, more than 34 million Americans are now enrolled in HMOs, 10% of them in plans where patient evaluations help set doctors' income.

Employers, too, are pushing HMOs to cut costs and improve service to their employees. Xerox, for example, has created a network of six HMOs, which compete with each other. Based on such criteria as the number of doctors available per patient member, rate of physician turnover, patient access to care, and waiting time, Xerox will direct its employees to the better performers.

IN BRIEF
- Many health-care insurers and employers are switching to "managed care," including HMOs.
- In an HMO, participants pay membership fees rather than insurance premiums.
- Those fees entitle participants (and dependents, if covered) to unlimited health care. There may be no additional costs or only token fees.
- Routine checkups and preventive care are included in HMO coverage, and patients are encouraged to take advantage.
- There are few or no claim forms to deal with.
- HMO members are largely limited to certain doctors and

hospitals. If they use others, they may have little or no coverage.

- HMO health care may involve inconvenience and the loss of intimate doctor-patient relationships.
- Although HMOs have performed well in studies, critics charge that their emphasis on cost control can lead to shortcuts in treatment.
- In response, HMOs are taking steps to provide more freedom of choice and to improve service.
- Before joining an HMO, closely question its financial strength and its operating record.

Chapter 10

PPOs Versus HMOs

"Managed care" is the catchphrase of the day in health insurance as payers attempt to manage their health-care costs. Almost all large companies now offer health-care choices to their employees. The same goes for government agencies. You may have to choose among indemnity plans, health maintenance organizations (HMOs), and preferred provider organizations (PPOs). In some large organizations, there may be a dozen or more choices. At General Motors, for example, 45% of hourly workers and more than 65% of salaried employees are enrolled in a managed-care plan.

HMOs, as mentioned, offer "all you can eat" for a fixed price, but you have to pick from a set menu of doctors. A PPO, by contrast, gives you a choice: column A or column B. Choose from column A, where the options are fewer, and you can cut your costs dramatically.

With PPOs you can use any doctor you want. But if you use a doctor on the PPO list—a preferred provider—you get a better deal.

You might, for example, have no obligation to pay a deductible for PPO treatments. You might get coverage for preventive health care (checkups, immunizations) not usually covered by an indemnity plan. In a PPO, you might have to pay only $10 or $15.

Therefore, signing up for a PPO can save you money, compared with a traditional plan, every time you use a preferred provider. Compared with an HMO, a PPO offers more choice. If you insist, you can see the best specialist in town, with the plan picking up some of the cost. With an HMO, you might get no reimbursement at all.

PPOs may offer broader coverage than HMOs. For example, HMOs often offer minimal treatment for "mental or nervous" disorders and treatment for substance abuse. PPOs might cover ongoing treatment, providing far more benefits.

JOIN THE NETWORK

The key to avoid confusion is to disregard the "O." An HMO, on the one hand, is a real organization. It may be a profit-making organization or a nonprofit group. But an HMO exists—it keeps records, and its income must exceed its expenses if it wants to survive over the long term.

A PPO, on the other hand, is not much of an "O." It may consist of 20,000 physicians, scattered throughout an entire state. A physician may belong to several PPOs. Say AT&T is putting together a PPO for its employees. It may ask Dr. James Johnson of Kansas City to join. At the same time, Metropolitan Life may be putting together a PPO for the health insurance plans it sells and those it administers. That same Dr. Johnson, by all accounts a fine physician, may be asked to join. There's no reason why he can't. In fact, he can belong to other PPOs as well.

Suppose he winds up signing up with six PPOs, with a total of 5,000 members in the Kansas City area. (Some doctors belong to as many as 10 PPOs.) Any of them could come to him for PPO treatment. And he can still see other patients who are not affiliated with any PPOs.

As you can see, a PPO is more of a network than a bona fide organization. Most of them serve group plans rather than individuals, but there is a trend to offering PPO benefits to individual and family policyholders. Each physician in the network makes a deal with the PPO's sponsor to charge less for PPO participants in return for being included on the list of "preferred providers" and thus likely to gain new patients. Many PPOs screen providers carefully, via computer. If Dr. Marcia Welby seems to be billing too much, to be using surgery for a certain procedure when most of her colleagues are prescribing medication, she may get a friendly visit from the home office. If she doesn't get the message, she may be dropped from the network. Increasingly, payers are playing hardball when it comes to health-care costs.

"CUSTOM" CARE IS CHEAPER

One of the first major examples of a PPO in action began in 1986, when Southwestern Bell was negotiating with its primary union. From 1975 to 1985, the company's spending on health benefits was up nearly 220%, with no relief in sight.

So the union agreed to a "custom care" plan. Networks of doctors and hospitals were set up; custom-care participants pay only $10 per doctor visit, and virtually nothing else, as long as they stay in the network. If they go outside the network, they must pay a deductible and coinsurance, up to nearly $2,500 per year for an individual, or $4,200 per year for a family of three.

At first, there was a lot of employee resistance to giving up their doctors. But, five years later, over 80% of eligible employees were enrolled in custom care, and nearly 85% of those told a survey that care was "excellent" or "very good." The payoff for Southwestern Bell: Health-care costs have been rising less than 10% per year, around half the national average.

Encouraged, other major companies are following suit. AT&T was struck by 100,000 workers in 1989 but wound up with a PPO in place. The 1,200 doctors in the PPO reportedly discount their regular rates around 20% in order to get on the list. A doctor in Atlanta, for example, gets $88 per year per employee assigned to him for primary care, plus a bonus if he holds down referrals to high-fee specialists.

Employees who use a PPO doctor in the AT&T system get 90%-plus reimbursement, while those who go outside the network get only 80% of what probably will be a higher fee. Deductibles are lower on PPO treatments, too, $150 versus $200.

IBM has gone a step further, setting up a PPO just for mental-health and substance-abuse benefits. IBM employees in the program can get 100% coverage of inpatient care after paying a deductible; outside the network, coverage is limited to only 90 days a year, and reimbursement is only 80%. For outpatient care, including psychiatrists' visits, PPO members will pay only 20% of costs up to $15,000 versus a 50% obligation if they go outside the network.

According to IBM, many of its employees appreciate the program because they want recommended therapists. Employees who already have their own care providers can nominate them for inclusion in the PPO.

Some individual health-care plans are adding a PPO option. For example, if you go to a preferred provider, you might pay 10% coinsurance rather than 20%. Or maybe you'll pay only $10 for an office visit.

How does a PPO stack up for the consumer? You give up some freedom of choice, but not much. You still can use any doctor you want, but there's a definite economic incentive to use preferred providers. In some cases, you may get extra coverage if you stay within the PPO network. That is, a checkup may be covered inside the PPO but totally paid for by you if you go outside.

PPOs vary so much from one to the next that it's difficult to give specific guidelines. You need to know the basic rules, of course: How much do I pay inside the PPO, and how much do I pay when I go outside?

THREE FOR THE MONEY

If your employer offers you a choice between fee-for-service, HMOs, and PPOs, which should you select? To a great extent,

---

CHECKUP

Here are some questions to ask before joining a PPO:

- Is there a primary physician "gatekeeper" procedure? If so, you give up a great deal of choice because all PPO-paid care must be approved by him or her.
- Are preexisting conditions eligible for PPO coverage?
- What happens when you're sick or injured while out of town?
- What sort of catastrophic protection is there? You'll want to be sure a stop-loss is in place, along with a $1 million + cap on lifetime benefits.

---

that depends on the quality of the plans. A good fee-for-service plan is better than a poor HMO or PPO.

Assuming that they're of equal quality, which should you choose? Start with the HMO. Your health-care costs, and those of your family, are virtually fixed. You can get all the preventive care and screening you want, which likely will pay off in better health over the long term. Plus, you won't get wiped out by a catastrophe.

But HMOs aren't for everyone. If freedom to choose physicians is vital to you, stay away from HMOs. The same if you insist upon a great deal of personalized attention from physicians. If you're concerned about large bills for psychiatric disorders or substance-abuse treatment, you probably won't find much coverage in an HMO.

An HMO that's far from your home or one with no nearby physicians may not serve you well.

If an HMO isn't for you, your decision may be between the PPO and the traditional fee-for-service plan. Again, start with the PPO, because that's potentially the less expensive choice. Look over the network of preferred providers. If you think you can take care of most of your health care from that list, take the PPO. (This assumes that the PPO offers adequate protection against catastrophes.)

However, if you feel that most of your visits will be to the doctors you have been using in the past, you won't get much benefit from the PPO. You'll probably wind up paying more, for non-network providers, so you might as well stick with the traditional fee-for-service plan.

For now, at least. The trend toward some sort of managed care is inevitable. For the overwhelming majority of Americans, the day is coming when you'll have to be treated by a doctor someone else has chosen if you want the costs to be paid by someone else.

IN BRIEF

- Health-care payers increasingly are focusing on "managed care." Besides HMOs, managed care includes PPOs.
- PPOs are networks of physicians and other health-care providers. Physicians in the network agree to give discounts when treating patients who are PPO participants.
- PPO participants usually can choose any doctors they want.
- When they choose doctors inside the PPO network, costs are modest or nonexistent. When they go outside the network, their costs may be substantial.
- If your employer offers you a choice of coverage, an HMO probably is the lowest-cost, lowest-risk option if you can stand the limitation on your choice of doctors.
- If you want more choice but are willing to use preferred providers to a substantial degree, a PPO can be less expensive than traditional fee-for-service health insurance.
- If you choose a PPO, evaluate the catastrophic coverage (stop-losses, lifetime cap on benefits) just as you would the coverage in a traditional plan.

Chapter 11

Medicare: Health Care's Safe Harbor

Love may be a battlefield, as Pat Benatar sang in the 1980s, but health care is more like a minefield. You crawl along from day to day, hoping you and your family can avoid a ruinous illness or accident. Health insurance, if you have some, must be approached with care. One expensive hospital stay and your premiums will explode: You may not be able to afford to carry insurance. Then all of your assets are vulnerable in case of another disaster.

At the other side of the minefield, though, is the promised land: Medicare. For most people, reaching age 65 means Medicare eligibility. Now Uncle Sam will take care of your health care, regardless of your health. You're home free.

Well, almost. It is true that people 65 and over generally are eligible for Medicare, which is available at a modest cost regardless of your health. (Some disabled people are eligible for Medicare before age 65.) It is also true that Medicare will pay some—perhaps most—of your health-care bills. However, Medicare does not cover everything. Even Medicare recipients can be wiped out by a health emergency.

So your need for health insurance doesn't end when you

reach 65. You probably need an insurance policy to supplement Medicare, popularly called "Medigap" insurance, because it fills the gaps in Medicare's coverage. Unfortunately, Medigap insurance has been replete with frauds and scoundrels who find the elderly easy prey.

Not all Medigap insurance is a scam. Indeed, some of America's best health insurers are in the Medigap market. But if you're buying a Medigap policy for yourself or advising an aging relative, you need to be able to separate the good guys from the bad guys. In order to do so, you need to know what Medicare provides so that you know what gaps a Medigap policy should fill.

"A" IS FOR AT THE HOSPITAL

You can apply for Medicare three months before you reach 65. Go to your local Social Security office with proof of your birthdate. As long as you've earned enough to be eligible for Social Security retirement benefits, you'll be eligible for Medicare. If you don't have enough earnings to qualify, you'll still be eligible if your spouse had the requisite earnings. (If you or your spouse didn't participate in Social Security because of government employment, that government agency likely has a retiree health insurance plan similar to Medicare.)

After you enroll in Medicare, you'll automatically be included in Part A, which is hospital coverage. Part A is free. (If, for some reason you don't qualify for Medicare, you can buy into Part A for around $3,000 per year, regardless of your health.)

HOW BENEFIT PERIODS WORK

To understand how Medicare A works, you need to become familiar with the concept of a Medicare "benefit period." A benefit period begins the day you enter the hospital. A benefit period ends after you have spent 60 consecutive days out of the hospital and out of any skilled-nursing homes.

Say Joe Jones goes into the hospital for a bypass operation on January 10. On January 20, he goes home. On March 20 (60 days later), his benefit period ends. If he needs another operation and reenters the hospital on April 1, he's into a new benefit period.

Janet Johnson, on the other hand, suffers a massive heart attack and enters the hospital on May 1. She's released on May 15 but has to go into a skilled-nursing home for a month. On June 15, she goes home. But she has a relapse on August 1 and has to spend the entire month of August in a hospital's intensive-care unit. In September, she is released to a skilled-nursing home, where she spends six weeks. By mid-October, she's judged strong enough for another operation, so it's back to the hospital until mid-November. She goes back to the skilled-nursing home until she is released in time to go home for the Christmas holidays.

All seems well, and Janet is once more able to compete on her senior citizens' ice skating race team. In early February (40 days after her release from the nursing home), she trips on the ice and breaks her ankle in three places. So it's back to the hospital for another operation and another release to the skilled-nursing home. On April 1, she gets out of the nursing home. Sixty days later, on May 30, her benefit period ends.

So Joe's benefit period lasts less than three months, while Janet's lasts over a year. Why is this important? Because Medicare A benefits are pegged to benefit periods. In each benefit period

• You pay a deductible. Currently, that's $652. (The numbers in this chapter are for 1992; they generally go up every year to match inflation.)

• After the deductible, the first 60 hospital days are paid for by Medicare.

• After 60 days in the hospital, you pay $163 per day for the next 30 days of each benefit period.

• Beyond 90 hospital days of each benefit period, each Medicare patient is entitled to 60 "reserve days" during his or her lifetime. Each of these days will cost you $326; reserve days are not replenished with each new benefit period. After you've used up your 60 reserve days, you're responsible for all the costs. Reserve days can cover hospital costs but not the costs of skilled-nursing homes.

NOT-SO-GRAND TOTALS

Going back to the above examples, Joe has to pay the $652 deductible, but Medicare pays for his 10-day hospital stint. (Joe, like many Medicare patients, also has to pay for some blood that he needed.) If he goes back into the hospital later, his Medicare clock starts over. There are no limits to the number of benefit periods he has.

Janet, though, has logged a total of 84 days in the hospital. So, in addition to her $652 deductible, she's responsible for 24 days (days 61 through 84) at $163 per day. That's nearly $4,000 in addition to her deductible. However, once she has spent 60 days outside of hospitals and skilled-nursing homes, the entire process starts over again. She has to pay another $652 deductible the next time she enters the hospital, but Medicare picks up the other costs for 60 days.

WELL COVERED

For hospital stays, Medicare A coverage is excellent. The cost of a semiprivate room is included. Intensive-care rooms are treated the same as other rooms in the hospital—that is, paid for—even though they're far more expensive. Meals, regular nurses, drugs, transfusions, and rehabilitation services are all covered. Usually, all you have to pay for, besides the deductible, is the phone and TV in your room. (Doctors' services performed in the hospital, including surgery, are covered by Medicare B, which is described in the next chapter.)

If you need a private room and your doctor says it's medically necessary, Medicare A probably will pay for that, too. Otherwise, you'll have to pay the difference between a private and a semiprivate room. Also, Medicare won't pay for private-duty nurses you hire.

UNCOVERED

Medicare is not immune from cost-control pressures. You don't have to be an avid follower of the daily news to know that the federal government, which pays Medicare bills, runs a budget deficit of hundreds of billions of dollars each year. To keep the deficit from growing even more, federal regulators are trying to rein in Medicare expenses.

The major weapon they're using is the DRG (diagnostic-related-group) system. Whenever you go into a hospital, your condition will be given a DRG number. Depending on that condition and the location of the hospital, Medicare will pay the hospital a flat fee. That fee might be $1,000, $2,000, $3,800, or whatever.

Now, the hospital is going to collect that $3,800 no matter how long you stay. Obviously, it's in the hospital's interest to get you out as fast as possible. After you're discharged, you won't be consuming costly hospital services; the hospital may get another patient to fill your bed and bring in more money.

Therefore, at a certain point, you'll receive a "notice of non-coverage" from the hospital. Generally, that means you have two more days of Medicare A coverage. On day six of your hospital stay, for example, the hospital will notify you that Medicare will pay for only eight days of coverage for your condition. If you want to stay longer, you'll have to pay for it.

A notice of noncoverage is not etched in stone. If you're not ready to leave, you can ask your doctor for help. He or she may be able to convince the hospital you need more time, covered by Medicare.

If this doesn't work, ask the hospital administrator for the phone number of your state's peer-review organization (PRO), an appeals court composed of doctors. You can call the PRO and officially appeal your notice of noncoverage.

In most cases, the PRO's decision won't come immediately.

In fact, it likely will come after you've been discharged from the hospital. If you have stayed beyond your notice of noncoverage, the PRO's decision will determine how much of the excess stay you'll have to pay for.

HALFWAY HOME

As you'd expect, the DRG system results in many patients convalescing outside, rather than inside, the hospital. Most people prefer to go home, but often they're not ready. Or there's no one at home to care for them. Consequently, the growth of DRGs has seen a parallel growth in discharges from hospitals to nursing homes.

Will Medicare pay for nursing-home care? Probably not. If the nursing care is purely custodial—feeding, bathing, dressing, dispensing pills—Medicare won't pay for the coverage. (In part III, nursing-home insurance is described.)

However, under certain conditions, Medicare A will pay for nursing-home costs:

• The patient has to be in the hospital for at least three days, not counting the day of discharge.

• Within 30 days of discharge, the patient goes into a nursing home for the same condition treated in the hospital.

• The nursing home must be a skilled-nursing facility and everyone—the doctor, the home, a Medicare reviewer—must agree that skilled care is necessary.

Skilled-nursing facilities are recognized by Medicare. In general, they are nursing homes or sections of larger nursing homes where licensed medical professionals care for patients.

These standards are not easy to meet—that's why Medicare pays for less than 2% of national nursing-home costs. If you do meet the criteria, though, Medicare A will pay for the first 20 days in a benefit period. For the next 80 days, you must pay

$81.50 per day. After 100 days, Medicare pays nothing, so you're fully responsible.

Janet Johnson, in our example, spends 150 days in skilled-nursing facilities in one benefit period. The first 20 days would be free. As many as 80 additional days would be covered by Medicare, after Janet has paid $81.50 per day. However, Medicare stops paying once the condition has stabilized and care becomes custodial. So Janet may find herself on the hook for thousands more, depending on her condition.

NOT HOME ALONE

Often people released from the hospital do go home rather than into a nursing home. In certain circumstances, Medicare will pay for a professional to visit you at your home. Generally, the circumstances are similar to those that apply to skilled-nursing care. Your care must be performed by a licensed professional, certified by Medicare, at your doctor's recommendation. You must be confined to your home and thus unable to go out to a professional's office.

Therefore, Medicare will pay for a nurse or therapist to see you at home and perform specific medical services. Such visits usually last less than an hour over a period of a few weeks. Medicare will *not* pay for someone to cook and clean for an aging parent while you go off to an eight-hour job.

Medicare A also provides hospice care for the terminally ill. In case you're not familiar with hospice care, it involves specially trained workers who help the ill finish out their days at home with a minimum of physicial and emotional pain. Hospice workers also help survivors cope with the trauma of a loved one's death. A Medicare recipient diagnosed as having less than six months to live is entitled to as much as 210 days of hospice care.

IN BRIEF

- When you reach 65 years of age, you're generally eligible for Medicare, health insurance provided by the federal government.
- There are no health requirements for Medicare eligibility.
- Part A of Medicare is free for everyone enrolled in Medicare.
- Part A covers most hospital costs. You may incur substantial costs if you stay in a hospital longer than 60 days.
- Cost-control pressures are forcing hospitals to release Medicare patients earlier. If you want to stay longer, you may have to pay for the extra days.
- In some circumstances, Medicare A also will pay for skilled-nursing homes, skilled health care at home, and hospice care for the terminally ill.

Chapter 12

"B" Is for
Besides-the-Hospital

When you sign up for Medicare, you're automatically enrolled in Part A at no charge. On the same application, you have a chance to decline Part B coverage. Most people don't decline; you're probably much better off accepting the coverage. If you accept Part B, around $30 per month will be deducted from your Social Security check. Your Medicare card, which you need whenever you receive medical services, will indicate whether or not you have Part B.

While Part A covers hospital costs, Part B covers other medical costs. Routine checkups aren't covered, but most other forms of treatment, including emergency-room services, are paid for under Medicare B as long as they're medically necessary. Medicare B works like a health insurance policy, with a $100 deductible and a 20% coinsurance responsibility.

LOOKING FOR DR. GOODGUY

You may recall the discussion of UCR (usual, customary, and reasonable) charges in health insurance policies (see page 55).

Insurers generally pay doctors based on UCR limits. If your doctor charges more, you're generally stuck paying the difference. A similar policy exists for Medicare B except that it's known as "accepting assignment." Medicare has a schedule of amounts it will pay for certain treatments per locality. Medicare will pay 80% of that amount. Let's say Medicare's idea of a surgeon's reasonable charge for a coronary-artery bypass is $2,900. Medicare B will pay the surgeon 80% ($2,320), while you're responsible for the other 20% ($580).

For some doctors, that's fine. They agree to "participate" in Medicare, accepting assignment for all Medicare billings. Your local Social Security office probably has a list of participating physicians; you may be able to get such a list from the insurance company that processes your Medicare claims. Participating doctors may display emblems or certificates in their office, showing that they're Medicare participants.

Other doctors may or may not participate. They may accept assignment for some patients or some procedures. And some doctors won't accept assignment at all. They always charge more than the Medicare rate.

Suppose you find participating physician Phyllis Doe, who always accepts assignment. Assuming the annual $100 deductible already has been paid, here's the cost breakdown on a $2,900 operation:

Operation costs	$2,900
Medicare pays 80%	(2,320)
You pay 20%	580

When Dr. Doe accepts assignment, she bills Medicare directly for the 80% share. All you would have to contend with is a bill for your 20%.

Suppose Paula Roe, the surgeon down the street, never accepts assignment. Under federal law, she may charge as much as 120% of the Medicare reimbursement rate (no more than 115% after 1992). Say she charges $3,400 for the same operation. Now

Operation costs	$3,400
Medicare pays 80% of $2,900	(2,320)
You pay balance	1,080

As you can see, Medicare pays a fixed amount. If you go to a more expensive physician, you're responsible for the difference. What's more, under this type of "balance billing" arrangement you will have to pay the full $3,400 yourself and wait for reimbursement of the $2,320 from Medicare.

PAPER CHASE

Under another new law, it's now the physician's responsibility to see that the claim forms are submitted to Medicare. This may help you if you've have a hard time with the forms. However, reimbursement may be slower this way.

In this example, if you're out of pocket $3,400 and are expecting a $2,320 check from Medicare, you can bet you'll file quickly. Your surgeon, though, already has your money; she won't get anything from Medicare. So where's her incentive to file promptly?

Doctors can take up to 15 months to file Medicare reimbursement forms. Moreover, they don't have to tell patients when they have submitted a claim. So it's up to you to follow up with your doctor. If necessary, you may still want to file yourself, on HCFA Form 1490S, available from your Social Security office or from insurance companies. Some Medicare "carriers" and "intermediaries" (insurance companies that process claims and make Medicare payments) say they'll pay on claims submitted directly by beneficiaries.

Obviously it's in your interest to see if a doctor will accept assignment. In some states, including Vermont, Massachusetts, Rhode Island, Connecticut, and Pennsylvania, accepting assignment for patients at certain income levels is mandatory. (Some other states, especially in the Northeast, are moving in this direction.) But in others, if you find cooperative doctors, you can save yourself hundreds or even thousands of dollars.

THE DOCTOR IS OUT

Medicare patients may find an unexpected problem: finding a doctor who'll treat them. As the paperwork burden increases and fees increasingly are being limited, many doctors are adopting this policy: They'll keep existing patients, including those who reach age 65, but they won't take any new patients on Medicare. Such patients tend to need more care than younger ones, and the payoff may not be worth it. A 1990 survey by the Association of American Physicians and Surgeons found that a *majority* of respondents plan to restrict their Medicare practices as a result of proposed or newly enacted regulations.

In 1992, a new Medicare payment schedule takes effect, slightly raising fees for basic medical treatment but slashing allowable charges for specialists' services. An ophthalmologist who performs an intraocular lens procedure, for example, might have charged over $1,300 under the old system. Now the new fee schedule puts a "reasonable charge" at around $800.

What's more, even if the ophthalmologist chooses not to accept assignment, there's a ceiling of $1,000 on the fee that can be charged under the new rules. This may sound great for Medicare patients, but you can see the potential danger. If the ophthalmologist can get $1,300 from private patients, why treat a Medicare patient for $1,000?

Suppose you're a Medicare enrollee who needs a new doctor because you moved or your doctor retired or you just decided to make a switch. You get sick and discover you can't get a doctor who'll take you as a patient. Or you need a specialized operation but can't find a specialist willing to perform it.

As physicians' dissatisfaction with Medicare increases, you'll have to make more of an effort to find a doctor you like. Start early, before you're on Medicare, if possible. If you are on Medicare, hunt for a doctor who'll accept you as a patient. Make an appointment for a routine checkup. Pay your bill promptly. Show the doctor you're a stand-up person. Then, in case of a health emergency, you'll already have a friendly physician on your side.

COORDINATING BENEFITS

Medicare isn't necessarily limited to retirees. Many professionals and business owners, for example, continue to work after 65. Often they have substantial earnings, so they're not entitled to collect Social Security benefits. Even in those cases, they're eligible for Medicare after they reach age 65.

Often people who enroll for Medicare while they're still working still participate in an employer's health insurance plan, such as Blue Cross/Blue Shield. Or they may continue their group coverage, after retirement, at bargain rates.

What happens when a Medicare recipient is covered by a group health insurance plan? Usually, the group health insurance is considered the "primary" carrier. You may have to file first with that insurer in order to get your claim processed. Then your doctor can file a Medicare claim that may cover unreimbursed expenses.

As you can see, the group health plan is supposed to pay first. Medicare hasn't enforced this procedure strictly in the past, but it is doing so now to save an estimated billion dollars per year. So be sure your physician has all the information needed to file claims properly. When your doctor files the first Medicare claim on your behalf, you must fill out a questionnaire describing the health coverage you have. Medicare has been rejecting claims in circumstances where there is a question of double coverage, so make sure full insurance disclosure is made on all of your claim forms.

On the other hand, when a Medicare patient is on a plan specifically designed to cover retirees, Medicare generally is the primary payer, and you look toward your retiree plan as a supplement. Often a retiree plan uses the "carve out" technique, which can leave you short.

Say you incur a $10,000 medical bill, of which Medicare will pay $8,000. In the absence of Medicare, your retiree health plan would have paid $9,000. Thus, your plan pays only $1,000 (its $9,000 obligation minus the $8,000 paid by Medicare), leaving you $1,000 out of pocket. For large bills, you can have substantial exposure.

These are known as "coordination of benefits" situations. If you run into one, check with your employer and with your doctor so that each knows who's filing what claim. In case of problems, call your Medicare carrier. If you don't know who that is, your local Social Security office can tell you.

THE *HMO* OPTION

One way to avoid paperwork hassles as well as the problem of paying excess medical bills is to join a health maintenance organization (HMO) (see chapter 9). Essentially, Medicare pays a premium to the HMO, which provides coverage to you. And that's about it. Your monthly premiums and coinsurance likely will be modest; you don't have to worry about doctors not accepting assignment. There is some variance among HMOs for the fees charged to Medicare enrollees, but you'll have few out-of-pocket costs as long as you stay within the HMO for health care.

However, you are limited yourself to the HMO's doctors and hospitals, so be sure the HMO has an extensive geriatric practice. As mentioned before, you need to check out the HMO's financial condition as well as its medical capabilities.

What if you're not happy with the HMO? You can quit and reenroll for regular Medicare coverage.

THE VERY END

Don't confuse Medicare with Medicaid.

Medicare is a nationwide program funded entirely by the federal government, primarily for the elderly. If you qualify, generally by reasons of age, you'll get the benefits regardless of your income or net worth. You are expected to pay part of the costs of Medicare either through copayments or some sort of insurance policy.

Medicaid, on the other hand, varies from state to state, with funding shared by the federal and state governments. Regardless of your age, you can qualify for Medicaid if you fall below the income and net-worth requirements for your state. Medicaid recipients essentially receive health care for which the government pays in full.

In the past few years, the practice of "spending down" (actually giving away most or all of your assets) in order to qualify for Medicaid has become more common among the elderly. Usually, this is done so people won't have to pay their own nursing-home expenses, as you'll see in chapter 25.

There's no reason you can't spend down so that Medicaid will pay for non-nursing-home medical expenses. However, there are many reasons not to do so. Medicaid patients often don't receive the best care because doctors are paid little to treat them; giving up all of your assets strips you of control over your own life; there are ethical problems in giving wealth to your family so that the government (all the taxpayers) can pay your medical bills. As long as you're covered by Medicare and can afford around $1,000 a year for a good health insurance policy to supplement Medicare, described in the next chapter, there's no need to impoverish yourself.

If you or an aged relative can't afford a Medicare supplement policy or if assets and income are virtually nil, you may be better off applying for Medicaid. But that's a step to consider after you've ruled out all other approaches.

In 1990, Washington passed a law calling for Medicaid to pay for out-of-pocket costs for Medicare beneficiaries whose incomes are below the poverty line. Generally, you need income of less than $6,620 a year and less than $4,000 in assets, not including a house, a car, and a burial plot. If you or someone you know qualifies, Medicaid will pick up the Part A deductible and coinsurance as well as the Part B monthly premium. The federal government hasn't been eager to promote this potential revenue drain, so you'll have to call your local Medicaid office if you're entitled to these benefits.

IN BRIEF
- While Part A of Medicare pays for hospital costs, Part B pays for doctors' bills and other medical expenses.
- The cost of Medicare B is around $30 per month, deducted from Social Security checks.

- After a $100 annual deductible, Medicare B pays 80% of the "reasonable cost" for each procedure.
- The other 20% is owed by the patient, along with any doctors' charges in excess of the reasonable cost.
- Doctors who accept Medicare's reasonable cost as payment in full are said to "accept assignment." Lists of participating physicians are available.
- If you exchange your Medicare benefits for HMO membership, you can avoid paying most or all out-of-pocket costs. However, you limit yourself to the HMO's doctors and hospitals, so check carefully.
- If you can't afford a Medigap policy, you may be able to qualify for Medicaid, a government welfare program that will pay your medical bills.

Chapter 13

Bridging the Medi-Gap

As you can see from the last chapter's discussion, Medicare is good but not great. The cost, around $400 per year, is excellent, especially for seniors who may be in poor health. However, if you rely on Medicare, you have several responsibilities of your own, including:

- Deductibles for Parts A and B, for a total of around $750 per year.
- Coinsurance for hospital stays of over 60 days.
- All the costs for extremely long hospital stays.
- Similar expenses for stays over 20 days in skilled-nursing facilities.
- All costs for stays in custodial nursing homes.
- All costs for custodial home care.
- Coinsurance (20%) for doctors' bills and related expenses.
- All doctors' charges in excess of what Medicare considers to be "reasonable."
- All charges for prescribed medication except for "shots" administered to you.
- All costs for routine physicals, eye examinations, etc.

Altogether, that can add up to a sizable exposure. Say you go into the hospital for a coronary bypass operation. The total bill comes to $100,000, split between Parts A and B. Part A might cover all $40,000 worth of hospitalization costs, except for the deductible.

However, suppose the doctors' bills come to $60,000, while Medicare considers $50,000 to be reasonable. Medicare would pay only $40,000 (80% of its reasonable rate) and leave the other $20,000, plus the deductibles, for you to pay.

To avoid such exposure, you can join an HMO. However, that means limiting your choice of doctors and hospitals, which seniors especially may find unappealing.

MORE THAN A GOLD WATCH

Some seniors have retiree health benefits from their former employers. If you retired after working for a large corporation or a government agency, you may have excellent coverage. However, government agencies have been feeling a financial pinch, so they've been cutting back on retiree health coverage. Similarly, corporations have been trimming retiree health benefits because of rising costs and changes in accounting rules, which make corporations with high health-care obligations report lower profits.

Buck Consultants, an employee benefits firm, recently surveyed 246 large corporations, the kinds of companies that have come to be counted on for generous retiree health-care plans. Of those corporations, 42% had already trimmed medical benefits, 35% were considering such changes, and 3% had made cuts and were considering further reductions. Only 20% of the companies were maintaining retiree medical benefits.

These changes are not only affecting future retirees; often people who are already retired have had their benefits trimmed.

Libbey-Owens-Ford, for example, now makes new retirees pay up to $1,100 per year before 100% coverage takes effect. AT&T is putting caps on the amount it spends for retiree health care. Gillette's retirees must pay a portion of their monthly premiums.

An increasingly popular plan calls for workers to pay their own money into a reserve fund, for health care after retirement, rather than employers making the commitment. Ball Corp., which employs around 7,000 people, is offering all new employees the opportunity to invest in these special accounts through payroll deduction. As long as the money is spent for postretirement health care, the earnings will be tax-free.

Other new wrinkles:

- Paying a fixed amount for retiree health insurance, leaving retirees to make up any difference.
- Cutting back benefits for early retirees who can't qualify for Medicare yet.
- Diverting money that would have gone into retirement plans into retiree health insurance plans instead.
- Restricting retiree health-care coverage to employees with at least 10 years of service.

So the trend is for retiree health benefits to be paid for increasingly by the employees and less by employers.

Things are not much different for government retirees. "When my mother retired from working for New York Sate, she didn't get much of a pension, but she had generous health insurance," says one middle-aged executive. "Recently, those benefits have been cut and cut, so she's paying more and more herself."

So if you or a relative has retiree health-care benefits, those benefits may or may not be adequate to supplement Medicare; if they are good, they may or may not be cut back. But if you are still working toward retirement, it's unlikely you can look forward to health-care benefits that will fully supplement Medicare.

The best retiree health-care coverage probably will be provided by major corporations. To get the most of their coverage, don't change jobs after you reach age 55. And be sure to save as much as you can in any employer plan where the company will match your contribution.

GAPPING WITHOUT GASPING

Most people won't be fully covered by Medicare and an employer's retiree health-care plan. Therefore, it's probable that you'll need a health insurance policy specifically designed to supplement Medicare—to fill the gaps. Such policies, familiarly called Medigap, are held by more than 20 million Americans, who pay $15 billion per year in premiums. A good Medigap policy will pay most of what Medicare doesn't pay for. More important, it will protect your assets from depletion in case of an expensive illness or sickness.

Unfortunately, not all of the dozens of insurers selling Medigap are scrupulous. Some insurers prey on the fears of the elderly, who may be terrified of the idea of impoverishing themselves and their families if their health fails.

Some Medigap insurers use deceptive phone and mail campaigns; some media promotions involving celebrities have been criticized. Many seniors buy duplicate policies—one purchased 15 different policies within three years. Even worse, the Medigap policies seniors have bought often turn out to be worth little or nothing because:

- They exclude certain diseases or conditions.
- They don't fill an important gap, such as the coinsurance requirements.
- They have caps on what they'll pay per day or per year or per lifetime.
- They can be canceled (or the premium can skyrocket) if a policyholder's health deteriorates.

RAISING THE STANDARD

In response to such excesses, a federal law was passed in late 1990 calling for the standardization of Medigap policies. By mid-1992, all 50 states are expected to have the necessary rules in place. Anyone selling a nonstandard Medigap policy will be fined up to $25,000.

Now there will be one "core" Medigap policy of basic benefits that all Medigap insurers must sell. After an insurer has a core policy ("A") in place, it can add up to nine other policies ("B" through "J") to its list. Each of these policies will have certain other features. An insurance company can offer none of them, all of them, or any number in between. No other Medigap policy ("K," "L," etc.) can be sold (see table 6).

The new Medigap policies must be guaranteed renewable. That is, the insurance company can't cancel a policy if you keep paying the premiums. However, if you make a "material misrepresentation" (lied about your health when you filled out the application), the insurer can cancel you.

All Medigap buyers must fill out a form stating that they're not eligible for Medicaid, because Medicaid recipients don't need Medigap insurance. On this form, buyers indicate what other health insurance they have. If you already own a Medigap policy, you must agree to drop the existing policy when the new one takes effect. Insurance companies and insurance agents selling duplicate Medigap policies, without the promise of canceling the older policies, are subject to fines and up to five years in jail!

For six months after you enroll for Medicare Part B, generally at age 65, you're entitled to Medigap coverage—at the standard rate—regardless of your health. Thus, when you first qualify for Medicare, you can shop around for the best coverage then available and lock it in for as long as you pay the required premiums. If you wait until after that six-month window to get Medigap coverage, you may be required to have a physical (and pay higher premiums).

For new Medigap policies, exclusions on coverage for pre-existing conditions are limited to six months. For policies that replace another Medigap policy, no new exclusions for pre-existing conditions can be added.

CORE-CARD

When the new rules are all in place, each Medigap policy must have core benefits, including:

Table 6: MEDICARE SUPPLEMENT COVERAGE

Medicare supplement insurance can be sold in only 10 standard plans. The table shows the benefits included in each plan. Every company must make available Plan A. Some plans may not be available in some states.

	A	B	C	D	E	F	G	H	I	J
Basic benefits	X	X	X	X	X	X	X	X	X	X
Skilled nursing coinsurance			X	X	X	X	X	X	X	X
Part A deductible		X	X	X	X	X	X	X	X	X
Part B deductible			X			X			X	X
Excess doctors' charges						100%	80%		100%	100%
Foreign travel emergency			X	X	X	X	X	X	X	X
At-home recovery				X			X		X	X
Prescription drugs								Basic Drugs*	Basic Drugs*	Extended Drugs†
Preventive care					X					X

* $1,250 limit. † $3,000 limit. *Source:* National Association of Insurance Commissioners.

- Hospitalization: Part A coinsurance plus coverage for 365 additional days after Medicare benefits end.
- Medical expenses: Part B coinsurance (20 percent of Medicare-approved expenses).
- Blood: first three pints of blood each year.

That's the basic policy, and the one that would have the lowest cost. Under the previous system, Medigap policies cost anywhere from $700 to $2,000 per year. Right now it's too soon to see what the new price range will be, but core policies likely will wind up on the low end of that range. In fact, some companies might be able to come out with a core policy selling for $500 or $600 per year.

If you want other benefits (see table 6), you'll have to pay more. As you can see on the table, picking up the hospital deductible for Part A ($652 in 1992) will likely be a popular option. The same if you want coverage for medical emergencies during foreign travel. Also, most of the option plans would pick up your obligation to pay coinsurance during long stays in skilled-nursing homes. Other options are less likely to be included and may greatly increase the costs.

Judging from the early reactions, some insurance companies will offer all ten policies, while others will be selective—Mutual of Omaha, for example, will sell policies A, C, F, and I.

Which policies make the most sense? Policy A may work if you're on a tight budget. Policy B adds the deductible for hospital stays: $652 in 1992. But this is essentially a dollar-trading device: You'll pay a few hundred dollars extra each year on the chance that you'll save $652 if you're hospitalized. Policy A is closer to pure insurance.

Both A and B leave some large exposures, such as medical expenses incurred during foreign travel, which can be a major risk for Medicare recipients. If you're traveling out of the country, even to Canada or Mexico, your medical expenses probably aren't covered by Medicare. Policies C through J all pay 80% of medically necessary expenses incurred outside the U.S., after a $250 annual deductible, up to a $50,000 lifetime benefit.

Similarly, policies C through J cover skilled-nursing coinsurance. Medicare picks up all costs for the first 20 days in an

CHECKUP

Follow the same rules for buying Medigap insurance as you would for any type of health insurance:

- Work with an agent you know and trust. It's true that many organizations, especially the American Association of Retired Persons, sell perfectly acceptable Medigap policies by mail or phone. Still, if you have an insurance agent or financial planner you can rely upon, buy your Medigap through him or her. If a question arises, you'll have a real person to fight your battle with you.
- Buy only through reputable insurers. Check how long a company has been around and how it's rated by A. M. Best, Moody's, or Standard & Poor's.
- Read the policy before you buy. See what's included and what's excluded. If you can't decipher the policy, buy Medigap from a company with a policy written in plain English.

---

approved facility, but patients owe $81.50 (in 1992) for each of the next 80 days. This exposure, over $6,500, is worth covering. Therefore, you probably should go beyond policy A if you can afford a few hundred dollars more per year.

Some of the other optional benefits, such as preventive care ($120 per year) and the $100 Part B deductible, relate to meager exposures that needn't be covered. The at-home recovery feature has some value but there's a benefit cap: Reimbursement is pegged at up to $40 per visit, up to $1,600 per year. Although these features have limited value, you may have to buy them in order to get more valuable protection, such as coverage during foreign travel or skilled-nursing care.

How can you choose from policies C through J? There are two key screens: prescription drugs and balance billing.

Are you likely to need several thousand dollars' worth of prescription drugs a year? With policies H and I, you pay the first $250, then the policy pays 50%, up to a $1,250 annual limit. Policy J works the same, except that the upper limit is $3,000.

Balance billing (doctors charging more than the Medicare rate) may not be a problem. As mentioned, some northeastern states have banned balance billing or are moving in that direction. In some other areas of the country, medical fees may be so low that balance billing isn't a significant problem.

So here's how to play the new Medigap game. If you are likely to spend much more than $3,000 worth of prescription drugs a year, buy J. No matter what sort of health condition you're in, you can take advantage of the open enrollment period and buy this policy within six months of signing up for Medicare Part B. Then the Medigap policy will pay for up to $3,000 worth of prescription drugs a year.

If your prescription-drug need is smaller, but still well over $1,000 per year, H or I may be the best bet. Choose I if there's likely to be a balance billing problem, H if balance billing isn't a concern.

What if you don't anticipate a heavy reliance on prescription drugs? If you may run into a balance billing problem, G looks like the best choice because at-home recovery is included. If you're neither a heavy user of prescription drugs nor vulnerable to balance billing, you can choose the cheapest policy among C through J and receive good catastrophic protection.

What if you already have a Medigap policy—should you switch to the new, standardized versions? Not necessarily. In some instances, existing policies offer greater benefits or better values. You should read each policy carefully, old and new, before making any decisions. Insurance companies will continue to renew and service their existing Medigap policies.

ETERNAL VIGILANCE

The Medigap market is changing now because of the new rules. There probably will be less fraud and misrepresentation in Medigap, but no government law will wipe it out completely.

"Standardizing" Medigap policies doesn't mean they'll all be the same.

Remember, even under the new rules, there is one gap virtually no Medigap policy will fill: custodial care in a nursing home. If you'll want that coverage, you'll need special long-term-care (LTC) insurance (see part III).

IN BRIEF
- Even if you're enrolled in Medicare, all of your medical bills won't be covered.
- You may be exposed to extremely large bills, on top of what Medicare covers.
- For protection, "Medigap" insurance policies can be used to supplement Medicare.
- In the past, some Medigap insurers took advantage of the elderly, selling them policies of little real value.
- Under a new federal law, Medigap policies are becoming standardized.
- All Medigap insurers must offer a noncancelable core policy to all buyers, with few limits on preexisting conditions.
- More expensive policies, with extra features, also may be offered.
- The new Medigap policies are available to everyone, regardless of health, in the six months after enrolling in Medicare Part B.
- Even with the new Medigap standards, you need to check policies closely before you buy. Policies from strong insurers are preferred.
- It may make sense to buy a policy that will pay for coverage during foreign travel and for skilled-nursing homes if you can afford to pay more than the "core" policy costs.

Chapter 14

Stayin' Alive

BENDING THE RULES

Many doctors and patients engage in practices that bend the rules, and some regularly break the law. Insurance fraud costs an estimated $60 billion per year, $60 billion that everyone winds up paying for through higher fees and higher insurance premiums. Some of these practices are so commonplace that it's easy to overlook that they're clearly illegal. You should know about them so that you can identify fraud if you see it and choose not to participate.

Everyone Has a Disease

Most health insurance policies won't pay for routine checkups but will cover treatment of an illness. So if a doctor reports your visit was to treat a cough, you may be reimbursed. (Of course, a doctor whose practice consists of hundreds of coughers and no routine checkups is likely to raise a few eyebrows.) Similarly, some doctors will report a "breast lump," which is covered, rather than a mammogram to screen for cancer, which isn't covered.

Flagging Waivers

A more complex subject is the waiver of copayment or coinsurance. In most health insurance policies, including Medicare, patients are required to pay something toward the cost, with 20% probably the standard. If you see your doctor when you have stomach flu and you're charged $100 for the visit, you may have to pay $20, while the insurance company pays $80. (That assumes you've already met your deductible for the year.)

There's a reason for the copayment. Obviously, the insurance company would rather pay $80 than $100. Moreover, insurers feel that the $20 cost helps cut down excess doctor visits. If you had no coinsurance to pay, you might run to the doctor's office every time you sniffled; that $20 you pay makes it more likely you'll go only when you genuinely need care.

Some doctors, though, "waive the copayment." That is, they put down a $100 fee on the claim form, so they collect $80 from the insurance company, but they wink at you and tell you to forget the $20. Some doctors do this routinely; others do it only for patients in financial distress.

To the doctor, this is a private matter between physician and patient. The insurers, though, think this places the entire system in jeopardy. As for you, you're certainly better off financially if you don't have to pay your fee. As for participating in schemes to waive copayments, that's between you and your conscience.

WATCHING FOR OVERCHARGES

Even if you have health insurance, a stay in the hospital can be a financial drain. Some policies won't cover all categories of expenses; others require you to pay a certain amount of coinsurance.

If you know you're heading for the hospital, spend $9.95 to buy *Take This Book to the Hospital with You*, published by the People's Medical Society, 462 Walnut Street, Allentown, PA

18102. Charles Inlander, the society's president, found himself charged for $1,000 worth of vitamins and medical treatment that were never delivered after his wife gave birth to a baby in a local hospital. You can avoid being swindled like this if you know what to look for.

The first rule is, never assume anything in a hospital is free. Whenever you're offered something, such as a baby pacifier or paper slippers, ask how much it will cost. Then decide whether or not you'll need it. (Are you sure Blue Cross will pay $15 for a pacifier?)

Then, when you check out, don't sign anything before you read your bill. If you don't get an itemized bill, insist on one. If it's long and involved, take your time reading it. The American Hospital Association has a "Patient's Bill of Rights" that entitles you to all the time you need to examine your bill. If you don't understand any items, ask the hospital or your doctor for an explanation.

Naturally, you can't be expected to tell whether or not $700 is a reasonable fee for the surgeon who removed your gallbladder. But you should be able to tell if you're being charged for services you never received. Or if you're being charged, for example, for the same test twice in the same day. Or if two different departments in the hospital are charging you for the same item.

If you spot overcharges, insist they be removed. That's true even if you're well insured. Don't forget, insurance companies may audit your bill and refuse to pay certain charges. In that case, doctors or the hospital may dun you for the money the insurer won't pay.

What's more, some health insurers are offering a reward for your diligence. A "medical bill audit" procedure may pay you 50% (up to, say, $1,000) if you discover excess or inappropriate charges that eventually are eliminated from your hospital bill.

CLAIM JUMPING

In the future, filing health insurance claims may be much simpler. The Travelers uses a computerized "Health Link" system for its health maintenance organizations (HMOs) and preferred provider organizations (PPOs). Each patient in this system receives a plastic card resembling a credit card. Before treatment, the card is run through a terminal to see if the patient is covered for that doctor's services. After treatment, a claim is electronically filed with The Travelers.

Eventually, such systems will connect with other insurers' payment systems. In time, health-care insurance payments may be faster and more accurate.

While you wait for that glorious day, help may be closer to hand. You probably pay a CPA several hundred dollars to cope with your federal and state income-tax returns. So why not do the same with all the health-care paperwork? Professional Claimcare of York, Pennsylvania, will help you deal with your health insurance and reimbursement claims. Annual membership is $110 per year. The founder, John Lohrman, got the idea after he broke his neck in an auto accident yet had to cope with mounds of paperwork while still injured. For details, call Professional Claimcare at (717) 741-4599. For the names of other health-care paperwork firms, including those in your area, call the National Association of Claims Assistance Professionals at (708) 963-3500.

Summary of Health Insurance Goals

If your employer provides you with unbreachable health insurance, even if it costs you hundreds of dollars per month, you have one less worry. But if you have no employer coverage or poor employer coverage, here are the ground rules:

1. You need health insurance to obtain quality health care.
2. The first goal of health insurance is risk control. You want to avoid the risks of a huge medical bill that will cost you everything you own.
3. After that risk has been elminated, you can decide how many smaller risks you're willing to assume and what you're willing to pay to minimize those risks.

With those ground rules in mind, here's the order of battle.

• HMOs are a good place to start because your costs are nearly fixed.

• Before considering an HMO, be certain that its plan will cover you, at all costs, in case of illness or accident.

• Check on an HMO's financial status.

• HMOs sound great in theory, bu the reality often is disappointing. If you're not prepared to give up freedom of choice in doctors, don't join an HMO. Be ready for inconvenience and a lack of personal attention.

• If you're willing to put up with some aggravation in return for financial security, a well-managed HMO may be your best choice. "I've carried my own health insurance for years," says one free-lance photographer with a wife and three small children. "High-deductible plans, low-deductible plans. I switched to an HMO to save money. My wife didn't like the inconvenience at first, but she's gotten used to the longer driving times to get to the HMO. Now we think we have a good deal."

• If an HMO isn't for you, see if you can find an individual or family plan affiliated with a PPO. You have more freedom of choice here, but if you stick within the PPO network, you'll save money.

• A PPO plan is only as good as its catastrophic coverage. Therefore, a PPO plan must be analyzed the same as a fee-for-service (indemnity) plan, where you choose your own doctors and file claims for reimbursement.

• You want to be sure a fee-for-service plan protects you in case of a serious accident or illness. Generally, that means a major medical plan with few exclusions, a stop-loss on your annual obligation, and at least $1 million in benefits that policyholders can collect.

• Hospital-only major medical plans limit benefits to costs incurred in a hospital or outpatient surgery. With these plans, you have exposure for many doctor-related expenses. You may get hit with a $5,000 or a $10,000 medical bill. However, you're unlikely to suffer the $50,000 or $100,000 killer bill because those expenses are virtually always incurred in a hospital. If you're willing to absorb your own doctor bills, you may save $1,000 or more per year in health insurance.

• If you're not willing to absorb the $5,000 or $10,000 doctor bill, you need a comprehensive major medical policy. Expect to spend several thousand dollars per year for this type of family protection.

• To reduce your health insurance premiums, you can take a higher deductible and pay higher coinsurance. In effect, you're paying the first couple of thousand dollars of health-care expenses yourself. The insurance will take effect only in serious situations. If you spend thousands of dollars per year on food for your family and on your family's cars, why not realize that health care deserves an equal place in your budget? Don't fret that your neighbor works for the state government and gets first-dollar coverage. She's taking health care as a form of compensation, earning less than she would have without health insurance in her contract.

• The same principles apply when shopping for Medigap coverage. You want to join an HMO or buy a Medigap policy that will cover you in case of a financially crippling disaster.

• If you or a family member is in poor health and can't purchase standard health insurance, join either a group that offers coverage or your state's high-risk pool or get a job where health care is a benefit. You need some sort of health insurance coverage.

Part II

DISABILITY INCOME INSURANCE

Chapter 15

Insurance for You, Not for Your Doctor

THE NEED FOR DISABILITY INSURANCE

Alan, who drives a truck in New England, knew he was having a heart attack. "If you want to see me a while longer," he told his wife, "you'd better call the ambulance." She did, it came, and Alan made it to the hospital in time.

He then began a long series of tests and operations. For several weeks he was in the hospital, running up a bill well over $50,000. Fortunately for Alan, he had decent health insurance through his employer. Although he wound up out of pocket several thousand dollars, most of the medical expenses were covered.

That is, the surgeon and the cardiologist got their money. The hospital got paid, so it could meet its payroll and make the payments on its expensive scanners and diagnostic machines. Thanks to Alan's health insurance, everybody had the income they were expecting.

Except Alan. After his operation, he was bedridden and then housebound for months. As it turned out, it was more than a year before he could go back to work. And it was nearly two years before he was able to drive the 16-wheelers he used to handle with ease.

What happened during those two years? Alan's mortgage payments came due each month. The same with his car payments. He still had to pay for heat in the winter, for air-conditioning in the summer. And his family still had to eat every day.

So Alan's expenses didn't stop, but his income did. During those two years his family went through all their savings, his wife struggled with two jobs, and they cut back on every expense that wasn't absolutely necessary.

That's the flip side of many serious illnesses and accidents. If you have health insurance, your medical bills may be largely covered. After treatment, though, you may not be able to work for months or years. Or you may be permanently out of work. Little or no income flows in. Some of your expenses may be reduced—your membership in the squash club, for instance—but you may have additional expenses, such as domestic help or an in-house elevator.

There is a solution to this problem—disability income (DI) insurance. If you have DI coverage, you have some protection when you're not able to work. Your policy will pay you income.

Suppose, in our story, Alan had a DI policy. He might, in some cases, have to go for 90 days without income. After that 90 days, benefits would begin. Maybe he'd collect $3,000 per month, depending on the policy. After he goes back to work but is only able to work half-time (and earn half a salary), the DI policy might continue to pay $1,500 per month.

So you can see the value of DI insurance. A long-term disability can be a "living death," draining your assets slowly, week by week and month by month. DI insurance can help you survive.

But there are two drawbacks to DI insurance. Coverage is expensive and complicated. To get good value, you have to know what you're buying.

DI: *Deciding Whether to Take It or Leave It*

Do you need DI insurance? Maybe not. Health insurance is a "no brainer"—you gotta have it. Your need for DI insurance depends on your individual circumstances. But many recent trends are turning DI into the "Don't Ignore" category.

Medical science, for one thing, has advanced. "Mortality" rates from hypertension, diabetes, cerebral arteriosclerosis, and heart disease have decreased, but "morbidity" rates from these conditions are up around 60%. We're more likely to survive illnesses but lose our productive abilities.

Bernice, for example, thought she had protected her family because she had $500,000 worth of life insurance. Then she suffered a massive brain seizure. Just a few years earlier, Bernice would likely have died. But she was rushed to the hospital, where a sophisticated operation saved her.

So Bernice is still alive. From a financial point of view, her life insurance serves no purpose. (If she had died, the life insurance proceeds would have been available.) She can't earn income, however, so her family must meet its daily expenses without help from her.

Similarly, medical advances have made it more likely you'll survive a severe traffic accident, only to face a long spell of disability.

Debt burdens have also changed in recent years. In the 1980s, many Americans borrowed heavily, increasing the ratio of debt to current income. If you have a large pile of mortgage debt, auto debt, credit-card debt, and so on, you may not be able to survive a six-month or one-year spell of no income without going into bankruptcy. UNUM Life Insurance Co., which sells DI insurance, reports that 48% of all home-mortgage foreclosures are due to disability of the homeowner versus 3% due to a homeowner's death.

A third trend affecting the need for DI is the increasing numbers of working women. If you and your spouse both work and your life-style depends on two incomes, then a disability for either of you could be financially crippling. Now there are two incomes that may need protection. From the early 1970s to the late 1980s, the percentage of individual DI contracts sold to women increased from 9% to 23%.

Scare Stories

What are the chances your income will need DI protection? IDS Financial Services, another DI insurer, has a presentation designed to scare you into buying coverage. (Virtually all DI insurers use similar messages.) According to IDS, if you're in your mid-20s, you're seven times more likely to suffer a disability (three months or longer) than death. In your mid-30s, disability is five times more likely. In your mid-40s, you're still three times more likely to be disabled than to die. The sales pitch, then, is why buy life insurance but not disability insurance?

Quoting from the Society of Actuaries, IDS says that more than 50% of all 35-year-olds will suffer at least one 90-day disability before age 65. Even among 50-year-olds, more than 35% will be disabled at least once by age 65 (see Table 7).

Table 7: CHANCES OF BECOMING DISABLED FOR 90 DAYS OR MORE

Out of 1,000 people at age	25	30	35	40	45	50	55	60
Number disabled by age 65	572	548	503	461	439	377	290	193

Source: IDS Financial Services.

What's more, if you're not back to work within three months, you may be out for much longer. IDS says that the average duration of these long disabilities is over five years at age 35, over six years at age 50.

Historically, those numbers have been boosted by the relatively high proportion of people working on farms, in factories, on construction sites, etc. Those doing manual labor naturally got most of the ruptured disks and wrenched backs that caused long-term disability. White-collar workers, who lifted nothing heavier than a box of paper for the photocopier, had a chance of long-term disability around 4%.

Still, that's not negligible. And it may no longer be the case. AIDS and other epidemics don't differentiate on the basis of what color collar you wear. Stress-related illnesses, including heart attacks, may be more prevalent among executives and managers. Today's white-collar workers may spend their day hunched over a computer terminal or performing repetitive motions that eventually will lead to severe pain.

For a lawyer, a persistent back cramp might hurt but wouldn't necessarily wipe out all income. That same back pain might make it impossible for a telephone switchboard operator to work a full day. If that happened to you, how would your family manage?

If your spouse has a secure, well-paying job, you might get through a disability with only a crimp in your life-style. The same goes if you have a wealthy family you can rely upon or an investment portfolio that generates sizable amounts of interest and dividends.

But suppose you're like many people, living from paycheck to paycheck. Maybe you have enough money in the bank to carry you for a month or two. After that, a long stretch of no income would cause extreme financial distress. Skip a few mortgage payments and you might lose your house. Especially if you have dependents, it's a chance you shouldn't take.

HOW TO CALCULATE YOUR NEED

You can check your vulnerability to a long-term disability by calculating your need (generally, your family's need) if you couldn't work.

Step 1: Determine Your Need

Start by determining how much income you must have each month in order to get by. Look at your canceled checks for the past year and your credit-card statements. That, along with cash outlays, will show you how much you spent. For each item, how much would you need to keep spending in case of a long disability?

Your mortgage loan and credit-card debt payments likely

would continue. If you have two auto loans, you might be forced to sell one car in the event of severe disability.

Utilities and property taxes would continue as before. You'd probably have to keep paying premiums on your life, health, homeowner's, and auto insurance.

You'd still have to eat, although grocery bills could be cut by shopping down (fewer luxury items, more store brands). Dining out and other forms of entertainment could be cut, along with vacations. New clothes could largely be deferred unless you have growing children.

Kids in private school could attend public school or apply for financial aid. Kids in college could apply for financial aid or get jobs to pay their own way. And so on. The whole exercise is almost exactly like the calculation you use to determine how much income your family would need in the event of your untimely death and how much life insurance you need to buy. Worksheet 1 will help you figure out what your ongoing expenses will be.

Step 2: Determine Your Potential Income

The next step is to see how much income you can expect in the event of a long-term disability. Can you expect income from a spouse's job or from an investment portfolio? Make a reasonable estimate and adjust for changing circumstances.

Suppose you have $50,000 worth of mutual funds, heavily weighted toward stock funds. Dividends generally are reinvested. If income was needed during your long-term disability, you could convert that portfolio into bond funds and take out dividends as they're paid. Assuming an average yield of 9%, that would be $4,500 per year, nearly $400 per month, without having to invade the principal.

Do you have money in IRAs or Keogh plans? You'd probably withdraw your funds during a long-term disability. If you have a vacation home or some investment real estate, you'd likely sell the property and invest the proceeds in CDs (certificates of deposit) or high-quality bonds.

When you figure your ongoing income, don't forget to use after-tax amounts. It's true that your tax bracket will be low if

Worksheet 1: Expenses Your Family Will Have If You're Disabled

Expenses	Per Month
Debt mortgage	
home equity	
auto	
credit cards	
other	
Rent	
Utilities telephone	
electricity	
oil/gas	
Insurance life	
health	
homeowner's/auto	
other	
Other car-related expenses	
Home maintenance	
Education	
Unreimbursed medical expenses	
Groceries	
Dining out/entertainment/ recreation/vacations	
Clothing	
Other	
Total anticipated expenses	

you're unable to work, but anticipate that state and federal income taxes (plus Social Security tax on your spouse's earnings) will take 10%–20% of gross income.

There are three other sources of possible income in the event of a disability: your employer, Social Security, and workers' compensation. They'll be covered separately. For now, though, be sure to check on your tax-deferred retirement plan at work to see if you can make penalty-free withdrawals if disability strikes.

Step 3: Income and Outgo

After you have all this information, then, you can make a guess at preinsurance disability income (worksheet 2). The gap between what you're likely to need and what you're likely to have is the amount of DI coverage you should buy.

Suppose your family now earns $5,000 per month, $4,000 after tax. You think that your family can get by on $3,000 per month should you be disabled. From all the sources listed above, you expect income would be around $2,500 per month, or $2,000 after tax. Thus, you need DI protection of $1,000 per month.

Your neighbors might have an identical income and an identical need for $3,000 per month. However, they might have virtually no investments, no spousal income, no employer support. So they might need DI protection of $3,000 per month.

In some ways, DI is more like life insurance than health insurance. A health insurance plan typically reimburses you for all or part of the health-care expenses you incur. When you buy a health insurance policy and pay $3,000 or more per year, there's no way of knowing how much the insurance will pay if you get sick or injured.

With life insurance, you pay so much for a fixed amount of "face value," or "death benefit." If you buy a $250,000 policy, when you die, your beneficiaries will collect $250,000.

Similarly, with a DI policy you pay so much for a fixed amount of disability benefits, which usually are expressed as a monthly income. Thus, you might buy a policy paying $1,000 per month, $4,000 per month, or even $2,250 per month. If

Worksheet 2: Income Your Family Will Have If You're Disabled

Income	Per Month
Spouse's earnings (after tax)	
Interest from bank accounts, bonds	
Dividends from stocks, mutual funds	
Interest on outstanding personal loans	
Property rental	
Assets you can sell, with net proceeds invested @ 6% per year, after tax	
Other income	
Social Security disability benefits	
Workers' compensation benefits	
Employer sick leave	
Employer disability benefits	
Proceeds from retirement fund withdrawals, invested @ 6% per year, after tax	
Total anticipated income	

The gap between the total anticipated income and expenses is what your family will need to live, without hardship, if you're disabled. That gap is the amount of DI benefits you need to buy.

you buy a $1,000-per-month DI policy and you become disabled, you'll receive $1,000 per month.

Naturally, the higher the benefit, the more the policy costs. So the trick is to buy as much as you need for protection but to avoid overbuying so you won't pay more than you need to. That's why you should start with worksheets 1 and 2.

The insurance industry's "rule of thumb" is to buy enough DI to replace 60%–70% of your predisability income. Insurers made up that rule so they could sell you as much DI as they could, without making benefits so generous that you'd malinger rather than work. (If your DI benefit was 100% of earned income, you'd have that much more incentive to discover throbbing but undetectable back pains.)

As you can tell by the above example, this rule of thumb is far from a rule. Each family's circumstances are different. If you make your calculations carefully, you can buy enough DI coverage, but not too much.

TAKING THE LONG VIEW

After you work through the calculations, you'll probably discover that you need some sort of DI coverage. But how to select the right policy? Many of the principles mentioned in the first section, on health insurance, still apply. You want to try to find a good agent to work with. (Many agents who sell health insurance also handle DI insurance.) And you want to check on the insurer's financial strength. If you're covered through an employer policy, you should check that policy just as you'd check on employer-provided health insurance.

Similarly, the same ground rules apply in selecting the type of coverage. In health insurance, you should be resigned to pay the little bills yourself while buying protection from the five- and six-figure calamities. Ditto for DI insurance. If you're out of work for a couple of months and then take a couple of months more to regain full speed, you should be able to bridge the gap through your own resources (savings, credit lines, belt tightening). DI should be used to get you through an extended period of time when virtually no income is coming in.

If you think you can do without DI insurance, consider the story of Bob, a financial executive who was earning $41,000 per year in 1982. His company stopped paying the premiums, so Bob assumed the payments himself. A few months later, Bob had a heart attack and has not worked since. Thanks to the DI policy, Bob has collected $1,700 per month (over $20,000 per year) ever since, and payments will continue another 11 years, until he's 65. Thanks to DI, Bob's kids went to college, his bills are paid up to date, and he still has his retirement nest egg. Without DI . . . ?

IN BRIEF

- If you have a serious illness or injury, good health insurance will pay most of the costs.
- If that illness or injury keeps you from working for a long time, you likely will lose income while your bills keep coming in.
- DI insurance can provide cash if you're unable to work.
- The chances of a long-term disability are much greater than your chance of dying, especially at an early age.
- The more vulnerable you are to a loss of income, the more you need DI coverage.
- Buying DI insurance means paying $X in annual premiums for $Y per month in disability benefits.
- To buy enough coverage but not too much, closely figure your income needs and your ongoing income in the event of disability.
- As in health insurance, shopping for DI insurance should begin with a good agent and a financially strong insurance company.
- Insure against catastrophic long-term disability, not against short-term inconvenience.

Chapter 16

Social Security
Disability Insurance:
Help Wanting

SOCIAL SECURITY DISABILITY BENEFITS

For the past 60 years, people increasingly have expected "the government" to "do something" to help "the downtrodden." If you're disabled, you naturally may expect some assistance from the government, to which you've loyally paid your taxes over the years.

At the federal level, there are Social Security benefits. The same Social Security system that will send you checks when you're retired from your job also may pay you if you can't get to your job.

Notice, however, the word "may" in the above sentence. Of all the applicants for Social Security disability benefits, only about 30% actually receive benefits from their initial applications. And those benefits, while welcome, are scarcely enough for most families to live on.

Who Is Eligible?

To be eligible for Social Security disability benefits, you need enough "work credits"—years in which you earned money and contributed to the system. If you're younger than age 24, you must have worked at least a year and a half in the previous three years. As you get older, the work requirement increases (e.g., 5 years at ages 31–42) until it reaches 10 years at age 62.

Plus, you have to be unable to perform virtually any type of work. This is a tough hurdle to clear. You may not be able to perform your usual job as a schoolteacher or a carpenter, but you might be able to, say, work in a retail store. If that's the case, you won't be eligible for Social Security disability benefits.

Short-term disabilities don't impress Social Security. You won't collect anything until you've been out of work at least five months. Even so, you still have to demonstrate (generally through a doctor's diagnosis) that you'll be out of work at least a year. If you can't make a convincing case, you won't receive any benefits.

Therefore, Social Security disability benefits are mainly for those who are severely crippled or bedridden. A back pain that may seem all too real to you might not be convincing.

Benefits If You Qualify

Even if you do qualify for Social Security disability, the benefits are hardly lavish. Depending on your age, your family situation (dependents may get extra benefits), and the earnings you've contributed to Social Security, you may get as much as $1,800 per month. However, you may get much less. Average benefits are around $600 per month for singles, $1,000 per month for a disabled worker with a family. When you're totally disabled for a year or more, such benefits aren't likely to go far enough, especially if your family is used to a relatively high living standard.

If you earn the minimum wage, Social Security disability benefits will pay you about 60% of your predisability income. For workers earning $50,000 and up, though, DI benefits from Social Security will replace only about 25% of normal income.

The Payoff from SSDI

Once you qualify for Social Security benefits, you'll receive them until you're back at work, earning at least $500 per month or judged to be recovered. However, there is a "trial work period," nine months in which you can earn as much as you can without affecting your benefits. If your earnings are over $500 per month, you generally will get another three-month grace period before your benefits stop.

After your trial work period, if your earnings drop below $500 per month within the next three years, you'll probably be considered still disabled, so your benefits will resume.

There are even "fringe benefits." Once you have been getting Social Security disability benefits for two years, you'll automatically be enrolled in Medicare. Beyond your trial work period, you'll get 39 more months of Medicare coverage. And, if you reach age 65 without recovering, Social Security disability benefits become retirement benefits, with the amount remaining the same.

Taxes May Bite

What about taxes? Social Security disability benefits are taxed just like Social Security retirement benefits. If you have little or no other income, Social Security payments aren't taxed. But if you have substantial other income (more than $25,000 or $32,000 per year, single or joint tax returns), you'll owe tax on a portion of your benefits. The most you'll owe, if your income is well over those thresholds, would be income tax on half the Social Security benefits you receive.

If You're Denied

To say that Social Security disability standards are not cast in stone is putting it mildly. Although the money comes from the federal government, administration is left up to each state. Thus, there are wide differences from state to state on eligibility for disability benefits and the amounts involved.

As mentioned above, about 30% of applicants receive benefits from their initial applications. But there's an appeal process for those who don't, consisting of: (1) a reconsideration stage; (2) the chance for a hearing before an administrative law judge; (3) a special "appeals council" that may review your case; and (4) a final appeal to a U.S. district court. You may have to hire a lawyer before you're through. Nevertheless, persistence pays: Many applicants succeed in winning benefits at these later stages (probably because you can show you've been out of work for over a year by the time you run the gamut of appeals).

Don't Count on Anything

At present, an expansion of Social Security disability benefits is unlikely because of budget pressures. Indeed, cutbacks are possible. In 1991, the Bush administration announced that applicants will be required to take an exercise test, which would disqualify enough people to save $220 million per year by 1995.

Therefore, it likely will become harder, rather than easier, to qualify for Social Security disability benefits. Don't count on them. Put a "0" on that line in worksheet 2. If you are seriously disabled, you can apply, and any amount you receive will be a welcome bonus.

OTHER GOVERNMENT DISABILITY PROGRAMS

There are a few other government programs that may provide disability benefits. Veterans, active members of the armed forces, and federal civil servants may be entitled to disability benefits, which are worth checking into. If you have virtually no assets or income, you may qualify for Supplemental Security Income (SSI), which provides disability payments the way Medicaid provides medical care for the poor.

Several states—including Hawaii, California, Rhode Island, .New York, and New Jersey—pay "cash sickness" benefits, funded through employer contributions, with California deemed the most liberal. These benefits are designed to provide payments in case Social Security or workers' compensation won't. Therefore, they tend to pay benefits soon, but for relatively short periods, perhaps up to 26 weeks.

If you have such protection, consider yourself fortunate. However, this is short-term coverage, so you won't get much comfort in case of long-term disability.

Another possible source of benefits is no-fault auto insurance. Many states will pay disability income (DI) to people injured in auto accidents. However, because you can't know your disability will come from an auto accident, you can't plan on the income.

WORKERS' COMPENSATION

Although only a few states have DI programs, every state plus the District of Columbia offers workers' compensation. If you suffer from an on-the-job injury, you're entitled to benefits.

"On-the-job" injury conjures up visions of a warehouse worker dropping a pack of steel tubing on his foot. Those injuries certainly are covered. Recently, there has been a trend extending workers' comp to cover certain conditions, such as stress or heart attacks, if the victim can show that the work environment helped to bring it on. So workers' comp may cover a wide range of disability.

Although each state has its own workers' comp rules, there are similarities. Employers are required to fund the program through regular premiums to an insurance company or a state fund. Companies can choose to self-insure, effectively putting all their assets on the line if they have to pay claims. (As is the case with health insurance, you should check to see if your employer has a bona fide workers' comp plan in place.)

No Fault

To collect workers' comp, you must be an employee. Self-employed workers (independent contractors) aren't eligible. If you suffer a work-related injury, you collect regardless of who was at fault. It doesn't matter if you dropped the steel tubing on your toe or if your co-worker failed to secure it properly.

There's a catch to this no-fault approach. If you're injured on the job, you can't sue your employer for causing the accident or contributing to it. You're limited to workers' comp benefits.

Benefits

What are those benefits? A combination of health and DI insurance. Under workers' comp, virtually all medical bills from work-related injuries are covered. That includes doctors' bills, hospital bills, prescriptions, and so on. There's usually no deductible or copayment to fulfill. In many states, you can choose any doctors you want; in others, your employer or a state board may limit your choices if you want to collect under workers' comp.

After medical treatment, workers' comp will pay for physical rehabilitation to get you ready to go back to work and, if necessary, for retraining so you can work in another line. If you have to travel to a training center, workers' comp will pay.

In addition to payments for medical care and rehab, workers' comp will pay you disability benefits while you can't work. Workers' comp pays for short-term as well as for long-term disability.

Typically, the waiting period before you can collect benefits is short, usually less than a week. After that, you'll collect what the state determines, usually 60%–80% of your basic wage. The more dependents you have, the greater the benefits you'll receive. What's more, workers' comp benefits are not subject to income tax. So far, so good.

However, each state puts a cap, or maximum, on the workers' comp you can receive. Often, that cap is between $200 and $400 per week, although some states pay over $600. So, if you were taking home $3,000 per month after taxes, $1,200 per month in workers' comp may leave a considerable gap to fill.

Workers' comp covers long-term disability, too, paying the state rate for as long as you can't go back to work. In some cases, you may receive a large lump sum instead of regular monthly benefits. You also may receive a lump sum if you suffer a partial disability.

If you receive Social Security benefits for long-term disability and workers' comp as well, you're "capped" at a total of 80% of predisability income. So you may be better off taking a lump sum from workers' comp and continuing to receive Social Security disability payments.

The Obstacle Course

You can collect workers' comp regardless of who was to blame for an injury, but that doesn't mean you'll collect automatically. On the contrary, you may have to clear quite an obstacle course in order to collect.

If you are injured at work or suffer an occupation-related disease, you should tell your employer or your supervisor. Just to make sure you get your message across, put it in writing. You may not be entitled to benefits if you don't report the injury within 30 days.

The next step, filing a formal claim, takes place after you have received medical treatment. Get a form from your employer or your union. Again, a delay may jeopardize your benefits.

By now, you should have an idea of how your employers will react. If they agree that you've been injured and that the injury is work related, they'll turn the claim over to the insurance company. Again, if the matter is clear-cut—you broke a leg when you tripped while loading a delivery truck—the insurer will begin to pay your benefits.

Today, though, few insurers are eager to pay claims (and few employers are eager to acknowledge injuries that may drive up their future premiums). Justifiably or not, employers and insurers feel the workers' comp system is being abused by some workers: Claims of headaches, stress, and bad backs are hard to prove or disprove. Total costs of workers' comp doubled, from $30 billion to $60 billion, in the period between 1986 and 1992. Therefore, states and insurers are aggressively citing "fraud" and denying claims.

Thus, you can expect an investigation before a hearing officer or judge to determine your eligibility. Often special administration systems—set up outside of state court systems—are used to hear cases. There may be not one hearing but a series of hearings, medical examinations, and appeals before a final determination is made.

When you find yourself in this situation, you're going to need a lawyer. Not the family lawyer who drew up your will or handled your house closing but a specialist in workers' comp. Before you hire anyone, ask for the names of clients the lawyer has represented in the past. Then check with those clients to see if the lawyer has been successful in workers' comp cases.

Workers' Comp and Fringe Benefits

If you're truly disabled because of a work-related injury and can prove it, you can collect benefits indefinitely. In some cases, your employer may decide you can work at a less taxing job. Federal Express, for example, has a policy of giving disabled delivery workers desk jobs at full pay rather than having them sit home and collect 70% of their pay.

As long as you're collecting workers' comp disability benefits, your employer must keep your fringe benefits, including health insurance, in force. So if you're offered a large lump sum instead of ongoing weekly payments, don't jump. Find out what will happen to your other benefits. Especially if you think your disability will be permanent, don't give up your health insurance, which may be hard for you to replace on your own.

When it comes to planning, workers' comp is similar to Social Security. The benefits are nice to have if you become disabled, but you can't plan on them. When it comes to deciding how much DI you'll need, you should enter "0" after workers' comp on worksheet 2.

IN BRIEF

- Social Security disability benefits are available if you can't work at all for a year or more.
- Because of stringent eligibility requirements, only about 30% of all applicants receive benefits on their first application.
- There is a four-stage appeals process that awards benefits to more applicants.

- Payments vary, but no one receives a great deal from Social Security disability benefits.
- A few states have "cash sickness" programs to provide short-term disability benefits.
- Every state has a workers' compensation program.
- Workers' comp covers job-related injuries and illnesses.
- Benefits are available for medical expenses, rehab and training, and DI.
- You can collect workers' comp, but you can't sue your employer for causing your injury.
- Workers' comp disability benefits tend to have low upper limits.
- You may have to go through a battery of medical exams and hearings, aided by a lawyer, before you can collect workers' comp disability benefits.
- Because eligibility for Social Security and workers' comp disability benefits is so uncertain and the amounts to be received unknowable, you can't count on them when deciding how much DI insurance you'll need to buy.

Chapter 17

DI from Your Employer

COMING UP SHORT

About 20% of American workers have long-term disability income (DI) insurance, according to an industry association. Most of that insurance is employer provided. So if you're one of the lucky 20%, you have some DI coverage. However, even more so than health insurance, employer-provided DI coverage may be inadequate.

Group DI policies provided by employers generally are not rip-offs. If you can't work, you'll receive benefits. However, the benefits you receive from a group DI policy may come up short for several reasons:

• Caps on benefits. Few group plans pay more than $5,000 per month. Some won't pay more than $2,000 or $3,000. High-income workers with heavy obligations may find it hard to live on such a reduced income.

• Skimpy benefits. Many group DI policies pay 60% of wages or salary. But some workers receive a great deal of their income from commissions and bonuses, not to mention contributions to retirement plans. Group plans may not cover everything.

Mary Malloy, a sales manager for Universal Exports, earned the following in 1991:

Salary	$75,000
Overrides on salespeoples' commissions	25,000
Annual performance bonus	40,000
Company's contribution to her retirement account	10,000

Thus, Mary considers herself to have earned $150,000 and she has a life-style to match. But suppose she has a nervous breakdown and can't function in her high-powered job for a couple of years. Her company's DI insurer might make this calculation:

Salary	$75,000
60% of salary	45,000

So the policy would pay her less than $4,000 per month. That would be a huge comedown from what Mary's used to.

• Income taxes. If your employer has paid the premiums for DI insurance, you'll owe income taxes on the benefits you receive. In our example, Mary's $45,000 would be treated as fully taxable income.

• Coordination of benefits. Suppose Mary qualifies for Social Security or state cash sickness benefits of $12,000 per year. Under most group plans, the DI benefit would be reduced by $12,000, so Mary still gets a total of $45,000. (Actually, her after-tax cash flow might be a bit higher if the Social Security benefits are partially tax-free.)

• Long waits. In many group plans, you have to pay for up to 180 days of disability yourself, before benefits kick in.

• Definition of disability. Mary, with her nerves shot, may not be able to handle a multinational sales manager's job, but she might be able to teach marketing at a business school. In some group plans, this would disqualify her from DI benefits, even if she earned $20,000 or $30,000 per year rather than $150,000.

• Short periods. Often group plans won't provide benefits beyond a couple of years. This won't help in case of a truly long-term disability.

• Postretirement benefits. Most group plans stop paying DI benefits after age 65, when retirement benefits take effect. Some people, though, would prefer lifetime DI benefits.

• Inflexibility. Many group plans stop benefits if you return to work, even if you're only working part-time, with sharply lower earnings.

• Fixed benefits. Under most group plans, the $45,000 per year that Mary receives will stay at $45,000 per year, even if Mary is out of work for 5 or 10 years or longer. Over that time, her purchasing power will erode.

• Immovable objects. If you change jobs, your group DI coverage won't change with you. You'll have to buy a new individual policy. The older you are, the more expensive that policy will become.

• Impermanence. Group policies often can be canceled or altered by the insurer. Employees may not have long-term protection.

SHOULD YOU GET SUPPLEMENTAL *DI*?

Virtually all of those problems can be solved with an individual DI policy. That's not to say they should be. Some of the options available on individual DI policies, such as lifetime benefits, have limited value compared with the increased cost they generate.

Some problems, though, are serious. Most of all, will your group DI be adequate? Suppose you calculate (from worksheets

1 and 2) that your family will need $5,000 per month, over and above expected income, if you're disabled. Your group DI benefit, you learn, will pay only $4,000 per month. What's more, that $4,000 will be taxable, shaving the net benefit to less than $3,000 per month.

Thus, you need extra DI coverage of more than $2,000 per month to make sure you're covered.

Fortunately, these situations are by no means uncommon. DI insurers will sell supplemental policies—in this example, a DI policy that will pay another $2,000 or $2,500 per month, in addition to what the group plan will pay.

What's more, a supplemental policy may offer more generous terms. You may, for example, have a 90-day waiting period, so some benefits will start within three months rather than six. And you may be able to buy coverage that will pay in case of partial disability.

Here's an example, courtesy of Sidney Madlock, IDS Financial Services:

Larry Underwood, rising young executive, earns $125,000 per year, with a $45,000 bonus. His group DI policy calls for 60% of his $125,000 salary.

Annual Salary	$125,000	
Bonus	45,000	
Total cash income		$170,000
DI benefit (60% of $125,000 salary)		75,000
Income-replacement coverage		44%

So Larry decides to shop for supplemental DI coverage. The DI issuer, he discovers, will include many executive "perks" as income: the value of his company car, his club membership, his company-provided life insurance, his retirement savings, and so on. Altogether, his "insurable" income is calculated at over $230,000.

With this much income, the insurer decides that Larry qualifies for a total DI benefit of $9,525 per month, over $114,000 per year. Here's how the calculation works now:

Group DI monthly benefit	$6,250	
Assumed Social Security disability benefit	(925)	
Group DI would pay		$5,325

Amount of DI Larry qualifies for   9,525
Minus group coverage   (5,325)
Supplemental individual DI benefit   4,200

Now, if Larry suffers a long-term disability, he'll receive an extra $4,200 per month, over $50,000 per year. His total DI benefit could go as high as $125,000 per year, nearly 75% of his pre-disability cash income. In addition, the $50,000 he would get from his suplemental individual policy will be tax-free because he pays the premiums himself. (If you buy DI insurance either as a supplement to a group plan or as your only DI protection, any benefits you receive from that policy will be tax-free.)

How much does Larry pay for this extra protection? Nearly $2,200 per year. And, as you'll see in the next two chapters, if he wants special options, he could wind up paying over $3,000 per year for coverage.

Not everyone will have Larry's "problems," with total compensation over $200,000 per year, including fringe benefits. But, on a smaller scale, many people will face situations in which group DI plans fall short of full coverage. Then you have to decide if it's worth an extra thousand dollars or two each year for full peace of mind.

BENEFITS OF SUPPLEMENTAL *DI*

Portability

In addition, the supplemental DI benefits you buy, like all individual DI policies, are "portable." If you leave your employer, your group coverage will end, but your supplemental plan travels with you. While you're unemployed, you generally won't be able to buy DI insurance. If you join a new company and there's a waiting period before you qualify for benefits, your supplemental DI plan remains in force, giving you some protection.

Suppose you decide to set up your own business. It may take you a while to demonstrate earning power and qualify for new

DI coverage. If you have a supplemental DI policy in place, that will provide protection in the interim.

Splitting the Difference

Your employer may offer to pay a DI insurance premium on a "split-dollar" basis, meaning that you'll split the costs. The premium may be divided so that your employer pays for DI insurance that runs for a year or two and you pay for long-term DI coverage, perhaps to age 65. Because most disabilities last for less than two years, your employer's share of the premium will be the larger one.

If you're disabled and you receive DI benefits, you'll owe taxes up until you reach the end of the benefit period for which your employer paid. If the employer bought a two-year benefit period, you'll owe income tax on two years of benefits. After that, benefits will be tax-free.

Flex Plans

As mentioned on page 62, many large employers offer flexible plans from which you can choose fringe benefits, such as health insurance. DI insurance may be included in a flex plan—the plan may offer a monthly benefit of 45% of pretax income.

Flex plans will often give you the option of increasing coverage to 60% or 65% of pretax income. You can pay with "credits" under your flex plan or with taxable dollars.

If you want the extra coverage, pay with taxable dollars. If you use tax-free flex-plan credits, all DI benefits you collect will be taxable. If you use your own money, part of each DI benefit check would be tax-free.

	Per month
Your pretax income is	$5,000
Your flex plan offers, as a basic benefit, 45% DI coverage	2,250
You have the option of increasing DI coverage to 65%	3,250

If you pay for the extra $1,000 coverage with taxable dollars, about 30% of any DI benefits you will receive will be tax-free.

IN BRIEF

- Less than 20% of all American workers have long-term DI insurance.
- Group DI coverage, provided by employers, may have severe shortcomings.
- Most of all, group plans may not provide all the income you'll need in the event of a long-term disability.
- Benefits from employer-provided DI insurance are subject to income tax.
- You may be able to purchase supplemental DI coverage to fill the gap left by a group plan.
- All benefits you receive from a DI policy that you buy yourself are free of income tax.
- If you buy a supplemental DI policy, you can take it with you if you leave the group plan.
- In split-dollar and flex plans, the DI insurance you pay for with your own money will generate tax-free, not taxable, DI benefits.

Chapter 18

The Basics of Buying DI

If you're one of the lucky 20% with employer-provided, long-term disability income (DI) coverage, you may want to buy supplemental coverage, as described in the last chapter. More likely, you're among the 80% with no long-term DI coverage. If you want to protect yourself and your family, in the event of a severe disability, you'll have to shop for your own DI insurance.

PASSING INSURERS' *DI* TESTS

Beyond a good agent and good insurance company, what you need in a good DI policy is, first, the right amount of benefits. But you don't automatically qualify for any policy you'd like. Insurance companies will examine your income, health, and age, among other factors, before they determine whether you qualify for the policy you seek.

Income

Suppose your analysis from worksheets 1 and 2 shows that you'll need $3,000 a month in DI benefits. You need to find a company that will sell you that policy. To qualify, you'll probably need to show $5,000 per month in income. (Remember, insurance companies won't want to sell you DI coverage that amounts to more than 60% of your income.)

Or suppose you're self-employed, reporting income on a Schedule C. You may have $5,000 per month ($60,000 per year) in gross income, but by the time you get through deducting all your business expenses, you may be reporting a net income of only $3,000 per month ($36,000) per year on your tax return.

Naturally, an insurance company won't be eager to sell you a $3,000-per-month DI policy in these circumstances. You might be tempted to complain of a nonexistent disability and collect $3,000 per month tax-free. Judging from the records the insurer has, that's as much as you were earning full-time, so you might prefer to stop working and pocket the cash.

Therefore, you may have to shop around a bit for an insurance company that will sell you as much DI coverage as you want if your income isn't easy to demonstrate.

What if you're unemployed or just out of school looking for your first job? You won't be able to buy DI insurance unless you demonstrate that you work, earn an income, and need DI coverage to make up most of that income if you're disabled.

Glowing with Health

Besides income, you'll have to demonstrate your health to an insurance company in order to qualify for DI insurance. In this way, applying for DI is similar to applying for life insurance or health insurance. The less you need DI insurance (the better your health and the less likely you are to become disabled), the easier it is for you to get DI insurance at favorable premiums.

There are, however, differences when it comes to "underwriting" DI, which is the insurance-industry term for select-

186 YOUR MONEY OR YOUR LIFE

ing those it will insure. For life insurance, there is a great deal of data, developed over the years, indicating what effect diabetes, for example, or high blood pressure will have on life expectancy.

Statistics on disability aren't as well developed. True, musculo-skeletal disorders in an applicant's back or joints will raise a red flag, and all insurers are super cautious about AIDS these days, but it is very difficult for an insurer to point to a specific condition and say, this probably will cause disability 5 or 10 years from now.

Therefore, DI insurance underwriting tends to be more subjective than other kinds of insurance. One company may accept an applicant whom its competitors deny. It pays to look around. An experienced agent may be able to help you find the right company while keeping you from an outright rejection that will hamper your future efforts to get coverage.

Age

Your age counts, too. Insurers have found that the likehood of your becoming disabled increases as you grow older. Plus, the older you are when you're disabled, the longer the disability is likely to last. Therefore, the older you are when you apply for DI coverage, the more you can expect to pay.

In 1991, for example, Guardian Life was charging a 30-year-old around $1,100 per year for a policy with a $3,000-per-month benefit. That same policy would cost a 50-year-old nearly $2,000 per year. New York Life showed an even greater age-related price difference: $1,800 at age 50 for a policy costing only $750 at age 30.

If you think you need DI coverage, don't wait to apply. Standard DI insurance is level premium, meaning the amount you'll pay now is what you'll pay next year and the year after, and so on, as long as there is no change in the level of benefits you want. So it pays to buy while you're young and lock in the low premium.

Here are some typical rates for a $2,000-per-month DI policy, with a waiting period of 180 days, as quoted by IDS Life:

Your Age When You Buy the Policy	Level Premium You Pay Each Year
30	$644
35	760
40	944
45	1,192

If you keep the same policy in force until age 65, here's how much you wind up paying:

Your Age When You Buy the Policy	Total Premiums Paid to Age 65
30	$22,540
35	22,800
40	23,600
45	23,840

The differences are minor, to be sure. Plus, there's a "use-of-money" benefit to paying later. If you buy DI at age 45 instead of age 30, you have 15 years to invest the money you're not paying in insurance premiums.

But by the same token, you're not protected from disabilities during those 15 years. And you wind up paying about the same for the much less protection.

If you start at age 30, you get 35 years worth of protection with a policy that pays benefits through age 65. At $2,000 per month, you could collect as much as $840,000. If you wait until age 45 to buy, you get only 20 years of coverage and only $480,000 in maximum benefits.

If you wait until too late, you might not be able to buy DI coverage: It's very hard to buy after age 60, for example, and may be difficult to purchase in your late 50s. That doesn't mean, though, that DI insurers only want college students. The ideal applicant, from an insurance company's point of view, is a married professional over 30 years old who owns a home and has been in his or her present occupation more than three years. Such people, history has shown, are least likely to file questionable claims. So the closer you are to this profile, the more likely you'll be looked upon favorably if you apply for DI insurance.

CHOOSING FEATURES FROM THE MENU

Assuming that you are in good health with demonstrable income, you probably will qualify for the DI benefits you'd like. Now you have to decide which policy features you want and which ones you don't want. Here are the standard features you'll find in a good DI insurance policy:

Cause of Disability

Don't buy a policy that pays only if you're disabled in an accident. You should get one that will pay for illness as well. According to Social Security claims statistics (table 8), accidents are not the most likely causes of long-term disability:

Table 8: LEADING CAUSES OF DISABILITY

Males	Females
1. Heart Disease	1. Cancer
2. Cancer	2. Heart disease
3. Accidents (primarily job related)	3. Accidents (primarily auto related)
4. Respiratory disorders	4. Nervous disorders
5. Digestive disorders	5. Mental disorders
6. Nervous disorders	6. Attempted suicide
7. Mental disorders	7. Diabetes
8. Diabetes	8. Respiratory disorders
9. Attempted suicide	9. Digestive disorders
10. Infective and parasitic diseases	10. Infective and parasitic diseases

Renewability

The best policies are noncancelable, meaning that the company can't cut you off from coverage as long as you keep paying the agreed-upon premiums. By the same token, the company can't raise your premium, which might effectively force you to drop the coverage.

Some DI policies are "guaranteed renewable," which is slightly less desirable. Here your premium can be increased as long as it's raised for an entire class of policyholders. You don't have as much protection here as you have with a noncancelable policy.

Other types of DI insurance aren't worth buying because your coverage can be dropped if your health deteriorates.

Definition of Disability

This usually is the key to DI insurance, so it pays to read the policy closely. Avoid policies requiring total disability. In such policies, a lawyer who could work as a janitor wouldn't collect.

Most people are adequately served by "any occupation," or "any-occ," disability policies. Such a policy might state that if you can work at any job for which you are "reasonably suited by education, training, and experience," you are not considered disabled. Mary, the burned-out marketing executive forced to teach at a business school, would not be considered disabled under an any-occ policy. But if Mary were judged able to sell newspapers at the corner newsstand, that wouldn't disqualify her for benefits. Her education, training, and experience suit her for more demanding work.

In recent years, DI insurers have offered "own-occ" policies in which you're considered disabled if you can't perform your "own occupation," even if you can do other work for which you're qualified. The proverbial surgeon with the crippled hand who can teach or practice some other form of medicine is the usual example. These policies will have language saying you're entitled to benefits if you can't perform the "material and substantial duties of your primary occupation," for example.

Own-occ coverage costs more than any-occ, adding perhaps 10% to your premium. Is it worth it? Few of us are surgeons or in similar positions where we might not be able to perform a high-priced specialty but can perform a related, lower-paid task. If you're a corporate manager and can't get to your job for months at a stretch, you probably won't be able to teach or do other suitable work. Even if you have to take a lower-paid job, your family won't face a long period of total income loss.

That's the sort of catastrophe DI insurance is designed to prevent. So that's what you should pay for.

People in the DI business regard own-occ coverage as an appeal to the buyer's ego—you feel what you do is so special that you should have prime coverage. It's a "marketing gimmick," one executive has stated for publication. Unless your circumstances are truly unique, you should probably choose less expensive any-occ coverage.

Some DI policies provide own-occ coverage for a year or two, then shift to any-occ. That may be worthwhile if coverage is cheaper than a straight own-occ policy would be. But you need to read the language of the DI policy to see how it pertains to your particular situation.

Take the case of the 40-something Brooklyn pharmacist whose job consisted largely of twisting safety caps from bottles. He developed carpal tunnel syndrome, a severe injury to the nerves and tendons of his twisting hand, and found it impossible to work. However, his DI insurer refused to pay because he still could do other tasks in his pharmacy, such as carrying packages. The pharmacist, father of five children, is in court trying to collect. So if your work requires any special physical demands, besides reading reports and talking to people on the phone, discuss your situation closely with your agent to be sure you're really covered.

Waiting Period

No DI policy is going to pay you for the first day you can't work. At best, your benefits will begin after seven days of disability, but such policies are extremely expensive. If you can support yourself for 30 or 60 or 90 days of disability, you'll lower your premiums dramatically.

The most popular waiting ("elimination") period is 30 days, but 90 days often seems to be the most economically efficient waiting period. Equitable Life, for example, recently quoted a $3,000-per-month policy with a 30-day waiting period for a 25-year-old at over $1,000 per year. That same policy drops to around $750 per year if the elimination is stretched to 90 days.

So, by bearing some risks yourself, you can slash your DI cost by around 25%.

Beyond 90 days, however, there is little benefit to a longer waiting period. A one-year elimination period cuts only about 10% off the cost of a 90-day elimination period:

Length of Time Out of Work Until DI Benefits Begin	Annual Premium*
30 days	$1,000
90 days	750
One year	675

*Approximate rates for illustration purposes.

Most people, then, are well served with a 90-day waiting period. But the length of the desirable waiting period depends on individual circumstances. Say you work for a company that offers you three months of paid sick leave. In that case, you really don't need a DI policy that kicks in after 30 days. You can elect a 90-day waiting period, or perhaps even a six-month waiting period, if you have adequate savings.

Although it makes sense to reduce premiums with a long waiting period, don't take this route if you don't have enough of a reserve to see you through. A 90-day waiting period may actually be 120 days because of the lag time before you receive your first DI check. If you truly live from one paycheck to the next, you may need a 30- or 60-day waiting period.

A good DI policy will count total and partial ("residual") disability toward meeting the waiting period requirement.

Rehab and Retraining

DI insurers naturally want to get you back to work as soon as possible. Therefore, good DI policies will pay for physical rehabilitation, to help you heal, and possibly for occupational retraining, if necessary.

Benefit Period

As mentioned, DI insurance should cover you in the event of a catastrophe—if you can't work for several years of longer. So a policy that will pay benefits only for a year or two isn't adequate.

You may cut your premium by significant amounts if you limit your benefits period. In practice, only about 5% of all disabilities last longer than five years. But suppose you're one of that 5%? You and your family could be financially ruined. That's exactly the type of tragedy DI insurance is intended to prevent.

So you're probably best served by a policy that pays benefits until age 65. That is, if you're disabled at age 58 and are unable to go back to work, you'll collect benefits for seven years.

MORE FEATURES, MORE DECISIONS

Lifetime Benefits

By age 65, DI benefits may not be meaningful because you probably would have stopped working, anyway, so you won't be losing income if you're disabled. By then, you probably will be able to collect Social Security retirement benefits plus employer-provided retirement funds.

However, for an extra 10%–25% in premium payments, you can buy a policy that will pay you lifetime benefits. That may make sense if you're in your 20s or 30s and you haven't worked enough to qualify for Social Security retirement benefits or built up any sort of pension plan.

Some "lifetime benefits" clauses will pay that long only if you're disabled prior to age 60. Some are even more complicated: if you're injured after age 55, your benefit will decline by 10% per year after age 65.

Although these provisions are complicated, they make sense if they help trim your premium. As a practical matter, if you're not seriously disabled before age 55 or 60, you'll be able to qualify for Social Security retirement benefits and perhaps build up a pension fund, so you might want to drop this coverage along the way.

Some policies will put some sort of a catch on long-term benefits. They might, for example, say they'll pay you for two years if you can't work in a suitable occupation. After that, though, they'll pay only if you're totally disabled. Try to avoid DI policies if there's a chance you'll be denied benefits during a long-term disability.

Definition of Recurrent Disability

When you put together a DI policy's elimination period and its benefit period, you can see the need for further clarification. Suppose, for example, Bob White's DI policy has a 90-day waiting period before he can collect benefits. He has a heart attack and misses work for six months, collecting DI benefits for the last three of those months.

He returns to work then, but after a week he has a relapse. He winds up missing another three months of work.

The question is, does Bob have to start a new waiting period because he went back to work for that week? If so, he won't collect any DI benefits for the last three months that he's out of work.

Here's another situation. Sue Green buys a DI policy that provides no more than two years of benefits per disability. She suffers from severe back pains and can't work for two years, using up all her DI benefits.

Sue's employer, who's sympathetic, allows her to go back to work for a few days. Then she says she's become disabled again, and—after another waiting period—she collects DI benefits for another two years.

To avoid such abuses by insurers or insured individuals, a definition of "recurrent disability" should be included in the policy. Usually, any disability that recurs within six months is considered part of the original disability.

So, if you were in Bob White's situation, you could continue to collect benefits without going through another 90-day waiting period. The few days you spent back at work wouldn't be counted against you.

On the other hand Sue Green would have to show she's no longer disabled by working at least six months before another benefit period can begin.

Preexisting Conditions

Another question that needs to be answered in a basic DI policy is the treatment of preexisting conditions. This issue is similar to that posed by health insurance policies. If you are disabled because of a condition you had within two years prior to buying the policy, does the insurer have to pay benefits?

Typically, you'll be expected to fill out a medical history form honestly and to take a medical exam. Preexisting conditions that come to light may be specifically described in the policy; claims made as a result of such conditions, within two years of taking out the policy, likely will be contested. The same will happen if you hid or minimized a problem. But if you disclosed all the important information and the insurer didn't single out specific preexisting conditions, then resultant disability can't be challenged.

Suppose, for example, you mentioned dizzy spells. The insurer didn't specify that this was a preexisting condition. If your dizzy spells get worse and worse, to the point where you can't work and need to collect DI benefits, the insurer can't renege on its promise.

After two years of coverage, all conditions will be covered unless there's a specific exclusion. Most DI policies exclude benefits in cases of attempted suicide, drug abuse, and normal pregnancy.

PAYING FOR THE BASICS

A plain "vanilla" DI policy, then, should include the following features:

- Coverage for illness as well as accidents.
- Noncancelation clause.
- Benefits paid if you can't work at a suitable occupation.
- An elimination period to match your financial reserves.
- Payment of benefits until age 65.
- A definition of recurrent disability that allows six months for recovery.

- Clearly defined waiting periods and exclusions for pre-existing conditions.

What might such a policy cost? That will vary according to your age and your health, among other factors. But figure a 30-year-old will pay around $250–$300 per year per $1,000 in monthly benefits. Thus, a $3,000-per-month DI policy might cost $750–$900 per year.

A 50-year-old will pay more, as mentioned, perhaps $500–$600 per $1,000. The annual premium on that $3,000-per-month DI policy might be $1,500–$1,800.

IN BRIEF
- To qualify for a DI insurance policy that will pay the desired benefits, you will have to demonstrate a certain level of income.
- You'll also have to pass a medical exam to qualify for coverage.
- If you qualify, you likely will pay the same premium, year after year.
- That premium will be higher the older you are when you apply for coverage.
- An ideal DI policy can't be canceled or increased in price for any reason (including poor health); if you're disabled, it will pay benefits until age 65.
- Benefits should be paid if you can't perform work for which you're suited by training and experience.
- To cut costs, you can agree to wait a longer period before benefits start.
- The policy should specify when each benefit period ends, usually six months after a full return to work.
- Certain preexisting conditions may be excluded from coverage for two years or longer.

Chapter 19

Hold the Options

A "plain vanilla" disability income (DI) policy, described in the previous chapter, likely will be all that you really need. If you suffer from a long-term disability and can't earn a living, the policy will help you and your family pay the bills and maintain your standard of living.

But many insurance agents will discourage you from buying a vanilla policy. They want to sell you chocolate chips and cherries and Reese's Pieces and chunks of Oreos.

Unfortunately, shopping for DI insurance is a long way from loading up at the sundae bar. The purpose of offering all the extras, it seems, is to make it harder for you to figure out what's for sale. Then you'll turn to the agent for advice. Some agents, to be sure, are honest folk, but some will take advantage, selling you a $3,000 policy when a $2,000 policy will do and increasing their commission by 50%.

Certainly, many DI policy options provide valuable benefits. In an ideal world, you'd buy the best. But in the real world you're paying for life insurance and health insurance and auto insurance and homeowner's insurance, not to mention a few noninsurance expenses. You probably can't afford all the DI accessories you'd like.

Instead, you can cut your costs by buying only the features you need. Make sure you're buying enough coverage for a long enough time period. Most other extras, or "riders" to the policy, are there because the insurer expects to make more money by selling them. You'll probably come out ahead keeping your policy as lean as possible.

When you discuss DI insurance with your agent, here are some of the extra features likely to be offered:

HELPING YOU GET BACK ON YOUR FEET

Partial Disability

What if you can only work part-time? Your income will be reduced, but you may not qualify for full DI benefits. If your policy includes a partial-disability option, you'll receive a fixed amount if you can work part-time. Generally, partial-disability coverage pays 50% of the basic benefit. If your policy calls for $3,000 per month, you'll receive $1,500. This benefit usually is paid for a short time period, perhaps no longer than six months.

Today most DI claims are for partial disability. However, a short-term partial-disability feature won't provide much protection. Instead, you're better off with residual disability, defined below.

Residual Disability

In recent years, partial-disability clauses have largely given way to residual disability provisions. This is a more sophisticated concept, with benefits based upon your lost income. After a disability, most people likely will go back to their own occupation. But what happens if you can only work part-time? If you're not strong enough to put in the 40- or 50- or 60-hour week that you're used to?

That circumstance can be covered by a "full recovery benefit" feature, sometimes called "residual disability benefit." If your earnings are reduced, you will receive partial compensation, generally up to 80% of the full DI benefit.

For example, suppose you suffer through a period of total disability, receiving a benefit of, say, $3,000 per month. Then you go back to work. However, you can't put in a full day; many of your customers have taken their business elsewhere. So your income is only 25% of what it was. Under a standard DI policy, you couldn't collect anything. With a residual benefit, you'd collect 75% of your basic benefit, or $2,250 per month.

As your income increases to 50% of the predisability level, your DI benefit decreases to $1,500 per month, 50% of your basic amount. And so on. Full recovery benefits will continue paying over varying lengths of time (6 months, 12 months), depending on the contract. The best policies pay as long as your income is depressed, up to age 65. Usually, when your income reaches 75%–80% of predisability earnings, residual benefits cease (see table 9).

In some cases, you have to be totally disabled first, before you can collect residual benefits. If this is the case, you'll want a policy for as short a "qualification period" as possible—30 or 60 days, rather than 180 days, for example. But you probably can find a policy with a residual disability rider that does not require a period of total disability.

Of all the options you can buy, this one may make the most sense. (Some individual DI policies include residual benefits as a standard feature.) A good residual benefits rider may add 15% to the cost of a basic DI policy, but it's money well spent. You don't want to feel that you can't go back to work because you'll lose all your benefits, and you don't want to lose all your benefits if you go back to work part-time.

HEDGING AGAINST INFLATION

Future Increase Option

Suppose you buy DI coverage when you're a rising young executive earning $3,000 per month, so you buy a policy that will

Table 9: HOW RESIDUAL DISABILITY BENEFITS ARE PAID*

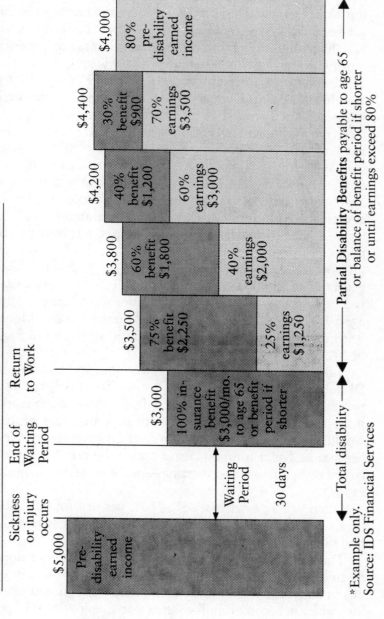

Sickness or injury occurs	End of Waiting Period	Return to Work					
$5,000	$3,000	$3,500	$3,800	$4,200	$4,400	$4,000
Pre-disability earned income	100% insurance benefit $3,000/mo. to age 65 or benefit period if shorter	75% benefit $2,250	60% benefit $1,800	40% benefit $1,200	30% benefit $900	80% pre-disability earned income
		25% earnings $1,250	40% earnings $2,000	60% earnings $3,000	70% earnings $3,500	

Waiting Period 30 days

◄─── Total disability ───►   ◄─── Partial Disability Benefits payable to age 65 or balance of benefit period if shorter or until earnings exceed 80% ───►

*Example only.
Source: IDS Financial Services

pay you $2,000 per month. Twenty years later, you're at the top of the heap, with a $200,000 income and hundreds of thousands of dollars in mortgage debt. If you can't work, your $2,000 per month in DI won't maintain your family's life-style, much less make the required monthly payments.

You'd like to increase your DI coverage to $10,000 per month, and you're willing to pay for it. However, in the interim, you've acquired more than a few pounds, a weak heart, and an ulcer. No insurer will sell you anywhere near $10,000 per month in coverage.

The insurance company has an answer to this problem. At the time you buy your first DI policy, while you're young and healthy, you also buy an option entitling you to step up your coverage. If you get a 10% raise, say, you automatically can increase your DI benefit by 10% if you pay a 10% higher premium. No physical exam is required.

You could, if your income justifies it, go from a $2,000 benefit to an $8,000 benefit, no health questions asked. Usually, you can increase coverage every year or every other year, up to age 50, as long as you can show the requisite income. Monthly benefit increases may be limited to $1,500 apiece, up to $6,000 or $7,500 over the life of a policy.

Take the example of Carl, a patent attorney who bought a DI policy with a future-increase option. Shortly thereafter, he needed back surgery. Although he didn't miss enough work to make a claim, he now has a health condition that probably would make it impossible to buy more DI coverage. However, because he has a future-increase option, he can buy more DI coverage as his income increases—without taking a medical exam.

Often you'll pay an extra 5%–10% per year for this option; in some cases, you must exercise it after the first year, or you lose the option for the future.

This feature may not be very expensive, but that doesn't mean it's worth buying. You might consider it if you're in your 20s or early 30s with a great career ahead of you. But later in life, when it becomes unlikely that you'll enjoy huge leaps in income, you're not facing much of a risk here.

Suppose, for example, you project that your family needs

$5,000 a month to live on if you're disabled. You expect $1,000 to come from other sources, so you buy $4,000 a month in DI insurance.

Several years later, when your income is considerably higher, you try to increase DI coverage to $6,000 per month, but you're turned down. Note that you're only turned down for the increased coverage. As long as you keep paying your premium and have a noncancelable policy, you'll still receive that $4,000 per month if you're disabled.

Now you're disabled, and you're receiving only $4,000 per month, not $6,000. Yes, there might be a restaurant dinner skipped, a new outfit not bought, but you're not likely to go begging. In a worst-case scenario, you might have to trade down from your expensive house.

Rather than guard against this possibility by paying an insurance company for the right to buy more insurance, you should be a bit cautious about the debt you take on, especially if you know you have health problems.

Even if you don't buy this type of rider, some policies automatically will adjust your monthly benefit upward, regardless of your income, to reflect changes in the consumer price index. Of course, the premium goes up, too. You should be sure you have the option of not paying for increased coverage you don't want.

Cost-of-Living Adjustment (COLA)

Don't confuse COLA options with future-increase options. A future-increase option gives you a chance to increase coverage before you're disabled, while COLAs increase your coverage after you're disabled.

Mort bought a $3,000-per-month policy with a COLA option back in 1987. In 1990, he was disabled and collected $3,000 per month from his policy.

After a year, he was still disabled. According to the index used by his insurance company (possibly the consumer price index), the cost of living rose by 5% that year. Therefore, his benefit automatically increased by $150 (5% times $3,000), to $3,150 per month.

Another year passed, and Mort still can't work. This year, the insurance company finds the cost of living has risen by 6%. Starting at $3,150, the monthly benefit now is pegged at $3,339, up another $189 (6% times $3,150). And so on, every year while Mort is disabled. If Mort collects residual benefits, those, too, will be indexed for inflation with a good COLA option.

Suppose Mort recovers from his disability and goes back to work. A year or two later he's disabled again, collecting benefits. Where do the monthly benefits start? In some DI policies, the initial monthly benefit would start over, at $3,000 per month; in other policies, Mort will be able to buy the higher-indexed benefit, without passing a medical exam, if he's willing to pay the higher premium.

COLA certainly is an option that sounds necessary. Who wants to collect that same $3,000 year after year?

However, a COLA option can be expensive. A 45-year-old executive buying $4,000 worth of monthly coverage might pay $2,000 per year for the base plan and more than $800 per year for the COLA option: a premium increase of over 40%. In some policies, this option will increase premium by more than 60%. Does it make sense to increase premiums 40% or 60% per year to get future increases of 5% or 6% per year?

What's more, a COLA might not really be necessary. Often, your greatest obligation if you're disabled is debt repayment: home mortgage, auto loan, credit-card account. These are usually fixed obligations that won't rise over the years, no matter what happens to inflation. Thus, if you are disabled, your expenses won't rise in lockstep with the cost of living. COLAs, in DI insurance, often are a luxury you can live without.

CUT YOUR COSTS BY SHAVING YOUR INSURANCE

Social-Benefits Rider

This feature is billed as a cost cutter. It allows the insurance company to reduce the monthly benefit it pays you by the amount Social Security would pay if you were eligible for SSDI benefits. In return, you pay a lower premium.

Let's say you want to receive $3,000 per month in DI benefits. Instead of buying a basic $3,000-per-month DI policy, you could buy a $2,250-per-month base policy plus a $750-per-month social-benefits rider. If you're disabled, you'd collect

	per month
From your base DI policy	$2,250
From your social-benefits rider	750
Total	3,000

Suppose several months go by and you qualify for $600 per month from Social Security. In this circumstance, you'd collect

From your base DI policy	$2,250
From Social Security	600
From your social-benefits rider	150
Total	3,000

If you collect $500 a month from Social Security, the insurance company would owe you $250 a month on the rider. And so on. As you can see, the insurance company's risk is reduced because it may make smaller payments if you qualify for "social benefits." Such a policy will be less expensive than a DI policy that would call for the insurance company to pay $3,000 per month no matter what.

Certainly, saving money is a fine idea, especially if you're going to get your desired $3,000 per month, anyway. The question is, how much do you save and how much do you give up in potential benefits?

In some DI plans, a $3,000-per-month policy that would cost $1,675 per year drops to $1,580 per year if you include a social-benefits rider. That's $95 per year in your pocket. Considering the odds against your being disabled and qualifying for Social Security benefits, you might as well save the $95.

In other situations, though, the annual premium only drops from $1,115 to $1,105. So you're saving only $10 per year, but you're giving up a chance for up to $750 per month in benefits.

That is, if you pay the extra $10 and buy the straight $3,000-per-month policy without the social-benefits rider, you could receive $3,000 per month from the insurer *plus* any benefits you receive from Social Security.

Social Security Supplement

Don't confuse this feature with a social-benefits rider. With this supplement, you get an extra payment, perhaps $500 per month, until Social Security disability payments begin. This can add anywhere from 10% to 25% to your premium. Again, this is a gimmick because you don't know when or if or how much you'll collect from Social Security. If you'll need income while you're disabled, buy it as part of your basic benefit.

In a variation, some policies will have a fairly long waiting period (say, 180 days), then offer a supplement that pays a smaller benefit—maybe $1,000 per month—for a 10% increase in premium. This seems like classic push me, pull me. Why go to a long waiting period to reduce premium costs and then increase premiums with an option that shortens the waiting period?

Stick to basics. If you have enough resources to support yourself for 30 or 90 or 180 days, that's the waiting period to choose.

Nonoccupational Coverage

Here's a variation on the social-benefits rider. Some DI policies cover only off-the-job injuries and illnesses. If a person can collect workers' comp, these policies won't pay DI benefits. Because the insurer's risk is reduced, your premiums will be lower.

Such DI policies usually are aimed at low-income, blue-collar workers. In fact, they may be the only DI policies such people can buy. But if you're not in that category and you're looking for DI benefits of $2,000 per month and up, such policies aren't appropriate. Saving premium dollars won't help if you're locked in to low workers' comp DI benefits.

APPROACH WITH EXTREME CAUTION

Waiver of premium

This is an option commonly added to life insurance and DI policies. In effect, if you suffer from a disability and need to collect DI benefits, you don't have to keep paying the premiums on your policy until you're back at work again. If you pay premiums annually or semiannually or quarterly, you may be entitled to a partial refund of premiums you've already paid, once you're declared disabled.

This is definitely a nice feature to have—there will be one less bill to pay in case you're disabled. The question is, is it cost-effective? Suppose, for example, you want a DI policy paying $2,000 per month. Your agent shows you a policy that costs $1,200 per year, or $100 per month. If you had, in this example, $2,100 per month in DI benefits, you could use the extra $100 per month ($1,200 per year) to pay the premiums on your DI coverage. So you should choose whatever is cheaper: buying the waiver of premium or buying an extra $100 per month in DI coverage.

You should go through the same exercise when deciding whether to buy a disability waiver of premium on life insurance policies. If you are disabled, moreover, you should check all of your insurance policies to see if you're excused from paying premiums.

Presumptive Disability

In some policies, you're considered disabled if you lose your sight, your hearing, your speech, two limbs, etc. Even if you continue to work, you'll collect DI benefits.

Such a feature is acceptable if included in the basic policy, but you shouldn't pay extra for it. The purpose of DI insurance is to protect your income no matter what the cause, not to participate in a morbidity sweepstakes.

Special Hospitalization Benefits

Some DI policies will waive the waiting period if your disability begins with a hospital stay. Others will pay you an extra amount, above your DI benefit, while you're in the hospital.

These are the kinds of features from which insurance companies make money. You should cover hospital stays with health insurance; use DI to make up for lost income.

Accidental Death and Dismemberment

Some policies will pay a relatively large sum either to you or your beneficiaries if you die in an accident or lose a limb, eyesight, etc. Again, accidental death is no different from any other kind of death, so it should be covered by life insurance. Accidental dismemberment can be covered by health insurance and regular DI benefits.

Medical Reimbursement

Another feature covers specific types of accidents or sicknesses where hospitalization is not required. Your medical expenses will be repaid. Again, you should cover these possibilities with health insurance. Such features amount to no more than gambling with the insurance company, which knows the odds and sets the prices in its favor.

Return of Premium

Of all the DI insurance extras, here's the most gimmicky: free insurance. With this feature, if you never collect from a disability claim, you get your money back, or 80% of your money back. Or, if you make very few claims, you get part of your money back. In some policies, you'll get this refund every five years or so. In others, you have to wait until age 65.

Not all DI insurers offer this feature, but the list has been growing and now includes Mutual of Omaha, Maccabees Mutual, Mutual of New York, National Life of Vermont, and Provident Life & Accident. Policies differ; in one variation, you have to pay DI insurance premiums for 10 years. After that time, the insurer will calculate the difference, if any, between the premiums you've paid and the payments you've received. You'll get a check for 80% of the difference.

Annual DI premium	$3,000
10 years of premiums	30,000
Disability benefits collected	0
Net cost to you	30,000
Return of premium – 80%	24,000
10-year net cost of DI insurance	6,000

Typically, return-of-premium (ROP) policies are more expensive than standard DI policies, perhaps 50% higher. Coverage comparable to what you bought for $3,000 per year might cost only $2,000 per year without the ROP feature. Still, paying $6,000 over 10 years obviously is better than paying $20,000 even if you figure in the interest you could have earned on your extra $1,000 per year in premium payments.

Getting your premium back, however, isn't a sure thing. Every claim you make reduces the amount of premium that will be returned. If you're disabled for a year or so, depending on the policy, you may get no refund at all.

In the meantime, ROP policies commonly have "surrender charges" until age 65. If you've had such a policy for, say, 10 years and decide to change it, you might get back only 25% of what you paid, not 80% or 100%.

ROP sounds attractive, but it's a gimmick. You're locking yourself into a much higher premium for many years. If you want DI coverage, buy it. It's expensive enough without overpaying on the chance that you'll stay healthy and get your money back.

Cash for College

Some DI policies will include payments for college. You buy a maximum benefit, perhaps $40,000 or $50,000. If you suffer a long-term disability—over one year—you'll collect benefits for college expenses.

Suppose you buy a $40,000 college benefit and become disabled when your child is 14. For the next four years, you can't work. There is a one-year waiting period, then three years (36 months) during which benefits are accrued. When your child reaches 18, you'll receive a lump sum of around $25,000, representing those 36 months' worth of disability payments.

If you can go back to work then, benefits will cease. But if you're still disabled or if disability recurs, you'll collect around $670 per month until you reach your $40,000 limit.

This is a feature you might buy if money is not a concern. You should provide for your kids' college education.

Most people, though, don't have that luxury. If you're on a budget, money set aside for college should go where it certainly will be available, not into insurance that may never be used. If you are disabled, not being able to pay for your children's college education will be a disappointment but not a disaster. Your children may have to go to a less expensive public university or rely on their own earnings and on financial aid.

IN BRIEF
- DI insurance companies often offer a series of added benefits at an added cost.
- When comparison shopping, it's worth looking into the prices of these features.
- With residual disability, if you're not totally disabled, you can work part-time and collect partial benefits.
- With a future-increase option, if you're very young and expect your earnings eventually will increase substantially, you might want a future-increase option, which gives you the right to buy extra DI coverage in the future without taking a physical.
- With a waiver-of-premium option, if you're disabled, you won't have to keep paying for DI insurance. It may be cheaper, though, to skip this option and buy extra basic coverage instead.
- With a social-benefits rider, you pay a lower premium if you agree that the insurer can cut its payments while you receive Social Security benefits.

- Many other "extras," though, offer coverage you don't really need or benefits that should be covered by health and life insurance.
- A plain "vanilla" policy with few added benefits can give you disaster protection at moderate cost.

Chapter 20

Down with DI Costs

If you don't have a disability income (DI) policy or if you want to increase your coverage, you may be in for a shock. After a competitive period in the early and mid-1980s, when rates were relatively low, DI premiums started to rise in the late 1980s. Today it may be difficult to get a DI policy at all.

Although insurers deny it, many attorneys say that they can't get DI coverage. They contend that insurance companies are afraid lawers will claim disability at the drop of a tort and that laywers know their way around the paperwork well enough to make their claims stick. So they don't want to give lawyers a chance to play the game.

Even if you're not a lawyer, you can expect the premium you pay for DI insurance—and the availability of coverage—to depend on the kind of work you do. Today DI insurers' greatest reluctance doesn't concern people who make a living hauling piles of masonry around. Instead, the insurance companies have taken a beating from stress-related claims: high blood pressure, psychiatric disorders, depression, substance abuse, and so on. The companies have isolated occupations most likely to file those types of claims, each company maintaining its own list; if you work in an occupation a company deems high-stress, be ready to pay high DI premiums, if you can get any coverage at all.

FIVE TECHNIQUES FOR LOWERING *DI* COSTS

What can you do about the increasing cost and decreasing availability of DI coverage? Here are some basic techniques:

• Shop around. One insurer may have had a difficult experience with your occupation, while another may not have the same problem. The difference will be reflected in the rates you'll be asked to pay.

• Look for discounts. The pricing trends aren't all negative. Some insurers offer discounts from their published DI rates. Paul Revere Life, for example, will give you a 5% discount if you demonstrate income by submitting last year's income-tax return and an additional 10% discount if you buy two years' worth of coverage in advance. Many DI insurers also give 5%–15% discounts to nonsmokers.

• Look for dividends. Buy from a mutual company that pays dividends on DI (Northwestern Mutual or Connecticut Mutual Life, for example). Mutual insurance companies distribute excess earnings to policyholders. If all goes well, you might get a "dividend" (actually a partial refund) of around 10% of the premiums you paid. Usually, you have to be a policyholder for a few years before you can collect dividends.

• Stick with even numbers. If you determine your DI insurance needs are an odd number—say, $2,700 per month—ask your agent for a quote at the next higher "price point." Sometimes larger policies actually cost the same as, or even less, than, a smaller one. For example, buying a $3,000-per-month benefit often costs less than a $2,700-per-month benefit.

• Buy what you need, no more. This should be your primary

approach: First, you need to determine how much DI insurance you need. Then shop for a DI policy that will meet those needs long-term.

The best way to avoid overpaying is to buy the coverage you need and nothing more. Avoid most if not all of the riders that are offered.

Sometimes you'll see a policy with some of these "extras" apparently built in. Don't be intimidated. In many cases, insurers can strip away virtually any feature and give you a price without it. All the company has to do is make a few adjustments on a computer. So ask for the coverage you really need. No less, but no more, either.

ARDI: WHAT YOUR AGENT WON'T TELL YOU

Another way to save money is to ask about "annual renewable disability income" (ARDI) policies. If you have life insurance, you may know that permanent life policies have level premiums while term life insurance policies have increasing premiums. However, term premiums are much lower than permanent life premiums, especially in the initial years of the policy.

ARDI is the disability insurance industry's answer to term insurance. Premiums start low and increase. If you're truly concerned about being able to afford DI, this may be the way to start.

However, after eight or nine years or so, ARDI premiums may be higher than regular, level-premium DI insurance. So ARDI is a short-term response, chosen in the hopes that your income will eventually increase and you can afford the level premium.

To buy a $5,000-per-month DI policy, for example, with a 90-day waiting period and many extra features (cost-of-living benefits increase, residual benefits, automatic increase option), you might pay $1,500 per year in premiums if you're 35. With ARDI, on the other hand, you might pay only around $1,000 the first year— a huge savings.

The ARDI premium might increase 8%–10% per year. At some point in the future, perhaps seven years into the policy, this premium might become so high that it pays to convert to a level-premium policy. Or if you're still in good health, you can shop around and begin all over with a new ARDI.

So ARDI may be an excellent way to save on DI coverage, at least for now. A few years from now, maybe you'll get a lower rate on a new ARDI policy.

However, buying ARDI insurance may not be as easy as it sounds. Commissions are much lower, compared to level-premium DI insurance, so insurance salespeople may not mention it to you unless you specifically ask about it.

A variation of ARDI is "step-rate" coverage, in which a multiyear schedule (usually five years) of increases is built into the contract. Initial premiums may be 25%–40% lower than traditional, fixed-premium contracts.

WAIVER THEORY

Do you own permanent life insurance? If so, you probably own DI coverage, too, even though you don't realize it. When you bought the policy, your agent said something like "If we add this waiver-of-premium feature, you won't have to pay premiums if you're disabled. The extra cost is only 6%." How could you resist?

Before you buy, check out the numbers. Say you're a 35-year-old male buying a $250,000 universal life policy. The annual premium is $2,000 per year. To add a waiver-of-premium feature costs an extra 6%, or $120 per year. So you'd pay $120 per year for a possible benefit of $2,000 per year: not having to pay the premium if you're disabled. This benefit can be used only for paying life insurance premiums.

A typical minimum benefit for DI insurance is $400 per month ($4,800 per year), which might cost a 35-year-old $150 per year. With that $4,800 per year, if you were disabled, you could pay the $2,000 life insurance premium (if you wanted to) and have an extra $2,800 per year left over. Or you could decide to revise your life insurance coverage (cancel it, trade down) and have as much as $4,800 per year to spend.

Paying an extra $30 per year, in this example, gives you much more money and flexibility:

Situation A: Buy $250,000 permanent life insurance policy plus waiver-of-premium rider.

	Per year
Life insurance premium paid	$2,000
Waiver-of-premium cost	120
Total paid	2,120
If you are disabled, you collect	paid life insurance premiums
You have left over	0

Situation B: Buy $250,000 permanent life insurance policy and $400-per-month DI insurance policy.

	Per Year
Life insurance premium paid	$2,000
DI premium paid	150
Total paid	2,150
If you are disabled, you collect	4,800
After paying the insurance premium of	2,000
You have left over	2,800

Every situation won't work out this neatly—it will depend on your age and the life insurance policy you're buying. But you may well find you get a better deal if you pass up the waiver-of-premium option and instead buy a little more DI coverage with that money.

CREDIT CRUNCH

Another form of back-door disability insurance is "credit life" insurance, widely sold by lenders who want to get repaid. Say you take out an auto loan or run up a balance on your credit card. The lender or issuer may offer to sell you insurance as an "option." If you die with those loans outstanding, the insurance will pay off the debt.

Often, credit life insurance really is credit disability insurance, too. If you're disabled, payments will be waived. (Don't confuse this optional coverage with "mortgage insurance" that many homeowners are required to pay for, often until their home equity reaches a certain portion of their loan balance.)

The problem with credit life or credit disability insurance is its tremendous expense. Marketing costs are extremely high in relation to the small value per policy (around $3,500, on average). Credit insurance policies typically have "loss ratios" of only around 40%–50%, meaning that 40–50 cents of every premium dollar is paid out in claims. That's far below what life or DI policies should pay. As a result, you generally wind up paying too much for so little coverage.

Recently, for example, Chase Manhattan's credit-card holders received a solicitation for credit insurance that included life and disability protection. The premium was 66 cents per month per $100 balance. Pretty cheap, right?

Well, 66 cents per month is nearly $8 per year. For a $100,000 balance, that would be an $8,000 annual premium. A reasonably healthy middle-aged person can buy $100,000 worth of term insurance for just a few hundred dollars per year. Although the comparison with DI isn't so straightforward, you can see the magnitude of the price difference, even allowing for the fact that you're buying multiple coverage.

Say you have $10,000 worth of auto or credit-card loans outstanding. At $8 per $100, that's $800 per year in insurance premiums. Maybe you're paying $2,400 a year, or $200 per month, on those loans. As mentioned above, you probably can buy DI that will pay you $400 per month for around $150 per year.

The bottom line: If you're worried about paying off loans in the event of death or disability, buy more standard life or DI coverage, not some flaky credit insurance.

DI WITHOUT THE *I*

Recently, DI insurers have been experimenting with a "long-term care" (LTC) rider. Say you buy DI coverage while you're working. If you're disabled, you collect benefits.

Now you reach retirement age with the policy still in force. If you want, you can convert your DI policy into a LTC policy. In essence, this means if you become disabled after retirement and have to enter a nursing home, the policy will pay nursing-home costs instead of replacing lost income.

These policies resemble other types of convertible insurances. As long as you keep paying the premiums, you can't be denied coverage no matter what happens to your health.

Do they make sense? It's too early to tell because DI insurers are still testing LTC coverage. But here are some points to consider:

• If the LTC option is free, why not take it? But don't buy a particular DI policy just to get an LTC option. Pick the best, most cost effective DI policy on its own merits.

• If you have to pay for an LTC option, check it over closely. The key selling point supposedly is cost: Buy now and lock in a low annual premium on LTC insurance 20 years in the future. So find out how much your future costs will be.

• Evaluate the LTC benefits under the guidelines explained in the next section, which covers insurance specifically designed to pay for LTC.

IN BRIEF
• The best way to hold down DI insurance costs is to determine the benefit you really need. Buy a policy that will provide that benefit, long-term, while avoiding most of the options offered.
• In certain occupations, you may have to shop hard to find reasonably priced DI insurance.
• Some DI insurers give discounts to nonsmokers, or for other reasons.

- DI insurers organized as mutual companies may give partial refunds to policyholders.
- Some DI policies are structured like term life insurance, with lower initial premiums.
- If you're asked to pay for a waiver-of-premium feature on permanent life insurance, you may be better off buying extra DI coverage instead.
- DI insurance sold to cover debt repayment may be wildly overpriced.
- DI insurers are now working on policies that convert to LTC policies at retirement.

Summary of DI Goals

Your goal is to have enough DI coverage to prevent a financial disaster if you can't work for many months or years. Here's how to reach that goal:

1. Make a realistic assessment of ongoing expenses in case you can't work for an extended time period.
2. Make a similarly realistic assessment of ongoing income from investments, spouse's job, etc.
3. If there's a projected shortfall, you need enough DI insurance to fill in.

How do you go about finding the extra $1,000, $3,000, or $5,000 per month you're likely to need?

• Look at your employer coverage, if any. If the benefits are enough to fill your DI gap and they'll be paid to age 65, you're protected.

• Few employer plans are that good. You may be able to purchase supplemental coverage at a favorable price. If you calculate a $4,000 monthly need, for example, and your employer's long-term DI will pay $2,000 per month, consider purchasing a supplemental DI policy that will pay another $2,000 per month.

• Whenever you have a choice, purchase supplemental DI insurance with your own, already taxed dollars. The DI benefits you purchase with those dollars will be tax-free.

• If you have no DI coverage from your employer and no opportunity to buy lower-cost group coverage, you need to buy your own DI insurance. Don't count on Social Security or workers' compensation.

• As is the case with any type of insurance, check into the insurer's financial strength. Top ratings from independent agencies are your best source of comfort.

• When you buy DI insurance on your own, be sure to read the definition of "disability" carefully to see how it applies to you. You want a policy that will pay if you can't do the type of work for which you're suited by education and training.

• DI insurance is expensive, especially if you're buying an individual policy. The best way to keep costs reasonable is to avoid most policy "extras." Expensive "own occupation" coverage, cost-of-living adjustments (COLAs), and "return-of-premium" features are among the options whose costs often exceed the benefits.

• To keep costs low, see if you can manage a 90-day elimination period. That is, agree to pay for the first 90 days you're out of work before the insurer has to pay.

• Long-term DI coverage should protect you at least until age 65. If you have an adequate retirement plan in place, you don't need to pay extra for lifetime DI benefits. (That is, in case of a long-term disablity, your DI coverage will run until age 65, after which your retirement plan and Social Security will provide income.)

• Some DI policy extras may make sense. For a relatively small amount, you may purchase the right to buy more coverage, if needed, without taking another medical exam.

• Another way to pay less for DI coverage is to agree to let the insurance company cut its payments if you qualify for Social Security DI or for workers' compensation. You'll still have full protection, but you give up the chance of a "windfall" through extra benefits.

• A DI insurance feature that's probably worth buying is "residual disability," partial benefits if you can work part-time. This protects you against loss of income. Be sure to check the definition of residual disability.

• Shop around for the lowest-cost DI policy, sold by a sound insurer, with the benefits you desire. There may be wide price differences from one insurer to the next. Some insurers may offer you a good deal on annual renewable DI coverage, where premiums start low and then increase.

Part III

LONG-TERM-CARE
INSURANCE

Chapter 21

Age-Old Problems

About $800 billion is spent on health care in the United States each year. Some of that money goes to accomplish the miraculous. People who might have died of a heart attack or a stroke are kept alive through great medical skill, which is amply rewarded. Many billions each year go toward compensating doctors who perform death-defying feats.

Then what? Patients who are brought back from the dead live to grow older. The phrase "graying of America" enters our daily discourse. By the year 2020, there are expected to be 50 million Americans over age 65, double the number in 1985. The 85-plus population is expected to grow even faster, from 3 million to more than 8 million. Already, the United States has more grandparents than teenagers.

People may be living longer, but they're not always living better. Unfortunately, most people become increasingly frail as they grow older. The man who is climbing mountains at age 65 may be having trouble climbing stairs at 75. At 85, he may not be able to fix his own meals or put his clothes on.

Eventually, many elderly people need help. They may need assistance with "activites of daily living," or ADLs, to use the current jargon. ADLs usually include bathing, eating, dressing, walking, and using the toilet. Other people, although they're physically healthy, suffer from Alzheimer's or some other mental disease, in which they lose memory or the ability to reason.

In these situations, the elderly need someone else to care for them. Who? Maybe it's a spouse or a sibling. That may be a possibility as long as the necessary care consists of fixing meals, say, or helping someone take a pill. But too often "care" evolves into "long-term care" (LTC). Now an elderly person needs attention most of the time, day after day, for months or years. This kind of a burden may be too much for someone else who's also elderly.

The next step may be to turn to a middle-aged son, daughter, or in-law. Again, this may be a feasible solution, at a distance. If you can stop by every day or so to check on your aging father or take him shopping, the task may be bearable.

But when LTC is needed, your dad may have to move in with you and your family. That's when the strain begins. Is there enough room in your house? What demands is the newcomer placing on your spouse? If you have a full day as it is, working and raising kids, can you manage an elderly parent, too? Your kids, you expect, will grow and go off on their own. You know your mom or dad isn't going to regain independence.

ENTER THE CAREGIVERS

Ideally, LTC for the aging can be handled by family members. Practically speaking, you may have to pay third parties to do the job. Paid LTC generally comes in two categories, home care and institutional care.

With home care, the elderly person stays at home. Someone comes in during the day or actually lives in the house. The third-party "caregivers" are paid for their services. The alternative to home care is to have the elderly person move into a nursing home where constant attention is available.

In 1991, statisticians from the federal Health and Human Services Department issued projections regarding the 2.2 million Americans who turned 65 in 1990. They predicted:

- Over 40% will spend at least some time in a nursing home before they die.
- Thirty-three percent will spend at least three months in a nursing home.
- Twenty-five percent will stay for over a year.
- Nine percent will stay at least five years.

The older you are, the more likely it is you will live in a nursing home. Already, more than 20% of the 85-plus population is institutionalized. As many as 8 million Americans—about 3% of the entire population—will need to stay in a nursing home by the year 2000.

Half of those nursing-home stays are relatively short, but the other half are extensive, lasting over six months. Long-stay nursing-home visits average two and a half years.

NURSING-HOME CARE AND COSTS

Although the distinctions aren't hard and fast, there are three levels of institutional care provided in nursing homes.

- Skilled care. Medical treatment is given to the patient by licensed health professionals in a facility specifically licensed to provide this kind of care. Often people who have been released from a hospital need such ongoing, intensive medical care.
- Custodial care. No medical attention is needed except perhaps help with dispensing medication. Instead, patients are assisted in coping with their daily tasks. This, by far, is the most common form of nursing-home care.
- Intermediate care. This category falls in between the first two.

Some nursing homes specialize in one of these levels of care. Other homes have all three levels, perhaps in different parts of the same building.

Aside from medical care, nursing-home residents pay for room and board and staff salaries. That's not cheap: The average stay in a nursing home now costs around $2,500 per month, or $30,000 per year. So a stay of two and a half years would cost $75,000, on average. In some parts of the United States, especially the Boston–Washington corridor, good nursing homes now cost $50,000–$70,000 per year. You can see how a nursing-home stay might cost a total of $75,000–$150,000. A few years from now, those costs likely will be even higher.

Now, that may not be a problem. If you (or your elderly parents) have a large portfolio of liquid securities, one that throws off $30,000, $40,000, or more after tax, you may have no problem with nursing-home stays. Say you have $500,000 to invest in Treasury bonds or CDs. Assuming a 6% return after tax, you'll earn $30,000 per year. Including your Social Security checks, you likely will be able to pay nursing-home bills out of current income.

Or suppose you or your parents receive a generous pension from a former employer. Combined with Social Security and investment income, you may enjoy a total income that's sufficient to cover nursing-home costs. In either case, the threat of a nursing home needn't be a financial worry.

But not everyone has a half-million-dollar investment portfolio or a fat corporate pension. For those who don't, a nursing-home stay can bring you face-to-face with some grim realities.

WHO PAYS?

Medicare probably won't pay your nursing-home bill. Medicare, as mentioned, is a federal *health insurance* program. Its focus, therefore, is on medical care. If you're discharged from a hospital and need acute care in a skilled-nursing home or if you need intensive rehabilitation, Medicare may pay most or all of the bill.

However, such stays are relatively rare. Medicare actually pays for less than 2% of total nursing-home costs.

What about private health-care insurance, including Medigap policies? What about employer-sponsored retiree benefits? Again, the emphasis is on reimbursement of medical expenses. Money spent for custodial care—keeping nursing-home residents clean and fed—won't come from Medicare, from Medigap, from a health insurance policy, or from a health maintenance organization (HMO).

So where will the money come from? From the nursing-home residents themselves. Or from their middle-aged children, who want to take care of their aging parents.

There's another possibility. The elderly patient in the nursing home may be poor enough to qualify for Medicaid, a welfare program paid for by the state and federal governments. Below the poverty line, Medicaid will pay for nursing-home care. Medicaid now spends over $20 billion per year on nursing homes, around one-third of all the money spent by Medicaid each year. About half of the national nursing-home bill is paid by Medicaid.

Nursing-home costs, then, are usually paid by residents, their families, or Medicaid (if the residents are certifiably poor). This presents a range of scenarios for the not rich and not poor, all unwelcome:

• You go into a nursing home and "spend down" all your assets until you're poor enough to qualify for Medicaid. If still living, your spouse may be impoverished. In fact, some elderly couples have been forced into divorces to avoid this disaster.

Nursing homes usually receive lower fees from Medicaid than they get from "private pay" patients. Though this isn't always the case, Medicaid patients may become second-class citizens, with lower levels of service. In fact, some nursing homes are reluctant to accept Medicaid patients.

• Even if you don't spend all of your assets, nursing-home costs may deplete your resources so that there is less for your children to inherit.

• To avoid the above situations, your middle-aged children contribute to your nursing-home care. Or, if you're middle-aged with aging parents in a nursing home, you help to pay the bill. In either case, the financial squeeze can be excruciating for people who are trying to put their own children through college while they support their aging parents.

HOW CAN YOU AFFORD NURSING-HOME CARE?

What can you do to ease these financial strains? A little advance planning can make your life easier.

• Find out how much decent nursing homes in your area actually cost. If the national average is $30,000 per year but some nursing homes cost $60,000 per year, there must be others that cost $20,000 or $25,000 per year.

• Estimate how much you'll pay for a nursing home. Consider age and adjust estimated costs for inflation. Someone likely to go into a nursing home in 20 years will pay more—much more—than someone who might go in within the next few years.

Nursing-home costs tripled in the 1980s. They're not likely to triple again in the 1990s (that would raise the average cost to $90,000 per year!), but they could double.

• Estimate how much income there will be at the time when you're likely to have to pay. How much will come from Social Security, which is indexed for inflation? From retirement plans, including IRAs? From investments?

The calculation is similar to that performed in worksheet 2, chapter 15, when figuring out how much ongoing income there will be in case of a disability. If your estimated income equals or exceeds your estimated nursing-home costs, this won't be a problem.

Are you willing to dip into assets? This is a tougher call. If you expect your mother to receive $10,000 per year from Social Security, $10,000 per year from a pension plan, and $10,000 per year from an investment interest, paying a $30,000 nursing-home bill won't be a sacrifice.

But what if there's an expected shortfall? As a parent, you likely want to leave as much as you can to your children, not spend your savings on fees to strangers providing custodial care. As a child, you naturally want to inherit as much as you can.

But suppose your mother transferred her assets to you in order to preserve them. That leaves her with virtually nothing, a ward of the state or a dependent on her own child. She could live another 20 healthy years, not confined to a nursing home but living on her own with only a few dollars to her name.

Later, you'll learn some strategies for dealing with such situations. For now, consider whether you'd be willing, say, to borrow against an old life insurance policy in order to raise money for nursing-home costs. (Outstanding policy loans reduce the amount the beneficiaries receive at the insured person's death.) Would you consider the sale of a vacation home, no longer used, so that the sale proceeds could be reinvested in corporate bonds, with the interest designated for nursing-home costs?

Finally, there's the question of the family home, perhaps an elderly person's greatest asset. No one likes to think of forcing that elderly person from home. But what happens when he or she goes into a nursing home for what seems like a long stay? Even if the nursing-home stay isn't permanent, that elderly person will probably have to find a small apartment rather than live in (and take care of) a large house.

When an elderly person goes into a nursing home, the personal residence might be sold and the proceeds reinvested. A $200,000 house, for example, might generate $12,000, $15,000, or even more in annual interest, which would go a long way toward paying nursing-home costs. Would you be willing to enter into that sort of sale and reinvestment, or are you determined to let the house pass from one generation to the next?

The more willing you are to dip into assets, the less you need to make any alternative plans. You may be able to pay for nursing-home costs out of current income or by dipping only slightly into capital. But if you're determined to preserve assets from one generation to the next, some careful planning is necessary, as explained in the next few chapters.

IN BRIEF

- Thanks to medical science, America's population is aging.
- Elderly people may need nonmedical help to carry on with their everyday lives.
- If family can't provide the necessary LTC, outside help must be hired.
- The help that's hired may care for the elderly at their own home or in a nursing home.
- Nursing homes are extremely expensive, costing an average of $30,000 per year, much higher in some areas.
- Neither Medicare nor health insurance plans will pay for custodial nursing-home care, the most common type.
- Nursing-home care is usually paid for by the elderly, out of their own resources, or by their middle-aged children.
- If the elderly spend or give away almost all of their assets, they can qualify for Medicaid and have the government pay for their nursing-home care.
- Advance planning is necessary to devise a strategy for paying for possible nursing-home costs.

Chapter 22

Care Packages

You worked your entire life. You paid taxes, you saved, you accumulated a modest amount of assets. And for what? To pay a nursing home for food you don't have to chew and for a change of bedpans? That's not what most of us have in mind for our life's work.

If you want to protect those assets, there is a choice: You can buy a long-term care (LTC) policy from an insurance company. Such policies are designed to pay benefits if you go into a nursing home, just as health insurance policies pay benefits if you're in a hospital.

Just 10 years ago, LTC policies were novelties. Now over 100 insurers, including some of the nation's largest (e.g., Prudential, The Travelers, John Hancock), sell them. Several Blue Cross and Blue Shield organizations also sell LTC policies.

Perhaps because these policies are so new, there's a bewildering lack of standardization. If you think health insurance and disability income (DI) insurance can be complicated, invite a few agents to hawk LTC policies.

Those agents may be part of the problem. LTC policies, by their very nature, are sold heavily to the elderly. Virtually since the first LTC commission check was cashed, complaints have piled up against sellers and selling practices. Even the most reputable insurers stand accused.

It may be that the nature of LTC policies confuses agent and buyer alike, leading to false impressions; it may be that the most venal agents gravitate toward policies sold to the elderly, who are often vulnerable to scare tactics and pressure pitches. (The same complaints frequently were voiced about Medigap marketing, which led to federal legislation, so Washington may eventually act on LTC policies, too.)

In 1991, two congressional committees, the Select Committee on Aging and the Committee on Small Business, combined to publish a report on LTC insurance. They found agents' knowledge of the product "appalling" and characterized such insurance as "not a good buy" because the policies won't pay when people need it. That's a hard knock.

Is LTC insurance a ripoff to be avoided at all costs?

Not really. Out of more than 100 policies on the market, some will be better than others. The trick is to find the better deals.

According to the federal General Accounting Office, these are the most frequent abuses:

1. Agents don't tell you what the policy really covers.
2. Insurance companies don't pay appropriate claims.
3. Agents engage in false or deceptive advertising.

If you steer clear of these pitfalls, you can find a decent LTC policy.

CREAMING THE CROP

Start your search by finding the right agent. With LTC coverage, this may not be easy. If you have an agent you can rely on, someone you work with on life insurance, health insurance, and DI insurance, ask whether he or she sells LTC insurance, too. If you're helping your parents shop for LTC insurance, be sure your agent is the one who works with them.

If you don't have an agent you can rely on, ask a local

community or religious group for recommendations. Many such groups are especially attuned to the needs of the elderly. You also may turn to the American Association of Retired Persons, which offers LTC insurance from Prudential—these policies are expensive, but coverage is solid.

If your LTC coverage comes from Prudential, you know the insurer will be around to pay off your claims. But what if the coverage is from a lesser-known company? Maybe, maybe not. Farwest American Assurance, a major LTC seller in the early 1980s, failed in 1990. So it's important to repeat the precautions recommended for health and DI insurers: Check that they have top ratings from A. M. Best, Standard & Poor's, Moody's, and Duff & Phelps.

Assuming you have a genuinely helpful agent and a sound insurer, you can turn to the policy itself. What are the loopholes in LTC coverage that allow insurers to avoid paying claims?

DIRTY DOESN'TS

The most common problem is the definition of what kind of LTC is covered by a given LTC policy.

• Some policies say that only "medically necessary" care is covered. However, LTC often requires no more than custodial care, which isn't covered under such policies.

• Some policies require previous stays in a hospital or a skilled-nursing home before custodial care is covered. Such policies are illegal in many states; most custodial care does not follow any medical treatment.

• Some policies try to evade responsibility for covering Alzheimer's by insisting that mental lapses be traced to a "demonstrable organic disease" in order to qualify for coverage. Alzheimer's patients often can't demonstrate that without undergoing brain surgery.

• Some policies won't cover care unless a facility has a physician or registered nurse on duty all the time, which isn't the case in all nursing homes.

• Some policies won't cover care in a custodial nursing home or "custodial facility." You have to be in a skilled-care or intermediate-care home to qualify.

• Some policies won't cover care in specific types of facilities, such as "homes for the aged" or homes with fewer than 25 residents.

Consider the case of Ted, who thought his LTC policy entitled him to two years of payments, for a total of $30,000. After he was in the home, he was told by the insurer that the two years of coverage were for "nursing care and therapy," which ceased after five months. Help with bathing and eating were covered for only 90 days. So the policy has paid only $6,000. Ted has had to make up the difference, and by now he has used up his life's savings.

WHAT TO LOOK FOR IN AN *LTC* POLICY

Naturally, your best choice is an LTC policy that pays for custodial care with no conditions about where you are or where you've been before that. Increasingly, LTC policies are written in terms of "ADLs," activities of daily living. These policies will pay if the insured individual can't perform a number of ADLs (usually two or three).

Even if he or she can perform all ADLs, if there's "cognitive impairment"—mental confusion—the policy should pay. That's particularly important because the elderly may suffer from Alzheimer's and still be capable of performing their ADLs. Alzheimer's can lead to long, costly nursing-home stays.

Don't neglect to ask about Alzheimer's coverage when shopping for a nursing-home policy. An LTC policy should specifically cover Alzheimer's diagnosed by a doctor.

A good LTC policy will cover purely custodial care, when

it's necessary, provided in virtually all types of nursing homes. What else should you be looking for in an LTC policy?

Guaranteed Renewability

The best LTC policies are "guaranteed renewable." That means that your coverage can't be cut off as long as you pay all the premiums on time. Your premiums can't be raised arbitrarily if you get sick, for example. If the insurer raises premiums for you, it has to raise premiums the same amount for everyone with the same coverage (and risk losing business if it jacks the rate up too high.)

Unfortunately, these policies are so new that insurers don't really know how to price them. The companies make certain assumptions about how many people will go into nursing homes, how long they'll stay, and how much each stay will cost. Three years from now, or five years, the insurers may discover their guesses were way out of line. In that case, premiums for all types of nursing-home insurance may go down or (more likely) go up.

Buying a guaranteed-renewable policy won't protect you in that situation. However, to avoid the worst price shocks, buy from the highest-quality companies: a Blue Cross/Blue Shield or a private company with a long history and top ratings from the ratings agencies.

Inflation Protection

Say you buy a policy that will pay $80 per day, or just about $29,000 per year. With an inflation clause, the benefit may go to $85 next year, $90 the year after that, and so on.

Naturally, you pay quite a bit more for this kind of insurance—perhaps a 50% higher premium. A policy that would cost $1,200 per year without inflation protection might cost $1,800 per year, including an escalator clause.

Nevertheless, if you're buying a policy at age 60 or 65, it's almost a necessity. The $80-a-day benefit you're buying might not go very far if you go into a nursing home in 2000 or 2005 or even later, when costs are $125, $150, or even more per day.

When shopping for inflation protection, look for the word "compounded" in the policy. Over a long time period, compounding the inflation increase results in a huge advantage. After 15 years, $80 per day increased by 5% per year, compounded, equals $166 per day. The same $80 per day increased by 5% per year, *not* compounded, equals only $140 per day.

A 5% annual increase, not compounded, is equivalent to a compound rate of 3.5%–4% per year.

After Six Months, No Holds Barred

Any restrictions on preexisting conditions should be for six months or less. Some policies, for example, won't cover you for a health problem that you already had when you bought the coverage. In a good LTC policy, six months after you buy the policy, you should be fully covered, for all types of conditions.

TRIMMING THE FAT

So you want an LTC policy from an established insurer, offering broad coverage and inflation protection. Such coverage will be costly. Suppose you want a policy that will pay $80 per day. If you buy a policy at age 65 and you're in reasonably good health, you might pay around $1,000 per year in premiums. But if you wait until age 75, when you're more likely to go into a nursing home, the annual premium might be over $3,000. (Most insurers won't sell you a new LTC policy after you reach age 84.)

Can you reduce these costs? There are a few things you should consider.

Waiting Period

Increase the waiting period. The principle here is the same as with DI insurance. The more of your nursing-home costs you agree to pay out of your own pocket, the lower the premium will be. A policy that costs $1,300 per year, with a 100-day waiting period, might cost $1,600 per year (20%–25% more) with a 20-day waiting period.

LTC policies have waiting periods ranging from zero to 100 days. If you can pay for 100 days (around $8,000, on average, at today's rates), go for the longer waiting period. Or wait 60 or 90 days.

Remember, the purpose of any type of insurance is to cut your exposure to catastrophic losses. Paying $8,000 for a nursing home (or even $10,000 or $15,000 in the future) probably won't be a disaster. The reason for the insurance is to guard against losing $100,000 or $200,000 because of a long nursing-home stay. Paying $1,300 per year rather than $1,600 may make it more feasible for you to continue to carry the insurance.

An insurance agent may press you to take a zero-day elimination period, arguing that many nursing-home stays are for only a few weeks. However, most short-lived nursing-home stays come after hospital discharges, when Medicare or private health insurance is likely to pay.

In LTC policies, the accent should be on "long-term."

If you choose a longer waiting period, though, take care with the wording of this provision in the policy. You don't want a situation in which the clock keeps starting over each time you go in and out of a hospital. Some mechanism for accumulating days is necessary.

Length of Coverage

You may be tempted to cut costs by choosing a one-year benefit period. Don't. That leaves you with too much exposure on long stays. However, you don't need to pay for lifetime benefits, or even benefits stretching 5 or 10 years.

Instead, choose a policy that pays benefits for three years, Later, you'll see why that's enough time to arrange your affairs so you can transfer your assets and arrange for the government to pay for anything beyond your three-year period.

Benefit Amount

Most people will be amply covered by an $80 daily benefit if it's indexed to inflation. (That's $29,000 per year, in addition to income from Social Security, interest, pensions, etc.) However, if you live in the Northeast or California, where nursing-home costs are much higher, you might want to buy a $100 daily benefit ($36,500 per year) or a $120 daily benefit ($44,000).

Home-Care Coverage

Some people who need LTC don't need to be institutionalized. It's usually cheaper to have someone come in to provide care, full- or part-time, than it is to pay for a nursing-home bed, meals, and support services. Besides the money, some people are happy with access to their own space, neighbors, stores they know, and other familiar aspects of their lives.

Social Security won't pay for home care. Neither will Medicare, in most cases. However, some LTC insurance policies cover home care as well as nursing-home care; a few policies are designed solely for home care.

If such coverage were unlimited, no insurer could afford it. Every time your Aunt Sophie's neighbor from down the hall stopped by to carry out her garbage, a claim could be filed.

Thus, home-care insurance usually covers only payments to skilled providers: nurses, therapists, licensed health aides, etc. Commonly, these provisions pay 50% of the nursing-home benefit. That is, an LTC policy might pay $80 per day in a nursing home and $40 per day for home health care. LTC policies offering home-care options might offer coverage for one, three, or five years, naturally requiring you to pay more for longer coverage.

Almost every company has a different wrinkle to its home-care coverage. Some companies provide coverage specifically designed to help you recuperate from a nursing-home stay. However, these plans assume (1) a medical visit to a nursing home followed by (2) convalescence at home. That doesn't help people who want to avoid nursing homes altogether.

Other policies cover you for home care after a hospital stay. Best of all are those that don't require any previous hospital or nursing-home stays.

Even so, these policies have drawbacks. Skilled-nursing care is probably covered by Medicare; what you really want from an LTC policy is payment for someone who'll come in and do household chores, take you shopping, etc.

Blue Cross of Western Pennsylvania offers a home-care policy that really covers home care: No prior institutionalization is required, and payments cover personal services and home-making as well as nursing care. If Blue Cross's geriatric experts determine that Aunt Sophie is unable to perform ADLs, she can collect the same amount as would be paid for a nursing-home stay. The insured has to pay for 100 home visits, after which the policy will pay for 10 home visits per week, up to the policy's limits on daily payments and duration of benefits.

Buying home-care coverage adds considerably to the cost of an LTC policy. A policy you might buy for under $750 per year, for example, might cost over $1,000 if it covers home care, too.

Is it worth paying the extra cost? Probably not. Remember the purpose of any kind of insurance: to protect against disaster.

If you have to go into a nursing home for a long stay, that will be a financial disaster. Figure $100,000+ for a three-year stay. When you need institutional care, your options are limited. There may be no way to avoid that $100,000 tab.

Home care isn't as much of a threat. For one thing, the costs are only half as much on average. Paying $15,000 per year for home care isn't going to deplete your assets as rapidly as paying $30,000 per year for nursing-home care.

Also, people who are healthy enough to receive care at home may have more choices. There may be a relative willing to help or even take them in. Part-time rather than full-time care may be adequate.

The problem of defining what's covered and what's not may be greater with home-care coverage. If you're in a nursing home, you're in a nursing home. As long as you've bought a policy that will pay for needed custodial care, you'll collect. Home-care coverage, though, is specifically designed to cover only professional care. Do you really want to tell family members not to come and help because your insurance policy covers only professional care?

You'll probably buy an LTC policy when you're around 65 or 70 and in reasonably good health. At that stage, your main risk is a long stay in an institution, so that's what you should be protecting against.

Waiver of Premium

If you can, buy a policy without the waiver-of-premium option to cut your costs.

Such waivers are commmon in life, health, and disability policies. The premise is that if you're sick or injured, you won't be able to work. If you can't work, your income will be sharply reduced. In those circumstances, your life/health/disability insurance will stay in force without premium payments if you have this waiver option.

With LTC policies, the premium would be waived while you're in a nursing home. You can see that buying this option makes little or no sense. More than likely, when you're confined in a nursing home for a long stay, collecting benefits on an LTC policy, you're well past the age of retirement. You're not losing any income because you're no longer working. So paying an LTC premium is no more difficult than it is at any other time.

In fact, paying the LTC premiums may be easier if you're in a nursing home collecting benefits. Your income (Social Security, investments, pensions) will continue as before; your living expenses will be lower while you're in the nursing home; and you'll receive LTC benefits. If you're collecting $30,000 a year in LTC benefits, you can keep paying your LTC premiums. Don't pay extra money for a waiver.

Return of Premium

You could buy an LTC policy at age 65, pay $40,000 worth of premiums over 20 years, then die without collecting a penny in benefits when you never need LTC. Some LTC policies, therefore, offer to give you your money back, in whole or in part, if you drop the policy after 10 or 20 years.

Such features are most common in group LTC plans, which will be covered later. However, some plans offered to individuals have a return-of-premium option. It's hard to see how this can be worth paying for: You pay a certain premium because you want protection against a long nursing-home stay. Getting back your premiums after 10 years won't reduce your risk.

To get a return-of-premium option, you pay a higher premium year after year. You're betting against the insurance company, and you're likely to lose. Save money by doing without this gimmick.

Some policies offer a "paid up" policy feature. After paying premiums for many years, part of the benefits are still available, even if you drop the policy. This may be worthwhile, but you have to look at the cost. If you can save several hundreds of dollars a year doing without these features, do without them.

Death Benefit

Premiums you've paid, minus any benefits, are returned to your heirs after you die. Sometimes there's an age limit (e.g., good only if you die before age 70).

This feature converts an LTC policy into pseudo–life insurance. Again, the amount you pay may be more than the benefit is worth.

LTC policies are expensive enough just to buy an $80 or $100 daily benefit for three years with inflation protection. Unless you have an oversupply of money, try to scrape as many extras off an LTC policy to keep the cost down.

IN BRIEF
- LTC policies are designed to pay benefits if you're confined in a nursing home.
- LTC policies have been harshly criticized by many experts.
- The main complaints are that agents misrepresent the policies, which often don't cover nursing-home stays.
- Some policies are designed to avoid paying the costs of purely custodial care.
- To get the best LTC policies, work with an agent you respect and buy from an established, highly rated insurance company.
- Insist on a policy that will cover all types of care in all types of nursing homes, without any conditions of prior institutionalization.

- A good policy will specifically cover Alzheimer's disease diagnosed by a doctor.
- Policies should be guaranteed renewable, meaning that coverage can't be canceled if you have a health problem.
- Especially if you're under age 70, you should look for an LTC policy with a provision to increase benefits to keep up with future inflation.
- LTC policies should pay benefits of $80 or $100 per day for three years.
- To cut costs, you can buy a policy with a longer waiting period before benefits begin.
- Another cost-cutting strategy is to avoid added features, such as home-care coverage, waiver of premium, and return of premium.

Chapter 23

Buying LTC Coverage You Can Afford in the Long Term

Making a good long-term care (LTC) policy affordable can be a challenge. As mentioned in the last chapter, you can cut back on costs by extending the waiting period before benefits begin and by doing without unnecessary options, such as home care and waiver of premium. This chapter will look at some other features of LTC policies to help you evaluate whether they make any sense for you.

POLICY FEATURES TO WEIGH

Attained-Age Policies

One way to cut costs is to buy an "attained-age" policy. However, that's not recommended for LTC insurance buyers.

Rather than charge a fixed premium each year, as most LTC policies do, attained-age policies charge more as you grow older, just as term life insurance policies do. A 65-year-old might buy an attained-age LTC policy for around $500 the first year, while a similar level-premium policy might cost $1,200 per year. However, attained-age policies increase dramatically over the years. By age 80, instead of paying $500 per year, the attained-age buyer might pay $3,500 per year; the level-premium policy would have remained $1,200.

	Per Year
LEVEL PREMIUM	
At age 65, an LTC policy costs	$1,200
At age 80, an LTC policy costs	1,200
ATTAINED AGE	
At age 65, an LTC policy costs	500
At age 80, an LTC policy costs	3,500

Although there may be exceptions, the rapidly escalating costs of attained-age policies make them poor buys.

You may have spotted some seeming inconsistencies in these recommendations. In the discussion of disability income (DI) insurance, inflation adjustments were not recommended. For LTC insurance, the last chapter stated that you should look for a well-priced policy that includes inflation protection.

Conversely, annual renewal disability insurance was mentioned as a possible way to cut DI costs. But attained-age LTC policies, which also offer increasing premiums, are not recommended.

Why the apparently conflicting advice? Let's look at the two issues separately.

Inflation Protection

In DI, the inflation protection won't kick in until you have been receiving benefits, usually for one full year. So you may be paying an extra 40% per year for 10 years for a benefit that will increase 5% a year starting 10 years from now.

Moreover, the object of DI insurance is to help your family stay afloat in case you're out of work for months or years. Many of the costs they'd have to face if you became disabled are fixed (a mortgage payment, for example). So the need for a rising DI benefit isn't great. Sure, $3,300 per month is better than $3,000 per month, but the differential isn't likely to lead to disaster.

On the other hand, inflation protection in a good LTC policy kicks in right away. Each year, your benefit rises. The $80 daily benefit goes up to $100, $125, $150, etc. If you ever have to collect benefits, you'll have real insurance, not something that will pay half the bill and leave you struggling to make up the difference.

Rising Premiums

The best prospects for ARDI (annual renewable disability income) coverage are young people who expect their incomes to rise. You can pay $700 per year when you're 30, expecting to pay $800 when you're 31, because you expect your income to be more than $100 higher then. Also, ARDI policies generally are designed for conversion into a fixed-rate policy.

With LTC, there's usually not much prospect of increasing income as you age from 65 to 70 to 75. Your income generally is fixed except for Social Security cost-of-living increases. Going from $500 per year to $3,500 per year can be a real financial hardship. However, if high premiums cause you to drop coverage at age 80, when you're extremely vulnerable, you run the risk of going into a nursing home for three years and spending $100,000+ or more.

In theory, there's no reason an age-based LTC premium couldn't work. You'd start very low at 65, when there's little chance of going into a nursing home, and increase until, say, 75, when your chances are greater. But such policies should reach a point where premiums level off and can be maintained indefinitely. (In the earlier example, in which the fixed premium was $1,200, an age-based LTC premium might level off at $1,500 after age 72. The insured pays more from age 72 on in return for lower initial premiums, but the policy never becomes so expensive it has to be abandoned.)

Perhaps the attained-age LTC policy will be refined so it's economically attractive. For now, be extremely careful of such premium structures. Ask for projections, on paper, of what future premiums will be.

Family Plans

The cost of LTC insurance is most severe for married couples. Each may need coverage, doubling the premiums paid.

Some insurers, such as CIGNA, are introducing family policies that cover both spouses. There's generally a price break, if both are in good health, because the odds are against both needing LTC.

Transamerica Occidental Life Insurance, for example, has a TransCare policy that covers both spouses. Under a "survivorship" benefit, when one spouse dies, the other owes no further payments as long as the policy has been in force for at least 10 years.

Spousal coverage likely will become popular in LTC policies. In addition, Transamerica offers policyholders access to advisers who'll help evaluate "overall medical, personal, and social service needs." That's another benefit major insurers probably will begin to offer along with LTC insurance.

HOW AGE AND HEALTH AFFECT *LTC* POLICIES

LTC coverage is like many types of insurance: You can't get it when you most need it. When you're old and frail, barely able to stand up, no insurer will sell you a policy and swallow a certain loss. The best time to buy is when you're relatively young, 55 to 65, and in good health. Premiums actually are lowest at age 50, the earliest age many insurers will sell an LTC policy. However, a healthy 50-year-old may be 25 or 30 years away from a nursing home. So much can happen in those years (government regulation, policy innovations) that you may not be "locking in" desirable benefits at a low rate. (Whenever you shop for an LTC policy, ask if you can convert to new, improved policies the insurer will come out with.)

The price break for buying before age 65 may not be all that great. A policy that costs $475 per year, if purchased at age 55, might cost $625 per year (an increase of around 30%) if purchased at age 65. However, if you wait another 10 years, until 75, the price might increase a further 100%, to $1,250 per year.

If you're self-employed or employed by a company that offers skimpy benefits, this is really moot. Not until you reach age 65, when you can discontinue disability insurance and trade in your health insurance for less expensive Medigap coverage, will you be able to afford an LTC policy, in most cases. If your employer picks up most of your health and DI insurance tab, you may want to start thinking about LTC at 55 or 60.

Avoid any insurer that will sell you an LTC policy just for the asking. If a company is doing that for you, it's likely doing the same for all policy applicants. Therefore, there's a good chance it will cover a lot of people in poor health, people who will wind up in nursing homes. By the time the insurance company gets through paying everyone else, it may not have enough left to pay you.

On the other hand, suppose you have to pass a tough physical to get coverage. Because that insurance company probably is going to wind up insuring healthy people, it won't have to meet as many claims, so it's more likely to have money for you if you have to go into a nursing home.

Therefore, the best LTC policies may be those that are hardest to qualify for.

A company that sells policies to virtually all comers likely engages in "post-underwriting." Suppose you buy an LTC policy from a company that does not require a full medical review or physician's statement; all you have to do is fill out an application saying you're not bedridden, you don't have Alzheimer's, you haven't had a stroke, etc.

With post-underwriting, after you file a claim, the insurance company will check your medical history. If there's a discrepancy between what you put down on your application and your record, the company will try to get your policy revoked. You may wind up with a return of premiums but no benefits.

Therefore, when you apply for LTC insurance, be sure to answer all the medical questions fully. Don't let the agent fill out the policy for you and check off "no" for all the questions about health conditions. If you do, your policy may be canceled retroactively when you enter a nursing home and apply for benefits.

That's what happened to Vickie, who "forgot" to mention

she had arthritis when she applied for an LTC policy. She had to go into a nursing home for reasons not connected with her arthritis, but the insurer denied her benefits on the ground that she had falsified her application.

EMPLOYER-SPONSORED *LTC* COVERAGE

Besides buying an LTC policy on your own, there are a few other ways to obtain coverage. For example, large employers increasingly offer LTC insurance as a fringe benefit.

Employer-sponsored LTC insurance is not a basic benefit like employer-sponsored health insurance. Instead, LTC insurance usually is offered on a "cafeteria" or "flex" plan. Employees can choose LTC insurance from a list that includes other benefits.

Thus, the employee usually winds up paying the cost of the LTC policy, with little or no subsidy from the employer. What's more, when you buy a group policy, you have no flexibility. If your employer chooses, say, a 30-day waiting period and a four-year payout period, that's what you're buying.

So why consider group policies? There are some "advantages," with some real and some illusory.

• With a group plan, someone else (your company's benefits specialists) is checking on the quality of the insurer and the breadth of the coverage.

• You're less likely to be defrauded. If, for some reason, the insurer doesn't deliver on its promises, your employer may feel obliged to step in.

• Group policies may be 20%–30% less expensive than individually purchased policies, mainly because selling costs are lower.

• Group plans may not require physical exams of employees. This can be valuable if you're in your 50s or 60s with diabetes, asthma, high blood pressure, or some other condition that usually discourages LTC insurers.

• You can cover your spouse and perhaps even a parent through your employer's plan. This is a limited benefit, though, because insurers usually check the health of spouses and parents before offering coverage.

• You can buy coverage when you're in your 30s or 40s. As mentioned, though, people in this age range are so young, with so many years before LTC is necessary, that they may be buying an insurance policy that will become outmoded.

• Many group policies offer a return of premium, sometimes called "nonforfeiture benefits." However, you pay a higher premium for this benefit.

How do the pluses and minuses add up? If your employer offers you an LTC policy, by all means look into it for yourself or for a parent. Compare what you can buy, at what cost, with what you can buy elsewhere. You should have the right to take an LTC policy with you if you leave the company or if your employer changes insurers. Don't ignore the coverage but don't automatically assume you should buy it.

As mentioned, group LTC policies may be most attractive if you're near retirement, with a health condition, and you can get coverage without taking a physical.

Group coverage also may be offered by associations. The American Association of Retired Persons, for example, has a deal with Prudential in which LTC policies are offered to members. These policies are expensive, but they offer compound inflation protection as well as coverage for nursing-home and home care.

Other "associations," though, are really bogus groups set up by insurers merely to push inferior LTC policies. So check an associations's LTC policy as carefully as any policy before you buy it.

HOW TO RESEARCH *LTC* POLICIES

Just as is the case with health insurance and Medigap policies, your insurance agent can use computerized data bases to help find LTC policies. Recently, Quotesmith ran a search on behalf of a 57-year-old man who wanted LTC coverage of $100 per day with a lifetime payment benefit.

Two policies are shown from the Quotesmith run (table 10). As you can see, both look extremely good on paper. Both the Bankers United Life and the PFL Life policies say that custodial care will be covered without a requirement for prior hospitalization. This coverage "primarily meets personal-care needs in activities of daily living . . . that can be provided by someone without professional medical skills."

Table 10: BENEFIT ANALYSIS*

CARRIER: 6160   BANKERS UNITED LIFE A
PLAN NAME: GOLDEN CARE PLAN III   ID: GC3-60 U

SKILLED-NURSING CARE

Benefit	$100 per day
Maximum daily benefit	100% of daily benefit
Waiting period	60 days

SKILLED-NURSING-CARE BENEFITS/REQUIREMENTS
No prior hospitalization required. Full benefits for skilled, intermediate, and custodial (personal) care given in skilled- or intermediate nursing facilities licensed by the state. Provides for treatment by a registered nurse under doctor's supervision.

INTERMEDIATE NURSING CARE

Benefit	$100 per day
Maximum daily benefit	100% of daily benefit
Waiting period	60 days

INTERMEDIATE-NURSING-CARE BENEFITS/REQUIREMENTS
No prior hospitalization required. Refers to occasional nursing and rehabilitative care under the supervision of skilled medical personnel.

CUSTODIAL NURSING CARE

Benefit	$100 per day

Maximum daily benefit   100% of daily benefit
Waiting period   60 days

CUSTODIAL-NURSING-CARE BENEFITS/REQUIREMENTS

No prior hospitalization required. Primarily meets personal-care needs in activities of daily living, such as help in bathing or eating, that can be provided by someone without professional medical skills.

HOME HEALTH CARE (OPTIONAL RIDER)

Benefit   Equal to plan's daily benefit
Maximum daily benefit   100% of daily benefit
Waiting period   10 days

HOME-HEALTH-CARE BENEFITS/REQUIREMENTS

This is an optional rider that requires an additional premium to be paid. The maximum lifetime benefit amount paid on this rider is unlimited. This benefit pays 100% of professional services and 50% of basic services up to the plan's maximum daily benefit.

ADULT DAY CARE (OPTIONAL RIDER)

Benefit   Equal to plan's daily benefit
Maximum daily benefit   25% of maximum daily benefit
Waiting period   10 days

ADULT-DAY-CARE BENEFITS/REQUIREMENTS

Payable for a maximum of 365 days. Care must be provided in a state-licensed or certified adult day care center. Elimination period will be waived if confinement occurs for 3 days or more in the 30 days immediately prior to receiving home health care or adult day care.

PLAN SPECIFICATIONS

Coverage for Alzheimer's   Yes
Preexisting conditions (months)   No preexisting condition limitation
Married couple discount   Yes—included in rates shown
Maximum benefit period   Lifetime
Waiver of premium   After 60 consecutive days of confinement
Terms of renewability   Guaranteed the right to renew for life

Minimum/maximum issue ages   40/80

Level of care required at entry   Any level

COMMENTS/OPTIONAL RIDERS
Inflation protection (benefit increase option) increases benefits yearly by 5%. This plan guarantees not to increase your premium for 3 years from the effective date of your policy.

FACTS ABOUT BANKERS UNITED LIFE A
Bankers United Life Assurance Company had a 9.72% return on invested assets before federal income taxes in 1989. The company has concentrated in the individual and group accident and health, annuity, and life markets. Their surplus position, relative to overall insurance risk, is above the average life insurance company. Bonds represent 74.0% of admitted assets and of the company's bond holdings, 92.0% are in investment-grade issues. Bankers United currently has no bonds in default.

		Annual Costs
Base plan:	$100 per day	$363.00
Alternate daily benefits:	$110 per day	399.30
	$120 per day	435.60
Options:	Optional inflation protection rider	312.00
	Optional home-health-care rider	153.00

CARRIER: 6095   PFL LIFE
PLAN NAME: SELECT CARE   ID: SC/L=30

SKILLED-NURSING CARE
Benefit $100 per day
Maximum daily benefit   100% of daily benefit
Waiting period   30 days

SKILLED-NURSING-CARE BENEFITS/REQUIREMENTS
No prior confinement required. Eligible benefits will be paid for covered confinement in any licensed and qualified custodial, intermediate, or skilled-nursing facility in the United States. The nursing home does not have to be Medicare approved.

INTERMEDIATE NURSING CARE
Benefit $100 per day

Maximum daily benefit   100% of daily benefit
Waiting period   30 days

INTERMEDIATE-NURSING-CARE BENEFITS/REQUIREMENTS
No prior confinement required. Provides for occasional nursing and rehabilitative care under the supervision of skilled medical personnel.

CUSTODIAL NURSING CARE
Benefit $100 per day
Maximum daily benefit   100% of daily benefit
Waiting period   30 days

CUSTODIAL-NURSING-CARE BENEFITS/REQUIREMENTS
No prior confinement required. Primarily meets personal-care needs in activities of daily living that can be provided by someone without professional medical skills.

HOME HEALTH CARE (OPTIONAL RIDER)
Benefit   Equal to plan's daily benefit
Maximum daily benefit   100% of daily benefit
Waiting period   0 days

HOME-HEALTH-CARE BENEFITS/REQUIREMENTS
This is an optional rider that requires an additional premium to be paid. No prior confinement of any type is required, and you may choose benefits of $20 through $120 per day. The lifetime maximum benefit period for each insured person under this option is 150% of selected benefit period.

ADULT DAY CARE
Benefit   Not available
Maximum daily benefit
Waiting period

PLAN SPECIFICATIONS
Coverage for Alzheimer's Yes
Preexisting conditions   3 prior/3 under
  (months)
Married couple discount   No discount available—
           individual plan
Maximum benefit period Lifetime

Waiver of Premium	Yes
Terms of Renewability	Guaranteed the right to renew for life
Minimum/maximum issue ages	50/79
Level of care required at entry	Any level

COMMENTS/OPTIONAL RIDERS

Premiums will be waived while you are confined in a convalescent-care facility beginning 90 days after the elimination period has been satisfied. Until age 85, this plan guarantees that upon each third anniversary date (every 36 months) of this plan those covered under the plan will be offered the opportunity to increase the original benefit selected by 15%. Home-health-care rates shown are for a 90-day benefit period. This plan also offers a 1-year, 2-year, and 4-year benefit period for home health care. Coverage under this policy is available on an individual basis only.

FACTS ABOUT PFL LIFE

Pacific Fidelity Life Insurance Company, NN Investors Life Insurance Company, and National Old Line Life are three companies that have merged together effective January 1991 and are now identified as PFL Life.

		Annual Costs
Base Plan:	$100 per day	$390.00
Alternate daily benefits:	$110 per day	429.00
	$120 per day	468.00
Options:	Optional home health care 90-day benefit	160.00

*Example only. The policies illustrated may not be available at the quoted prices.
Source: Quotesmith Corp.

However, you can't accept such descriptions without further investigation. You need to read the actual policies to see if there is any language that would give the insurer a way out if you're confined in a nursing home.

Otherwise, the policies seem very similar, although the PFL version is a bit tougher on preexisting conditions. The policy costs are slightly higher for the PFL policy ($390 versus $363 per year) apparently because the benefits will start after 30 days of care. If you agree to pay for the first 60 days (an extra 30 days), you can reduce your costs by around 7%, because the Bankers United Life policy costs $27 less per year.

Both policies, you'll notice, charge around $40 extra for a home-health-care rider. As mentioned, this may be a feature you can do without.

The two companies handle inflation coverage in different ways. Bankers United Life charges you 85% extra for a yearly benefit increase of 5%. Because the word "compounded" isn't included, you have to assume that the increase will be a flat $5 per year. PFL Life, on the other hand, offers you the chance to increase coverage by 15% every 3 years. If you take the extra coverage, you'll have to pay more then. However, even if your premium increases by 15% every 3 years, it will be only 75% higher after 12 years. Therefore, it will be many years before the inflation benefit costs you 85% of your original basic premium.

Most people would apply for LTC coverage after age 57, which would increase premiums. (The inflation protection would be a smaller percentage than 85% of the premium, though.) To cut costs, you could reduce the benefit from $100 to $80 and decrease the payout from lifetime to three years.

BASIC PROTECTION IS AVAILABLE

There has been a good deal of controversy over whether LTC policies are worth the aggravation. Is it true that they "aren't good enough," as some consumer advocates have charged?

Critics say LTC policies are dangerous because insurers rip off consumers. That is, they take in far more in premiums than they pay off in claims.

At the same time, the policies are disparaged because the level premiums aren't guaranteed. If future claims turn out to be greater than expected, insurers can raise rates across the board.

But if future claims turn out to be greater than expected, leading to increased premiums, that means insurers will be paying out more than expected. Consumers will be receiving greater-than-expected benefits from LTC policies. How can LTC policies be rip-offs if insurers are paying so much in benefits?

LTC insurance is terribly confusing. Prices vary widely, depending on the type of coverage you want. But if you start with the basics—good insurer, good coverage, $80 to $100 benefit, three-year payout—you can shop around for the best-priced coverage, including inflation protection. Such an LTC policy will protect your assets from the catastrophe of a long nursing-home stay.

Caught in the Middle

Some people won't be able to get LTC insurance or an LTC rider. If you have cancer, heart disease, Alzheimer's, or diabetes, for example, or have had a stroke, you may not find an insurer who'll cover you. Or the coverage may be so expensive it doesn't make sense.

The very elderly, those 85 and over, also are not likely to get LTC coverage if they do not already have a policy.

What can you do if you're that old or if your health is poor?

You can get rich. If your assets are great enough that your income is $30,000, $40,000, and up in retirement, you likely can pay for nursing-home care out of that income without depleting those assets. If you can afford a $60,000 up-front fee plus upwards of $1,000 a month, you may want to move into a continuing-care retirement community that provides nursing-home care (see page 266).

Or you can get poor. If you get rid of your assets in the right way at the right time, you can qualify for Medicaid. Then the government will pay your nursing-home bills. Getting poor is easier than getting rich, but you have to play by the rules, which will be explained in chapter 25.

IN BRIEF
- "Attained-age" policies start with low premiums that get higher as the insured person ages.
- Most increasing-premium LTC policies are not recommended

because they become too expensive for old people to pay for.

- Inflation protection is more important in an LTC policy than in a DI policy.
- Some insurers offer LTC policies with a price break for covering two spouses.
- The best time to buy a policy is when you're 55 to 65, near retirement but young enough to get a reasonably priced policy.
- The best LTC policies are those for which you have to pass a physical.
- LTC insurers who take all applicants may disallow subsequent claims on grounds you didn't disclose all of your health conditions.
- If your health is poor, don't lie on an insurance application. That will jeopardize your coverage.
- Employers are beginning to offer LTC insurance as a fringe benefit.
- Usually, employees have to bear all the costs of employer-sponsored policies, but the premiums may be lower than those of individual policies.
- All group LTC policies, including those offered by associations, need to be scrutinized carefully.
- Computerized data bases can help you locate LTC policies.
- Although it's not easy, you can find real protection in LTC insurance.

Chapter 24

Long-Term-Care Protection Without LTC Insurance

Only 4% of people over age 65 have long-term care (LTC) insurance. That's not surprising because the policies are expensive and there's no certainty that benefits ever will be received. People generally apply for these policies at age 65 or 70. Only those in good health are accepted. Then these healthy 65- and 70-year-olds pay $1,000, $1,500, or $2,000 every year for coverage. By age 85, they've probably paid $20,000 or more in premiums. Unless their health deteriorates markedly and they need long-term home care, they'll never collect any benefits.

From one point of view, that money is the cost of 20-year asset protection; from another, it's a waste of $20,000. If you take the latter perspective, you may prefer to buy life insurance with an "LTC rider." Or add such a rider to a life insurance policy you already own.

LTC RIDERS ON LIFE INSURANCE

What's a rider? It's a special feature that supplements your basic life insurance coverage. An LTC rider will pay some of the policy's death benefit while you're still alive.

For example, suppose you have $300,000 worth of life insurance coverage. You spend three years in a nursing home. Thanks to an LTC rider on that life insurance policy, $75,000 is paid out for nursing-home costs, $3,000 per month for 25 months, while you're still alive. When you die, your beneficiaries will receive $225,000 instead of $300,000.

LTC riders first came on the scene in 1988. Since then, they've been offered by over 100 life insurers, so they're not hard to find. Some companies are even modifying existing policies to add LTC riders. Typically, your basic premium cost will be increased by 5%–15% to pay for the rider, although some riders can increase the cost of a basic policy by as much as 33%.

When Riders Pay Off

LTC riders often will pay their "living benefits" when a serious illness occurs, even when no nursing-home care is needed. For example, victims of strokes, heart attacks, cancer, coronary artery surgery, and renal failure often can collect benefits while they're still alive. Sometimes the policyholder can receive 25% of the policy's face value up front rather than in regular monthly payments. That is, a stroke victim with a $300,000 life insurance policy may receive a $75,000 lump sum to help meet expenses.

Jackson National Life says that a male in his mid-40s has a 60% chance of suffering one of these disasters during his lifetime and that victims tend to live for an extended period, posing possible financial hardships. Thus, the lump sum from the insurance policy will come in handy. (However, insurers often won't issue these policies to people with a family history of heart attacks or cancer.)

LTC riders have their limits. They may not cover nursing-home stays outside the United States or LTC resulting from alcoholism, drug addiction, or attempted suicides. The main problem with many LTC riders, though, is that they'll cover nursing-home care only after a stay in a hospital or in a skilled-nursing home where medical treatment is dispensed. Most nursing-home residents enter the home directly, not after a stay in a hospital or skilled-nursing home.

Terminal Case

Just as is the case with LTC insurance, LTC riders vary widely from one insurer to another. Prudential, for example, boasts that its Living Needs Benefit Plan comes with no increase in premium. It's automatically added to all of its life insurance policies where the death benefit is $25,000 or more; it comes with all new life insurance policies for $50,000 or more.

In addition, Prudential claims that its policy is unusually generous. Many LTC riders limit so-called living benefits to 25%–50% of face value. On a $300,000 policy, for example, you might receive $75,000 to $150,000 for nursing-home costs, depending on the company. Prudential's Living Needs Benefit Plan usually pays 95%—up to $285,000 on that $300,000 policy.

But the Prudential plan has a couple of catches. It will pay living benefits only if a doctor stipulates you have less than six months to live. Or, if you have been in a nursing home for at least six months and the doctors expect you to stay there until you die, Prudential will pay early. (You don't have to take the money under those circumstances; it's your option.) Many LTC riders are far less restrictive on the conditions under which you can receive some cash.

Paying a Premium

When you reach the age when you're looking for LTC coverage, term life insurance is extremely expensive, if you can buy it at all. Therefore, LTC riders are added to permanent life policies. (That includes whole life, universal life, and variable life policies.)

Permanent life, as the name suggests, is a long-term commitment. Sales commissions are steep, so you have to be confident you'll hold on to the policy for many years to get your money's worth. If you change your mind and cancel the policy after a few years, you stand to take a beating from sales expenses, surrender charges, and income taxes.

Besides a long-term view, you need money. LTC policies cover "what if": The insurer pays only if you are confined to a nursing home. Life insurance covers "when": The insurer knows it will pay sooner or later.

Therefore, life insurance is much more expensive. Take the case of a 65-year-old man who wants three years of LTC protection at $80 per day in today's dollars.

Daily benefit	$80
Yearly benefit ($80 times 365)	29,200
Three-year maximum benefit	87,600
Estimated maximum benefit after 15 years of inflation	200,000
Estimated LTC policy cost, per year	1,000
Estimated total cost after 20 years	20,000

There are a lot of estimates here, but that's a rough guess of the cost of an LTC policy if home care isn't purchased.

Say that same 65-year-old, in good health, wanted to buy life insurance. Here's what he might be looking at:

Amount of life insurance desired	$200,000
Estimated annual premium	$10,000
Years of paying premiums	8
Total paid	$80,000

Again, there's a lot of guesswork involved. But an insurance company might quote you a price of $10,000 per year, for 8 years, for a $200,000 policy with an LTC rider. The $80,000 invested in the policy will, if all goes according to plan, generate enough cash to pay the annual premiums after 8 years.

Now you're paying $80,000 in 8 years instead of $20,000 over 20 years. So this option is much more expensive. But if you can afford it, you know that someone will receive the $200,000 at some time.

If you already have a permanent life insurance policy, you might be able to add an LTC rider. Or, if you're buying a permanent life insurance policy for unrelated reasons, you might ask about including an LTC rider. The younger you are, the lower the premium, including an LTC rider.

SPOUSECARE POLICIES

Recently, another innovative form of LTC policy was introduced by Golden Rule Insurance Co., which claims to be the nation's largest seller of individual health insurance policies. Its "SpouseCare" policy is a life insurance policy with LTC coverage as an integral part, not an add-on rider.

With SpouseCare:

- You can buy a paid-up policy with one premium, if you want.
- Coverage is for two people, usually spouses. The life insurance won't pay out until both spouses die.
- After one spouse dies, the other still is covered for LTC expenses.
- LTC covers all types of nursing homes, from skilled to custodial care, as well as hospice care and home care.
- Monthly benefits can be 2% of the first $200,000 worth of coverage and 1% for the next $300,000. (Home-care benefits are half that amount.)
- The full amount of the policy may be paid out for nursing-home care.

Golden Rule gives the example of a couple (he's 60, she's 52) who buy this policy in 1992, paying a $50,000 single premium. The original death benefit will be $165,000.

Assume the premium earns 8.75% per year. In the year 2002, the husband goes into a nursing home that costs $3,000 per month. He's there for a year, rolling up a $36,000 bill, all of which would be paid by SpouseCare. Then he dies.

His widow is still covered. In the year 2019, when she's 79, she goes into a nursing home, which by then costs $5,000 per month. She's there for four years, at a total cost of $240,000; again, all the costs are paid by SpouseCare.

In 2023, she dies. Even though $276,000 has been paid in

nursing-home costs, there is still $105,000 in life insurance proceeds for the policy's beneficiaries. If the tax laws in 2023 are the same as they are now, no income tax will be due on the $105,000.

Those are Golden Rule's numbers. Not everyone will have $50,000 to put into a life insurance policy; not everyone will enjoy 27 years of tax-free buildup before hitting a four-year nursing-home stay. And, of course, Golden Rule's examples of nursing-home costs ($3,000 per month in 2002, $5,000 per month in 2019–2023) may be on the low side. Nevertheless, you can see how life insurance and LTC protection can be combined.

LTC Q & A

Although LTC riders vary, here are the broad outlines of how they work:

How much money is available for nursing-home benefits?

The norm is 2% of insurance coverage per month. By this rule, a $100,000 policy would pay $2,000 per month. However, if your policy is over $150,000, you may get less than 2%. For example, suppose you have a $300,000 life insurance policy with an LTC rider, and you're confined to a nursing home. You might get 2% of the first $150,000 ($3,000) plus 0.5% of the next $150,000 ($750) for a total of $3,750 per month.

Some policies, though, cap the monthly payment at $3,000 per month. Even so, that will cover the cost at many nursing homes.

How long can you collect?

Some policies let you collect 100% of the amount of your life insurance, while others cut you off after you've received 50%.

How long do you have to wait before collecting?

Generally, you have to pay at least for the first 60 days of nursing-home care before an LTC rider kicks in. With some riders, you have to pay your own way for at least 180 days before you can collect.

Does the coverage take effect right away?

That's the standard now, but some LTC riders won't pay until you've been paying the extra premium for at least three years. That is, if you buy an LTC rider in 1992, in some policies you can't collect before 1995, 1997, or some other date.

Who really pays if LTC benefits are tapped?

When you collect LTC living benefits, you're really taking money that otherwise would belong to you and your beneficiaries. Let's say you have a $150,000 life insurance policy, with cash-value buildup of $50,000. You withdraw $10,000 worth of living benefits to pay for nursing-home costs. Now your cash value is down to $40,000; if you die, your beneficiaries will collect only $140,000.

In the above example, the insurance company has $100,000 "net amount at risk," while you start out with $50,000 in cash value you can access. Some LTC riders call for nursing-home payments to be shared by you and the company: In this example, only one-third of the amount would be taken from your cash value.

What's covered?

Most LTC riders will pay for skilled-care or intermediate-care nursing-home stays with no hassle. For custodial care, though, some riders won't pay at all, while others will pay only after three days in a hospital, say, or three weeks in a skilled-care or an intermediate-care home.

Is there a "waiver of premium?"

Again, this is similar to provisions offered by some disability income (DI) policies. While you're actually receiving benefits from an LTC rider, you're not obligated to keep paying premiums on that life insurance policy. As mentioned, you're generally better off avoiding this feature if you have to pay for it.

If you are shopping for life insurance with an LTC rider, you need to be just as careful as when shopping for LTC insurance. Find a sound insurer and check to see that the LTC rider will really pay if you're in a nursing home for custodial care, without any hidden escape clauses. Then check the numbers to see if LTC insurance or life insurance with an LTC rider works better for you.

BORROWING NOW AGAINST
YOUR FAMILY'S FUTURE

Buying life insurance at age 65 or 70 isn't easy and never will be inexpensive. You'll have to pass a physical to get any sort of coverage. However, you or your parent may have a permanent life policy already in force. If so, and if you have substantial "cash value" already built up, you probably can take policy loans to help pay nursing-home costs. Just as is the case with LTC riders, policy loans will reduce the amount your beneficiaries will collect.

Life insurance face value	$300,000
Policy loans	50,000
Compound interest on policy loans (not paid but added to loan balance)	20,000
Loan balance	70,000
Proceeds paid to beneficiaries ($300,000 minus $70,000)	230,000

There is a problem with using life insurance (LTC riders, policy loans) rather than straight LTC insurance. Say you have an LTC insurance policy with a three-year benefit. You go into a nursing home for a long stay. After three years, your policy has paid out all its benefits, and you have nothing left. If other qualifications are met (see next chapter), you can qualify for Medicaid, and the government will pay subsequent nursing-home bills.

If you use life insurance, though, you'll own a valuable insurance policy, which will disqualify you for Medicaid. In practice, this means the older insured person has to transfer ownership of the policy to someone else (preferably a child rather than a spouse) in order to qualify for Medicaid. Then the nursing-home resident has to rely on the child using that money for nursing-home bills.

If the insured person keeps the policy instead and doesn't apply for Medicaid, the policy's value may be entirely stripped away by a long nursing-home stay.

TAX CONSEQUENCES

What are the tax consequences of LTC coverage? If you borrow against the cash value of life insurance, you probably won't owe income taxes. That's the traditional treatment of life insurance policy loans. (There's an exception for life insurance bought since 1989 if a paid-up policy was purchased with one premium or a few premiums.)

But what if you receive benefits under an LTC policy or if you tap the death benefit of a life insurance policy, under an LTC rider, to pay nursing-home costs? You might receive $24,000, $36,000, or more per year. If that's considered taxable income, you could owe substantial income taxes.

The insurance companies generally say that LTC benefits and life insurance living benefits are exempt from income taxes, just as health insurance benefits are tax-free. But insurance companies don't make tax law; the IRS has yet to rule on this issue. So there may be a tax problem.

As a practical matter, though, if you're in a nursing home, you can tap your LTC coverage and decide not to declare the benefit as taxable income. Then it's up to the IRS to come after you, if it wants to. The behavior of the IRS is never predictable, but it may feel it has enough on its plate without hounding nursing-home residents (or their estates) for back taxes.

COMMUNITIES THAT CARE

Is there a way to protect yourself against ruinous nursing-home stays without insurance? About 250,000 people, mainly in their 70s and 80s, have chosen to reduce their exposure by moving into "continuing care" retirement communities.

Continuing-care communities are essentially apartment complexes for the elderly. They offer dining-room meals, housekeeping services, transportation to the local shopping mall or medical office building, swimming, golf, and a full range of social activities.

In addition, there's a nursing home—usually on the same

site—for residents who no longer are capable of independent living. Once you're in, you can stay there.

That sort of security doesn't come cheap. Typically, you have to pay an up-front fee plus a monthly rent. At some luxurious facilities, the entrance fee can be $250,000.

Most continuing-care communities are not in that league. Generally, they fall into three categories:

• Type A. For a one-bedroom apartment, the average entrance fee is around $60,000 plus about $900 per month in rent. You get unlimited nursing-home care and perhaps in-home care for bathing, dressing, etc.

• Type B. Costs here average around $45,000 up front plus $750 per month. Nursing-home care may be limited to so many days per year, with residents responsible for any excess.

• Type C. Fees are lower ($35,000; $600 per month), but you have to pay extra for nursing-home care, meals, housekeeping, etc.

Continuing-care facilities vary widely, so it's hard to say if they're "worthwhile" or not. If you (or your parents) have the means and you desire a certain life-style, then by all means check into continuing-care communities. If you like a place, you may enjoy your stay there.

But you need to check very carefully into what you'll get and what you'll pay. The monthly fees likely will increase; find out what the past record has been. Ask if there will be a refund of the up-front fee if you decide to leave or if your heirs will get a refund if you die without needing nursing-home care. If you're entering such a community with your spouse, find out what will happen if one spouse goes into a nursing home and the other stays in the apartment.

Most of all, don't give $30,000+ to a continuing-care community that's on shaky financial ground. You may never receive LTC there if it goes out of business. Have your accountant or another financial adviser review the community's latest statements to see if there's any doubt of its viability.

IN BRIEF

- Some life insurance policies offer LTC riders at a modest additional cost.
- These riders enable you to receive the policy's death benefit while you're still alive if you're in a nursing home.
- Features vary, but a typical LTC rider will enable you to receive $2,000–$3,000 per month.
- The benefits you receive while you're alive will reduce the amount of life insurance your beneficiaries receive at your death.
- Life insurance is more expensive than straight LTC insurance.
- However, with life insurance, you know that your beneficiaries eventually will receive the money you've paid plus interest.
- You need to evaluate LTC riders just as carefully as you evaluate LTC insurance to see if coverage is adequate.
- If you have an existing permanent life insurance policy, you may be able to borrow against the cash value to help pay nursing-home costs.
- The IRS has yet to rule on the taxability of money received under LTC policies and LTC life insurance riders.
- If you have ample means (perhaps after a house sale), you might be able to move into a continuing-care community that mixes social and athletic facilities with LTC services.
- Closely check the financial strength of a continuing-care community before making any commitments.

Chapter 25

Poverty Cases

You're not rich, but you're not poor. If you add up everything you own, the number would probably come out to be somewhere between $50,000 and $500,000. You're solid middle-class America.

Then, as the crowning achievement of your life's efforts, you give away everything so you can plead poverty and go on welfare.

Sound crazy? Perhaps, but that's what many elderly Americans are doing these days, often at the urging of their middle-aged children and some savvy lawyers.

Here's why. Medicare and private health insurance won't cover nursing-home costs to any meaningful degree. However, Medicaid will pay those costs in the right circumstances.

Medicaid, as mentioned (page 134), is a combined federal-state welfare program. If you meet certain standards, you're officially poor, and Medicaid will pick up your medical bills, including nursing-home costs. Medicaid now pays over $20 billion per year for nursing-home costs, about one-third of all Medicaid expenses. Altogether, Medicaid picks up about half of the national nursing-home bill.

How do people with a net worth of several hundred thousand dollars become poor? They give away almost all their assets. According to Medicaid rules, to qualify you can have a house, household effects, personal jewelry (including a wedding ring and an engagement ring), a car, term life insurance, a prepaid funeral, and a few thousand dollars in cash to cover burial costs. Everything else must go.

In addition, there are income limits. In most states, you simply have to have an income less than the nursing-home cost. (Considering how few assets you'll have left, that won't be hard to achieve.) In other states, you're allowed an income of no more than perhaps $1,000 or $1,200 per month from all sources.

When you give away assets, you won't be eligible for Medicaid immediately. Instead, there's a formula Medicaid applies:

A. Value of assets given away $60,000
B. Average monthly cost of nursing homes in your area $ 4,000
Divide A by B ($60,000 by $4,000)
Waiting period for Medicaid eligibility   15 months

In this example, you'd have to wait 15 months before Medicaid kicks in and pays your nursing-home bills. However, there's a maximum waiting period of 30 months.

IT'S NOT GREAT BEING POOR

So it sounds simple. You give away your assets to your kids, you become poor, you wait no more than 30 months, you qualify for Medicaid. Your kids have your assets, and the government picks up the nursing-home costs.

But real life isn't always simple. Here are some of the drawbacks to the Medicaid maneuver:

• *Loss of independence.* Once you give away virtually all of your assets and your income, you have to survive on what meager income you retain. You may not be able to live on $1,000 a month or so.

Generally, there will be some sort of tacit agreement between you and your children. You give them, say, $100,000 in CDs, earning $6,000 per year. They agree to turn over that $6,000 in interest income to you.

But such agreements can't be in writing if you want to qualify for Medicaid. You have to trust your kids. What happens if your children need that money for living expenses? To start a new business? To repay a loan? What if there's a divorce and that $100,000 worth of CDs is tossed into the pool that gets divided? Your children may be well intentioned, but your future income isn't guaranteed.

Besides the financial issue, there's a certain lack of dignity that's bound to follow after you've impoverished yourself and become a ward of the state.

• *Gift taxes.* This isn't an issue for most people, but if you have over $600,000 worth of assets (over $1.2 million for a married couple), giving everything away at one time probably will trigger taxes that otherwise could be avoided.

• *Medicaid liens.* As noted, you're allowed to hold on to a house and still qualify for Medicaid. In some states, though, Medicaid will keep track of how much money is spent on your behalf. At your death, when your heirs inherit your house, Medicaid will place a lien on that house for that amount. When the house is sold, Medicaid will collect. That essentially negates the advantage of the asset transfer.

• *Income taxes.* To avoid a Medicaid lien, you can give away your house, too. However, this forces you to lose two key tax breaks (the over-55 $125,000 exclusion and the step-up in basis*). Without going into all the technical details, that may mean a huge income tax bill for your kids when they eventually sell your house.

Similarly, suppose you give that $100,000 worth of CDs to

---

*Homeowners over age 55 can exclude up to $125,000 from capital-gains tax on the sale of a primary residence. When you die, all capital assets (including a house) receive a new cost for tax purposes, based on current value. An immediate sale, therefore, incurs no taxable gain.

your children. The $6,000 in annual interest income will be taxed at your children's income-tax rates, which may be much higher than yours. You might have retained $5,000 after tax. Your kids might have only $4,000 after tax to pass back to you.

• *Second-class status.* If you're on Medicaid, you won't be welcome at many nursing homes. In a state where a private patient pays $3,000 per month, Medicaid might pay only $1,500 or $2,000 per month. Thus, some of the better nursing homes won't take Medicaid patients at all. Others may take Medicaid patients but not make any great attempts to coddle them.

• *Spousal impoverishment.* If you impoverish yourself to qualify for Medicaid and avoid nursing-home expenses, what happens to your spouse? Does he or she have to become a poverty case, too?

Until 1989, that was basically the case. Then a new federal law, the Spousal Impoverishment Act, was passed. Now things are a little bit better for the healthy, stay-at-home spouse, but they're still not great.

Here's how the new system works. When one spouse goes into a nursing home, all spousal assets (except house, car, and other excluded assets) are added up. It doesn't make any difference which spouse earned the money, inherited it, brought it into the marriage, etc.

Say Eve and Steve married while in their 60s, the second marriage for each. Steve's total net worth was $40,000; Eve's was $400,000 plus the house in which they live. A prenuptial agreement, signed by Steve, says the house and the money will remain Eve's and will never be available to Steve.

No matter. According to Medicaid, the marital assets are $440,000. (There may be a problem with the house, too, as explained later.)

Under the 1989 law, for one spouse to qualify for Medicaid, the other can possess no more than half the marital assets. That means that Eve, who came into the marriage with $400,000, can have no more than $220,000 (half of $440,000) in order for Steve to qualify for Medicaid.

But that's not all. Under the federal law, there's a maximum amount of assets a spouse can retain, which takes precedence over the 50% Medicaid formula. Currently, the limit is around $70,000. (The numbers change each year, reflecting inflation.) If Eve possesses more than $70,000 in assets (not including the house and other permissible assets listed on page 270), Steve won't qualify for Medicaid.

So Eve can have no more than $70,000 worth of assets for Steve to qualify for Medicaid. Eve, who came into the marriage with $400,000, may have to spend or give away $330,000 before Steve qualifies for Medicaid.

• *The ethical dilemma.* When you transfer assets and go on Medicaid, you're asking other taxpayers, state and federal, to pay for your nursing-home care so that you can give money to your children. Is that fair? Not at all.

But life is unfair, John F. Kennedy once remarked. Is it fair for you to work all your life, pay your taxes, save, and so on, only to use that money to pay for a nursing-home bed when the man in the bed next to yours, who neither worked nor saved, gets the exact same service courtesy of the taxpayers? Most people, when push comes to shove, prefer to leave something to their children rather than spending all of it on a nursing home.

THE GIVEAWAY GAME

You have to resolve the ethics question yourself. The financial problems cited above can be handled, more or less, if you're familiar with the rules. Here's one possible strategy.

1. Do nothing. Keep your money and your independence as long as possible. (If you have substantial assets, you might want to give them away over time in order to reduce estate taxes, but that's a separate issue.)
2. If you can afford it, buy an LTC policy or a life insurance policy with an LTC rider, as described earlier.
3. If your health deteriorates and you have to enter a nursing home, go in as a private patient, paying the full rate. This

will enable you to select a first-class, well-regarded nursing home, based on recommendations. (If you plan on applying for Medicaid at some point, don't choose a nursing home that's entirely "private-pay.")

4. If you have LTC insurance or an LTC rider, those funds can pay some or all of the nursing-home expense. Otherwise, you'll have to use your own assets.

5. At that point, if it appears you're in for a long nursing-home stay, you can transfer your assets to your children. After an appropriate waiting period, but no longer than 30 months, you can qualify for Medicaid.

6. So you'll likely be responsible for up to 30 months of nursing-home bills. That's why a three-year payout period for LTC insurance is recommended.

7. Without LTC coverage, you'll have to cover the 30-month cost out of your assets or have your children pay the bills.

8. After the 30 months are up, you can apply for Medicaid coverage. From that point on, virtually all of your income will go toward the nursing-home bill, with Medicaid making up the difference:

	Per Month
Your nursing home has a Medicaid reimbursement rate of	$2,000
Your total income, after transferring assets, is	1,000
Your "personal needs allowance" is	40
You pay to the nursing home ($1,000 minus $40)	960
Medicaid pays the nursing home ($2,000 minus $960)	1,040

What have you accomplished?

- You're in a good nursing home. The quality of care shouldn't change when you shift from private-pay to Medicaid.
- You've managed to leave most of your assets to your children.
- From here on, you have virtually no assets, so you won't lose any more of your savings.
- Medicaid will pick up the future costs.
- If you never need nursing-home care, you never have to

transfer assets, and you retain your independence as long as you wish.

Is there a flaw in this seemingly win-win strategy? Suppose you have a stroke or otherwise become unable to handle your own affairs. Then, when you enter a nursing home, you won't be able to transfer your assets and start the 30-month Medicaid clock.

Therefore, you should work with a lawyer to create a "durable power of attorney." (You probably should have one whether or not you anticipate a Medicaid transfer.) This document gives someone else the authority to handle your affairs if you become incapacitated.

Naturally, you need to have absolute trust in the person you name to manage your assets. In some states, you can name more than one person; just be sure your "team" will work together.

Besides a durable power, draft a letter of instruction stating your intent. You might say that you want to transfer all of your assets, divided equally among X, Y, and Z, in the event you can't act on your own behalf. Be sure that your letter of instruction has all the details on your insurance, including where the policies are kept.

After you draft a durable power and letter of instruction, bring them up to date every two years or so in order to demonstrate that your intentions have not changed.

Although this isn't strictly on the subject, you should discuss a "living will" with members of your family. A living will spells out the conditions for "pulling the plug," cutting off your life support and sparing your family grief as well as unnecessary expense. You may give a family member a "medical power of attorney" so that he or she can confirm your wishes at the appropriate time.

KEEPING A HOUSEFUL OF BENEFITS

Medicaid permits you to keep your house, among other assets, and still qualify for public assistance. That's very generous. If you take advantage of this generosity, most of your planning may be wasted.

Let's say you give away all your other assets and qualify for Medicaid. Each month, Medicaid pays $1,000 on your behalf. (The amount may go up each year.) If you stay in the nursing home for another three years, that will be a total of at least $36,000. After your death, Medicaid can put a lien on your house and try to recoup that amount when the house is sold.

To avoid that, you give the house to your children. That takes care of Medicaid but not the IRS. Whenever you make a gift, the recipient also receives your "basis" (cost of the house for tax purposes):

You bought your house for	$40,000
You made capital improvements of	10,000
Your basis in the house is ($40,000 plus $10,000)	50,000
The house is now worth	150,000
Your children, though, retain your basis of	50,000
If they eventually sell the house for	150,000
They have a taxable gain of ($150,000 minus $50,000)	100,000
Assuming a tax rate of 35%, they'll owe the IRS	35,000

That's just about the same as paying the Medicaid lein. On some houses, the tax on the gain would be even greater.

So if it doesn't pay to keep the house and it doesn't pay to give it away, what can you do?

Life Estate Plan

One answer, according to Harley Gordon, a Boston attorney who specializes in "elder law," is to give away the house but retain a "life estate." That is, you keep an interest in the property for the rest of your life, giving you the right to live in the house. "This protects the house from a Medicaid lien," says Gordon, "because your interest ends when you die. Yet the house can pass to your children, for example, with a full step-up in basis."

Say you give your house to your children but retain a life estate. At your death, the house is valued at $150,000. That becomes your children's basis in the house. So if the house is sold for $150,000, there is no taxable gain, and no income tax will be due.

Naturally, you need to work with an experienced attorney if you're contemplating this strategy.

Downsizing

Another possibility is to sell your house. As you grow older and nearer the nursing-home stage, the task of keeping up a single-family home might be too much for you to manage. As long as you're over age 55, you're entitled to a once-in-a-lifetime $125,000 exemption from tax on the sale of your primary residence. In our above example, where the taxable gain would be $100,000, the exemption would more than cover the tax, and you'd owe nothing.

Then you could use the proceeds for a smaller place, perhaps a one-bedroom apartment in a top-flight continuing-care community (see page 266) that provides nursing-home services.

Or, if you keep the money, you could give it away when you transfer your other assets (step 5, above) and wait 30 months to go on Medicaid.

Married, Harried

The by-the-numbers planning process may not work so neatly when a married couple is involved, especially if it's a second marriage with two sets of children. What can Eve and Steve do, for example?

• Eve might decide to pay Steve's nursing-home bills. If Steve's income, from Social Security and his $40,000 in assets, is $12,000 per year, Eve might pay the other $18,000 a year in a $30,000 nursing home. With a $400,000 investment portfolio, she may be able to afford it.

• Eve can give away $330,000 to her own children from her first marriage to get down to the Medicaid limit.

- Eve can divorce Steve. Under the terms of their prenuptial agreement, she's entitled to $400,000 in the event of a divorce.

- Eve can choose to do none of the above. After Steve spends all of his money, Medicaid will step in, pay for his care, and possibly sue Eve for the money it's spending on Steve.

Will Medicaid file and win a suit? Different states have different policies in this regard and the outcome of a suit can't be known.

What about the house? If Steve owned the house, or a share of it, he could transfer his interest to his wife with no Medicaid penalty. Some lawyers say that the at-home spouse can sell the house without worrying about a Medicaid lien, but a lien will be imposed if both spouses die before a transfer is made.

Of course, if Eve sells the house to avoid a Medicaid lien, she'll have even more cash in her possession. Ultimately, she'll have to decide among the (1) pay, (2) giveaway, (3) divorce, (4) fight-Medicaid-in-court choices described above.

TRUST-WORTHY

There is another Medicaid strategy recommended by some attorneys: Give your assets to a trust rather than to your children.

First, a few trust basics:

- A trust is a fictional form of ownership.
- Besides the "maker" (the person who creates the trust and puts the money into it), a trust must have a trustee, who makes all the decisions regarding the funds, and a beneficiary, who receives the money disbursed by the trust.
- A trust can be revocable or irrevocable. An irrevocable trust, as the name suggests, is a more serious affair—it can't be canceled or materially changed after it has been established.

Some attorneys say that transferring a house to a revocable trust will avoid a Medicaid lien. You can act as trustee, retaining control over the house. Check with an attorney about the laws in your state.

For other assets, though, you have to use an irrevocable trust. After those assets are out of your hands and owned by the trust, you can qualify for Medicaid. Using the trust structure avoids the risk of an outright gift to a child, who might lose your assets in a divorce or a bad business deal.

So far, so good. But there's a disagreement as to how to structure Medicaid trusts. Some attorneys say that you can be the beneficiary, receiving the trust income as long as you're not in a nursing home. Some say a trust can shift income between spouses, so the wife gets the income when her husband goes into a nursing home. Others advocate "convertible" trusts, which become irrevocable, hands-off trusts only after the maker is in a nursing home.

However, some attorneys think that Medicaid may say these trusts are nothing but a subterfuge on the ground that you still have control of your assets. If Medicaid takes that position and is upheld in a hearing, you're back where you started, a long way from qualifying for Medicaid.

Attorneys with this point of view counsel a more conservative approach. They might advise, for example, that you appoint as trustee a nonrelated party who'll distribute the trust income to, say, your children. Then your children can give you that income, as long as you're not in a nursing home.

The latter approach may be more acceptable to Medicaid because you have no access to the trust assets or income. But without any control you're relying on the trustee and the beneficiary to maintain the income flow to you.

There are other concerns with Medicaid trusts. They're expensive to establish: on average, from $1,000 to $2,500. They take away your flexibility because the terms can't be changed after the trust has been established. And you have to be certain that the income the trust generates, along with other income (pensions, Social Security), won't put you over your state's Medicaid limits. So don't put your trust in a Medicaid trust unless you're certain your lawyer knows what he or she is doing.

SPENDDOWN TO THE BOTTOM

Suppose you don't have LTC coverage and you don't want to pay 30 months' worth of nursing-home bills, which can cost $75,000 and up. You can give away all of your assets way in advance of needing a nursing home so that you meet the 30-month waiting period for Medicaid eligibility. But that

1. Strips you of income and independence.
2. May be unnecessary if you never need LTC.
3. Labels you a Medicaid patient, whom many nursing homes won't admit.

There is another way to go—a "spenddown," with or without a prior asset giveaway. If your assets are modest, a spenddown may be your only path to a bed in a good nursing home.

As the name suggests, a spenddown consists of spending all of your money until you're down to the Medicaid limit. Suppose Frank, an elderly widower, has $20,000 in assets and a total monthly income of $1,050. The state where he lives permits Medicaid recipients to keep a total of $3,500, including an allowance for burial expenses.

Because Frank's assets ($20,000) exceed the Medicaid allowance ($3,500), he has to pay his own way when he goes into a nursing home. Of his $1,050 monthly income, he keeps a $50 personal-needs allowance and turns the other $1,000 over to the nursing home. Because the nursing home charges private patients $2,500 per month, Frank has to pay the extra $1,500 per month out of his assets.

After 11 months, Frank has spent $16,500 of his assets, so he has only $3,500 left. Now he can qualify for Medicaid. He'll continue to turn over $1,000 per month to the nursing home from his income, but now Medicaid will make up the difference.

Frank starts out with assets of	$20,000
His income is	1,050 per month
After a personal needs allowance of	50 per month
He turns over to the nursing home	1,000 per month
The nursing home charges	2,500 per month
So Frank has to pay out of savings ($2,500 minus $1,000)	1,500 per month

After 11 months, Frank has paid out of sav-
    ings (11 times $1,500)   16,500
Now Frank's assets are ($20,000 minus
    $16,500)   3,500
His state allows Medicaid recipients to keep   3,500
So Frank now qualifies for Medicaid.

Suppose Frank had $200,000 in assets. He could have given away $180,000 to his children and kept $20,000, anticipating this spenddown. As long as he does this at least 19 months before entering the nursing home, it won't make a difference. (Nineteen months plus 11 months in the nursing home equals the 30 months Medicaid requires after a gift of assets.) So he'll pay for 11 months in the nursing home, not 30 months.

As long as Frank is willing to live with just $20,000 to his name, and if he's confident a nursing home will accept him with those assets, this can save his family thousands of dollars ($28,500, in this example). You can save thousands with a spenddown plan; just be certain you know all the rules before you start the game.

IN BRIEF
- If you're poor, Medicaid will pay your nursing-home bills.
- To qualify as "poor," you're allowed a minimal income and few assets, as defined by federal and state law.
- If you give away assets, you'll have a waiting period (usually 30 months) before you can apply for Medicaid.
- Giving away assets has many drawbacks: loss of independence, second-class status as a Medicaid patient, possible tax costs.
- If one spouse qualifies for Medicaid, the other spouse will face strict limits on the assets that may be kept.
- A preferred strategy is to hold on to assets as long as you can. If you need LTC, enter a good nursing home as a private patient.
- Then you can give away your assets. After no longer than 30 months, you can qualify for Medicaid.
- In that 30-month period, you can use insurance or family contributions to pay nursing-home bills.
- A durable power of attorney, arranged in advance, will enable

someone else to transfer your assets if you're incapacitated.

- To avoid being hit with a Medicaid lien or income taxes when your house is eventually sold, work with an attorney on a transfer by which you retain a life estate.
- Married people with substantial assets have few choices if they want their spouse to qualify for Medicaid.
- Medicaid trusts can be a useful tool in asset protection as long as you work with a knowledgeable attorney.
- You may plan a spenddown to qualify for Medicaid if you object to paying full price for 30 months in a nursing home.

Summary of LTC Insurance Goals

Here are the steps that can prevent large asset losses in case you need extensive long-term care (LTC). They're presented as if you, the reader, are the one who'll need the care. However, the principles are the same if your concern is helping aging parents who may need LTC.

1. Find out the average cost of a first-class nursing home in your area. For example, a good home might cost $80 per day, $2,400 per month, $29,000 per year.
2. Make an appropriate inflation estimate. If you're in your 70s, you may need nursing-home care within the next few years, so the estimated cost might be 10%–20% higher than today's cost. But if you're in your 50s, with 20 or 30 years before you reach prime nursing-home age, you can expect to pay two or three times today's nursing-home fees.
3. Make a realistic estimate of the income you'll have when you're in your 70s and 80s. How much can you expect from Social Security plus retirement plans plus an investment portfolio? If you're in your 70s, for example,

and you enjoy a steady $50,000–$60,000 annual income, you likely will be able to cover nursing-home costs out of current cash flow.
4. If there's a shortfall, or a projected shortfall, you may be able to cut your risk by buying LTC insurance. (If you wait until you're age 75 or so, LTC insurance may be too expensive for you to afford. You'll get a cheaper annual rate if you buy a policy earlier, but it may not make sense to buy before you're in your mid-50s, because the unknowns are so great.)

LTC policies are extremely complicated, with great variations from one policy to the next. You can buy a good one if you proceed carefully and follow these suggestions:

• Buy from a financially strong insurer, one with top ratings from independent services.

• Be extra careful in examining a policy's definitions. Ideally, you want a policy that will cover custodial care in any type of institution if you can't care for yourself. No prior stays in a hospital or other medical institution should be required.

• Don't buy a policy unless there is specific language covering memory lapses, including Alzheimer's disease.

• A policy that will pay $80 a day probably is adequate. If you live in the Northeast or on the West Coast, where costs are higher, you may need at least a $100-per-day policy.

• Some sort of inflation protection probably should be included, especially if you're in your 50s or 60s when you buy the policy.

• You can cut your insurance premium by choosing a long waiting period before benefits begin.

• Another way to save money is to choose a policy that pays

benefits for three years rather than one with a longer benefit period.

• Other policy features, such as coverage for home health care, are costly and probably not necessary for preventing catastrophes.

• If you have a good LTC policy, you can pay your own way into a first-class nursing home. At that point, you can transfer virtually all of your assets to other family members, if you choose. This will qualify you for Medicaid (welfare), generally after a 30-month waiting period. So if your insurance policy pays for three years of nursing-home care, Medicaid will pick up after your coverage expires.

• Impoverishing yourself so that Medicaid will pay nursing-home costs is a complicated process, especially when married couples are involved. Be sure to work with an attorney who's experienced in this area.

• Another choice is to buy a life insurance policy with an "LTC rider." Such policies will pay benefits while you're still living if you're institutionalized. Any benefits paid for LTC will reduce the proceeds your beneficiaries will receive at your death. Life insurance is more expensive than LTC insurance, but there is a certainty that someone—either you or your beneficiaries—will collect benefits at some time. This strategy works best if you have ample income in retirement, enough to afford a hefty life insurance premium without cramping your life-style.

• Still another option is available if you have an existing "cash value" life insurance policy. Instead of buying an LTC policy or planning to impoverish yourself, you can rely on the cash value for protection. If you go into a nursing home, you can pay your way by borrowing against the policy.

Appendix A

Finding a Good Agent's No Secret

Nobody knows everything about everything. Certainly you, with many other matters on your mind, can't be expected to know everything about health insurance, disability income (DI) insurance, and long-term care (LTC) insurance.

When you need specialized help in medicine, in law, in tax preparation, you turn to a professional. The same should be true in insurance. When you want help, you should be able to turn to a professional insurance agent.

Unfortunately, not all insurance agents are very professional. In fact, it seems there are few real pros around, few people who really know what they need to know about health-care insurance. How can you find the few pros amid the incompetent and the downright dishonest?

It helps if you have a good life insurance agent. Most life insurance companies also sell at least some form of health-care insurance, so life insurance agents often sell other types of policies as well. A life insurance agent who knows you and your family situation may be the best person to handle your health-care insurance needs.

But what if you don't have an agent or don't particularly like the one who sold you your life insurance? Where can you go to find one that you will like?

Start by networking. Ask your friends and your friends' spouses.

Do they know of a good insurance agent for life or health insurance?

Do you work for a large company? Ask someone in the employee-benefits department.

Do you know someone who owns a small business? He or she probably has dealt with many insurance agents; ask for referrals.

Ask your accountant. Your doctor. Your lawyer. All of these people encounter insurance agents frequently. Find out which ones they would recommend.

Keep asking around and you'll surely come up with several names of prospective insurance agents.

FACING OFF

After you have the names of some recommended agents, call them. Once they get over the initial shock (most agents are surprised when a stranger calls them instead of the other way around), tell them you're interested in health or DI or LTC insurance. If that's a product line they handle, they'll be eager to come see you.

You'll be able to tell the good agents from the not so good in less than 10 minutes. The second-raters will do all the talking. They'll try to *sell you something.* Chances are, if you mention LTC insurance, they'll have the perfect policy for you right in their briefcase.

A real pro will have you do the talking. This agent will ask about your age, your health, your family, your financial situation, trying to figure out what you really need before coming up with a sales pitch.

Don't monopolize the conversation, though. Just as the agents wants to find out about you, you should be trying to find out about the agent. What's his or her educational background? How long has the agent been selling this type of insurance? What professional credentials have been attained? An agent who is a chartered financial consultant (ChFC), a chartered life underwriter (CLU), or a registered health underwriter (RHU) has met certain standards to earn those designations.

Ask for references. Before you buy anything, before you sign anything, you want to check on the agent first.

The agent may shy away from revealing clients' names. Fine. Say you understand if he or she wants to check with them first. After permission has been obtained you can get their names and phone numbers and call them.

What if an agent won't give you references, even with permission? You had better find another agent. You don't want to give anyone your business unless you can first determine that he or she is a true professional.

After you have references, call them. You don't want to ask personal questions (how much life insurance do you have?), but you want to know how they feel about the agent. What you're looking for is evidence of a relationship that goes back many years, one that covers some form of health-care insurance as well as life insurance.

Suppose you suspect that the references are "ringers"—the agent has given you a brother-in-law's name, for instance. Call, anyway. Any agent that gets kind words from a brother-in-law is doing something right.

PLAYING THE FIELD

Should you work with an independent agent? Probably. Agents who work exclusively with one company may be bright and diligent. However, it's not likely that one insurance company will have the health insurance policy and the DI insurance policy and the LTC policy that's best for you at the best price. An independent or semi-independent agent can scan a larger universe to come up with more choices for you.

Ask if the agent uses a computerized data base to search out policies for clients. That's not a knockout question—many good agents don't use these services—but an agent who does use a computer service may be one who tries hard to find the best deals for clients.

Finally, go with your instincts. An agent may have great credentials and excellent references, but there's something about him or her that makes you pause. Keep searching. A good insurance agent is someone you'll be working with regularly for many years. If the chemistry is lacking, you'll never feel the peace of mind you should enjoy when you know you have the right agent, the right insurers, and the right policies.

Appendix B

Keeping the Sure in Insurance

An insurance policy is only as good as the company that issues it. The following companies currently receive top ratings from all the major ratings agencies, and they all have at least 50 years of experience. They're listed by size, from Prudential (over $130 billion in assets) to Guardian Life (over $6 billion). Although these companies are primarily life insurers, they also sell health-care insurance.

If you buy a policy from these insurers, you won't have to worry about the company's financial strength. However, these companies got to be top-rated by being choosy about the people they insure. They're probably most appropriate if you're in good health.

Prudential	(201)802-6722
Metropolitan Life	(800)638-5433
New York Life	(212)576-7000
Connecticut General	(203)726-6000
Northwestern Mutual	(414)271-1444
Nationwide	(614)249-7111
State Farm	(309)766-2311
Guardian Life	(212)598-8000

The following insurance companies may not be as large or as well established as the ones listed above, but they have received favorable reviews for selling policies in at least one area of health care. Remember, fortunes can change rapidly, so ask about an insurer's current financial position before buying a policy. (This list is not meant to be exclusive; other insurers may sell excellent, well-priced policies.)

Health Insurance

Allstate	(708)402-5000
Blue Cross and Blue Shield of Minnesota	(800)382-2000
Blue Cross and Blue Shield of New Jersey	(201)822-4500
Boston Mutual Life	(617)227-5600
Continental American Life	(800)441-7004
Empire Blue Cross Blue Shield	(212)490-4757
Equitable Life Assurance Society	(212)554-1234
Fidelity Security Life	(800)821-7303
Pan American Life	(800)688-6800
Pennsylvania Blue Shield	(215)564-2100

Disability Income (DI) Insurance Policies

IDS Life	(612)372-3733
Maccabees Mutual Life	(800)678-6227
Massachusetts Mutual	(413)788-8411
Mutual of Omaha	(800)228-7669
National Life of Vermont	(802)229-3333
The New England	(617)578-6000
Paul Revere	(508)799-4441
Principal Mutual	(800)247-9988
Provident Life & Accident	(800)777-0116
UNUM	(207)770-9082

Long-Term Care (LTC) Policies

AIG Life	(302)594-2000
AMEX Life Assurance	(800)345-6600
Atlantic & Pacific	(800)537-1688
Blue Cross and Blue Shield of Rochester	(800)544-0327
CNA	(800)327-2430
Insurance Company of North America	(800)223-1481
John Hancock	(800)922-5050
Security Connecticut	(800)962-1652
Time Insurance	(800)624-5399
Transamerica Occidental	(800)772-5837
The Travelers	(203)277-0111

Life Insurance Policies with LTC Riders

Aetna	(800)243-2390
Connecticut Mutual	(203)727-6500
First Penn-Pacific	(800)323-1746
Golden Rule	(800)950-4474
ITT Life	(612)545-2100
Jackson National Life	(800)477-4099
Lincoln National	(800)248-6301
National Travelers Life	(515)283-0101

Glossary

Accepting assignment. The practice in which physicians agree to be paid in full for treating Medicare patients at posted rates. Doctors who accept assignment bill Medicare directly.

Activities of daily living (ADLs). Functions such as bathing, eating, dressing, etc. Some long-term care (LTC) insurance policies will pay if the insured individual can't perform two or three ADLs.

Annual renewable disability insurance (ARDI). Disability income insurance that starts with a relatively low annual premium that increases each year.

Cap on benefits. The maximum amoung an insurance policy will pay over the life of that policy.

COBRA. A federal law requiring employers to allow former employees to continue their group health insurance, for a certain time period, as long as the former employee pays the full cost of the insurance.

Coinsurance or copayment. The share of a medical bill that the patient is responsible for paying.

Continuing-care retirement community. An apartment complex for the elderly, frequently offering nursing-home facilities as well as independent living.

Custodial care. Long-term care (LTC), either at home or in an institution, that involves helping with routine tasks rather than skilled medical treatment.

Deductible. The initial medical costs, paid for by the patient, before the insurance coverage kicks in.

Durable power of attorney. Legal authority for one party to act on behalf of another in the event the latter becomes incompetent and can't care for him- or herself.

First-dollar health insurance. Coverage that pays all, or virtually all, of the medical bills for the insured and his or her family.

Guaranteed-renewable insurance. Coverage that assures the insured individual that a policy will stay in force as long as required premiums are paid, even if the insured's health deteriorates.

Health maintenance organization (HMO). A prepaid health-care plan. Individuals or families pay fixed fees for which they're entitled to virtually unlimited health care from affiliated doctors and hospitals.

Hospital-surgical health insurance. Coverage that applies mainly to medical bills incurred in a hospital, often with significant exceptions.

Indemnity health insurance. The traditional form of "fee-for-service" health insurance in which the patient chooses a doctor or hospital and the insurance company pays the medical bills.

Life estate. An arrangement in which one person, usually an elderly parent, gives a house to a child but retains the right to live in it.

Living benefits. Payments from a life insurance policy to an insured individual who is still alive, usually to pay for nursing-home costs or catastrophic medical care.

Living will. A formal document spelling out your wish to be disconnected from life support systems if there seems to be no chance of recovery.

Major-medical health insurance. Broad coverage for most types of medical bills.

Managed care. A term that describes many different strategies for cutting health-care costs, usually by limiting the patient's choice of doctors and hospitals.

Medicaid. A welfare system supported by federal and state governments that provides health care (including nursing-home care) for the poor.

Medicaid lien. A claim by the Medicaid system for reimbursement of costs incurred on behalf of a patient through sharing in the proceeds from the sale of the patient's house.

Medicare. A federal health insurance program primarily for those over age 65.

Medigap. Slang term for health insurance sold to the elderly to pay for charges not covered by Medicare.

Own-occupation. Form of disability income (DI) insurance that will pay you if you can work but can't perform the job for which you were specially trained.

Portability. The ability to take insurance coverage with you if you leave your employer.

Post-underwriting. The practice of some insurance companies to accept most applicants, then refuse to pay claims if the applicant did not reveal all health conditions.

Preexisting conditions. Health conditions you have before applying for a policy. In some circumstances, the insurance will not cover those conditions or will cover them only after a time lag.

Preferred provider organization (PPO). A network of physicians and hospitals that will give discount rates to participants in certain health plans.

Residual disability. A disability that forces you to work part-time, not full-time, with a significant loss of income.

Rider. Benefit added to a basic insurance policy, usually at an added cost.

Self-insurance. The practice in which an employer will retain insurance premiums and agree to pay out benefits rather than transfer that risk to an insurance company.

Stop-loss. The maximum amount an individual or a family will pay for medical expenses per year, before the insurance company pays all reasonable charges.

Third party. An insurance company or an employer that pays medical bills incurred by insured individuals.

UCR. "Usual, customary, and reasonable" charges are the maximum amounts an insurance company will pay for certain procedures.

Underwriting. The process in which an insurance company selects those applicants it will insure.

Waiting period. Also called an "elimination period." The time in which you have to pay all bills before the insurance takes effect.

Workers' compensation. Special insurance coverage for job-related injuries. Benefits are paid regardless of fault, but the amounts are limited.

Index